WILDFLO

along the Alaska Highway

**A
Roadside
Guide**

*Travel the Highway
Make stops where you may.
Explore some waysides
and woods on the way.
Walk to the mountains,
The lakes and the streams.
Fill your heart and your soul
With magnificent scenes.*

V.E.P.

THE ALASKA HIGHWAY

The Alaska Highway (ALCAN) which is a popular tourist route from the "Lower 48" to Alaska was built in less than 9 months in 1942 as a military supply route. The threat of a possible Japanese invasion during World War II prompted the United States and Canada to work together to build this rough, narrow, winding 1520 mile (2430km) gravel road from Dawson Creek, British Columbia to Delta Junction, Alaska.

In recent years many improvements have been made. The road is now completely paved except for small portions under re-construction and, because of the elimination of many curves, the overall length has been reduced to 1486 miles (2390km).

The Highway offers the traveler the experience of driving through beautiful changing countryside having a wide range of altitudinal and latitudinal differences, with a new experience and different plants around each corner. The wise traveler will take time to explore and enjoy.

As there are many publications about the Highway, its history and construction, already in print we have chosen to keep this section brief. We do, however, recommend a good Highway guide book that lists points of interest, as this will be indispensable to you. There are many side roads to explore and special things to do to make your trip more memorable. (Be sure to stop at Delta Junction to get your personalized "We Drove the Alaska Highway" Certificate).

Fireweed --- the Provincial flower of the Yukon Territory

WILDFLOWERS

along the Alaska Highway

Native Plants, Roadside, Delta Junction, AK
Arctic Lupine, Fireweed, White Oxytrope, Blue Fleabane, Fringed Fleabane, Bedstraw

Verna E. Pratt

Alaskakrafts, Incorporated
Anchorage, Alaska

First Printing-1991
Second Printing-1996

Library of Congress Catalog Card Number.......91-77654

ISBN 0-9623192-1-X

Printed in Korea by DNP (AMERICA), Inc.

All photographs are by Verna and Frank Pratt, unless otherwise credited.

Illustrations by Verna E. Pratt

General Editor—Frank G. Pratt

Technical Editor—Verna E. Pratt

Cover Photos:
FRONT COVER:
Upper Right ____ "Beginning of Alaska Highway" sign at Dawson Creek, BC
Top Row ______ Dwarf Fireweed---Northern White Lady's Slipper---Monkey Flower
Middle Row ____ Yellow Lady's Slipper (Photo by Gary Davies)---Paintbrush---Monkshood
Lower Row ____ Prickly Rose---Forget-Me-Not---Paintbrush
Lower Left _____ "End of Alaska Highway" sign at Delta Junction, AK
BACK COVER:
Photograph of the author by Jane Stammen

DEDICATED

To my husband, Frank, who encouraged me to pursue this project and who spends endless hours at the computer and trekking with me across the tundra and alpine slopes.

Open Woods, Glenallen, AK
Frank photographing White Calypso Orchids

ACKNOWLEDGMENTS

Our thanks to our many friends who so graciously tolerated our lack of time for them because of our busy schedule while putting this book together.

Special thanks to:

Dr. Marilyn Barker who willingly assists us in plant identification.

Alison Bodewitz, and Lynn and Mark Catlin for their untiring efforts with proofreading.

Sally Karabelnikoff for joining us and aiding us on our latest trip to complete this work.

Verna E. Pratt
Frank G. Pratt

Chugach Mountains, Anchorage,AK

Sally at her favorite pastime---taking time to smell the flowers. Moss Campion

INTRODUCTION

The purpose of this book is to aid the traveler and amateur botanist in having the joy of recognizing the plants most commonly seen along the Alaska Highway. My husband and I have explored pull-offs, public campsites, popular trails and other attractions along the way. It is, by no means, a complete listing of plants of the area. The avid hiker or explorer is sure to find plants not mentioned in this book. Separate check lists immediately follow the color section of the book, for the use of those who would like to keep track of their "finds".

The diversity of plants in this book is great as it covers a wide range of habitats and latitudinal differences from about 56 degrees north latitude at Dawson Creek, BC to 65 degrees north latitude at Fairbanks, AK. Because of the elevation and latitude differences, blooming times for any particular species may vary as much as 2 or 3 weeks. Other factors; such as, severity of winter, amount of snowfall and timing of snow meltoff also may alter blooming times. Plant species that grow at several different elevations and habitats may also vary in size depending on severity of weather.

Most alpine plants hug the ground for protection from the elements and develop deep root systems to reach for moisture and nutrients. Plants that grow in rich, deep soil usually do not need deep roots; but, frequently, they will grow taller reaching for sunlight.

Because re-vegetation along the highways often includes non-native (introduced) species, you will need to stop and explore the surrounding areas to see most native plants. Not all plants mentioned in this book are accompanied by photographs, but descriptions and comparisons of confusing species are included. Those with photographs and full descriptions are identified in the index by upper case text.

Information on the edibility of wild plants has been included in this book merely as points of interest to the reader, and/or use in field survival situations. The identification and processing of any wild plant for use as food requires reasonable caution and attention to detail since, as indicated in the text, certain parts of some plants are totally unsuitable for use as food and, in some instances, are even lethal. Personal allergies or sensitivities may also be cause for adverse reactions. Because attempts to use any wild plants for food depend on various factors controlled only by the reader, neither the author nor publisher assumes any responsibility for such adverse health effects as might be encountered in any individual case.

We sincerely hope that this book will inspire you to look more closely at fine details and will enhance your experience of travelling the Alaska Highway.

How to Use this Book

This book was arranged by color to make it as easy as possible to use. Some plants are difficult to place in this manner as their color varies and individual people see colors differently. Although some plants may readily be identified by a color photograph alone, it is strongly suggested that you also read the accompanying text for proper identification. Descriptions are as simple as possible and a glossary is provided for the more difficult terms. Both common and scientific names are given for each species where they are available. Not all plants have common names and some may be known by other names in different localities. Scientific names also change as further studies are made. We chose to use Hulten's *Flora of Alaska* as our source for scientific names. (Note: Within the field of botany; however, current protocol is to not capitalize the species portion of the scientific name). Blooming times may vary due to season, latitude, and/or elevation and plants may be found in habitats or places different from the ones listed. The "Comments" section of each plant description is used to present different or confusing species and other interesting information regarding the plant. To further your enjoyment, we have also included lists of plants that we observed, so that you may check off your "finds" if you so desire. These check lists are arranged by scientific name because not all plants have common names. For these lists, we chose to divide the Highway into 5 segments of about 300 miles each, and also included lists of places we feel are of special interest to plant enthusiasts. These are by no means complete lists and the avid hiker is sure to find other plants, especially in alpine areas.

No matter how much your time is limited, we recommend at least short excursions near picnic areas or campsites to fully appreciate the wide variety of plants that you may see on your journey along this wonderful Highway. Please take time to "smell the flowers" and identify them with the aid of this book.

Showy Oxytrope
(Buckinghorse River,BC)

Cut-leaf Anemone
(Champagne, YT)

Fireweed
(Anchorage, AK)

Color variations of some plants described in this book.

Table of Contents

Introduced Plants

Revegetation along roadsides frequently adds new plants (non-native) to the landscape. Here are a few not pictured elsewhere in the book.

Alfalfa
(Whitehorse, YT)

Red Clover
(Pink Mountain, BC)

Alfalfa
(Whitehorse, YT)

Iceland Poppy
(Robertson River Bridge, AK)

Artemisia dracunculus
(Whitehorse, YT)

Cow Vetch
(Fairbanks, AK)

BLUE & VIOLET-FLOWERED PLANTS

Sub-alpine slopes, Whitehorse, YT
Slender Beardtongue

Siberian Aster
(Dot Lake, AK)

SIBERIAN ASTER

Aster sibiricus

Family: Aster / Asteraceae

Habitat: River flats, roadsides, woodlands, and rocky sub-alpine slopes throughout the area.

Blooming Time: July and August.

Description: Stems, 8 to 16" (20 to 40cm) tall, with slightly hairy, coarse-toothed leaves that are broad at the base, tapering to a point and slightly toothed. Flower heads have light lavender ray flowers with yellow centers. Plant is shorter and more compact when growing in the sun.

Comments: Might be confused with some Erigerons which have narrower ray flowers. See page 32 in Pink Section.

Blue Fleabane
(Tok, AK)

BLUE FLEABANE

Erigeron acris

Family: Aster / Asteraceae

Habitat: Dry fields, roadsides and open woodland throughout most of the area.

Blooming Time: July and August

Description: This 12 to 20" (30 to 50cm) branched plant has somewhat rough, hairy stems. Basal leaves are somewhat broad, rounded at the end and tapering to the base. Stem leaves are nearly linear. Flowers are lavender and not as impressive as the fluffy dandelion-like, buff-colored, seed heads.

Comments: *Erigeron elatus* is a similar smaller variety up to 6" (15cm) with fewer flowers.

Blue Fleabane seed head
(Teslin, YT)

SMOOTH ASTER

Aster laevis

Family: Aster / Asteraceae

Habitat: Dry roadsides, fields, and margins of woods from Dawson Creek to the YT.

Blooming Time: July to early Sept.

Description: A tall, 2 to 4' (60 to 120cm) plant with rather coarse leaves that are broad near the base and tapering to a long point. Upper leaves are sessile (stemless), the lower ones have a short stem and frequently wither by blooming time. The leaves are very variable but, usually, have a few shallow teeth. Flowers are light lavender-blue 1" (2.5cm) across, and in loose, very showy branched inflorescences.

Comments: Other confusing species are:

1) Showy Aster, *Aster modestus*, see below.
2) Northern Aster, *A. subspicatus*, an aster of open woodlands. See below.

Smooth Aster (Wonowon, BC)

Northern Aster
(Liard Hot Springs, BC)

SHOWY ASTER

Aster modestus

Family: Aster / Asteraceae

Habitat: Open woods, fields and near streams from Dawson Creek to Watson Lake.

Blooming Time: August & September

Description: A very tall plant, 3 to 6' (1 to 2m) arising from a horizontal rhizome. The leaves are large, broad at the base, pointed, shallowly toothed and sometimes hairy. The upper leaves somewhat clasp the stems. The lower ones wither early. The numerous rosy-violet flowers are about 1.5" (3cm) across and are very showy with large, branched somewhat flat-topped inflorescences.

Showy Aster (Wonowon,BC)

Saussurea
(Snag Creek, YT)

SAUSSUREA

Saussurea angustifolia

Family: Aster / Asteraceae

Habitat: Moist places in the tundra or dry places in the mountains in AK and YT.

Blooming Time: Late June and July

Description: A coarse variable plant in regards to hairiness. The horizontal root sends up single stems 6 to 12" (15 to 30cm). The long, narrow, slightly acute leaves may be entire or slightly wavy. Flower heads are 3/8 to 5/8" (1 to 1.5cm) across.

KNAPWEED

Centaurea sp.

Family: Aster / Asteraceae

Habitat: Roadsides, pulloffs, etc. An introduced weed in BC.

Blooming Time: August and September

Description: Several species have naturalized along roadsides and disturbed areas. Most are 2 to 4' (60 to 120cm) tall with flowers that look much like a small thistle. Stems are usually coarse and rough. Leaves are linear to long, broad and pointed, the lower ones being pinnately divided.

COMMENTS: Bull Thistle and other introduced thistles may be seen along the highway. Leaves usually have sharply pointed, wavy edges, some spiny. Flowers are lavender. Seed heads are large, fluffy and usually tannish.

Knapweed
(Charlie Lake, BC)

Bull Thistle
(Pink Mountain, BC)

BELLFLOWER

Campanula aurita

Family: Bluebell / Campanulaceae

Blooming Time: July & August

Habitat: Rocky places. Seen at Summit Lake in area of interest.

Description: A weakly ascending plant, up to 8" (20cm). Basal leaves lacking, stem leaves lanceolate with some evidence of shallow, irregular teeth. The dark blue campanulate flowers are 3/4 to 1" (2 to 2.5cm). Petals are joined only at the base flaring out into a star shape.

Comments: A similar species, One-flowered Harebell, *Campanula uniflora*, with wider, more rounded leaves is found in similar areas. The flowers are lighter blue and petals are joined about half of the length of the narrow funnel-shaped flowers.

Bellflower
(Summit Lake, BC)

MOUNTAIN HAREBELL

Campanula lasiocarpa

Family: Bluebell / Campanulaceae

Habitat: Rocky alpine slopes and ridges throughout most of the area.

Blooming Time: July and August.

Description: A very small alpine plant, 2 to 4" (5 to 10cm), with small, oblong, toothed leaves at the base becoming narrow up the stem. Flowers are violet-blue, upright bells, usually singular, and are very large for the size of the plant.

Mt. Harebell
(Summit Lake, BC)

One-flowered Harebell
(Summit Lake, BC)

Larkspur
(Bougie Creek, BC)

LARKSPUR

Delphinium glaucum

Family: Buttercup or Crowfoot/ Ranunculaceae

Habitat: Moist meadows and woodlands from Steamboat, BC into Fairbanks, AK.

Blooming Time: Late June to early August.

Description: A very tall, 4 to 6' (1 to 2m), robust branched plant with many broad, deeply divided, 5-lobed leaves that are again divided into several sections, see below. The main stem, which is frequently purplish, is topped by many purplish-blue, 5-petaled, spurred flowers.

Comments: **A poisonous plant. DO NOT EAT.** Can be dried for use in decorative arrangements by hanging upside-down.

Small-flowered Columbine
(Summit Lake, BC)

SMALL-FLOWERED COLUMBINE

Aquilegia brevistyla

Family: Buttercup or Crowfoot/ Ranunculaceae

Habitat: Moist woods, fields throughout most of the area.

Blooming Time: June & July

Description: A perennial plant 16 to 28" (40 to 70cm) tall with a heavy tap root. Basal leaves have long stems, are divided into three 3-lobed sections. They are green and smooth above and whitish beneath. Upper leaves 3-lobed and nearly stemless. The nodding flowers are about 1" (2.5cm) across and have 5 pointed lavender sepals and 5 tubular white petals terminating in a lavender spur. The upright seed pod, which is divided into 3 parts, is very distinctive.

BLUEBELLS, LUNGWORT, LANGUID LADY, CHIMING BELLS

Mertensia paniculata

Family: Borage / Boraginaceae

Habitat: Woods and meadows throughout most of the area.

Blooming Time: June and July.

Description: A plant with many stems, 16 to 30" (40 to 75cm) tall, with hairy, dark green leaves that are broad at the base and tapering to a long point. The flowers are tubular (funnel-shaped), pink in bud, later turning blue; occasionally all pink.

Comments: The leaves are edible but somewhat fishy tasting.

Bluebells
(Wolf Creek, YT)

MONKSHOOD

Aconitum delphinifolium, ssp. *delphinifolium*

Family: Buttercup or Crowfoot/ Ranunculaceae

Habitat: Woodlands, meadows, into mid-alpine areas from Steamboat, BC to Fairbanks, AK.

Blooming Time: Late June to mid-August.

Description: A tall, branched slender plant, 2 to 4' (60 to 120cm), (much smaller in alpine areas). Leaves usually have 5 deeply-divided, narrow lobes which are divided again, usually into 3 narrow segments. Flowers which are scattered on a long stem above the leaves are shaped like a helmet and range in color from light blue to navy blue; and, occasionally, white.

Comments: **A poisonous plant, DO NOT EAT**. Once called wolfbane, as it was used in bait for killing wolves. Can be dried for use in decorative arrangements by hanging upside-down.

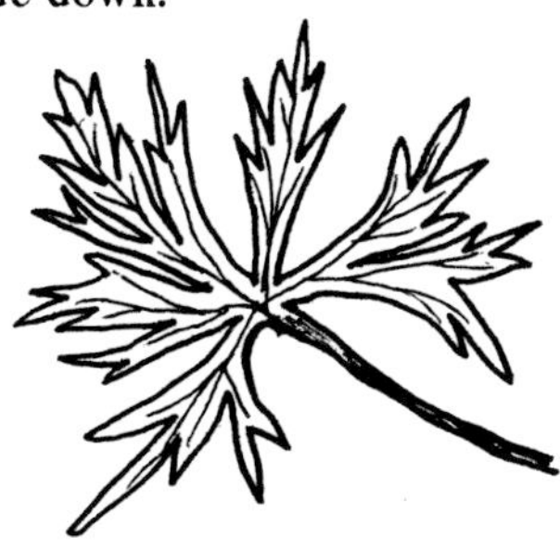

Monkshood
(Summit Lake, BC)

Blue-eyed Grass
(Buckinghorse Creek, BC)

BLUE-EYED GRASS

Sisyrinchium montanum

Family: Iris / Iridaceae

Habitat: Moist fields and meadows in BC.

Blooming Time: June and July

Description: A grasslike plant, up to 12" (30cm) tall. The long, narrow leaves are bluish-green. The bright bluish-violet flowers, which open on sunny days, are up to 5/8" (1.5cm) across and have 3 petals and 3 sepals that look alike. The seed capsule is round and is divided into 3 sections.

Wild Iris
(Delta, AK)

WILD IRIS, BLUE FLAG

Iris setosa ssp. *interior*

Family: Iris / Iridaceae

Habitat: Bogs, meadows and shores of lakes in AK.

Blooming Time: June and July

Description: A plant, 12 to 24" (30 to 60cm) tall, with broad, thin, swordlike leaves and a thick, round flower stalk. Flowers have 3 large, purple, blue or violet-colored (rarely white) falls (petal-like sepals) and 3 narrow, upright petals. The seed pod is large and divided into 3 sections. This is a large, showy flower, from 2.5 to 4" (6 to 10cm) across.

Comments: **A poisonous plant, causing vomiting. DO NOT EAT !** Individuals using edible plants should be careful not to confuse Wild Iris with edible cattail which also has long, narrow leaves and grows in standing water. See page 139 in Misc. Section.

Iris seed pod

BEAUTIFUL JACOB'S LADDER

Polemonium pulcherrimum

Family: Phlox / Polemoniaceae

Habitat: Dry, rocky areas, fields and roadsides throughout the area.

Blooming Time: Late May through July

Description: A low perennial plant, 8 to 14" (20 to 35cm), with many flowers on branched stems. The pinnately divided leaves have 10 to 15 rounded leaflets. The flowers are 5/8 to 3/4" (1 to 2cm) across, joined at the base and have 5 rounded violet-blue petals that are white at the base and have yellow centers.

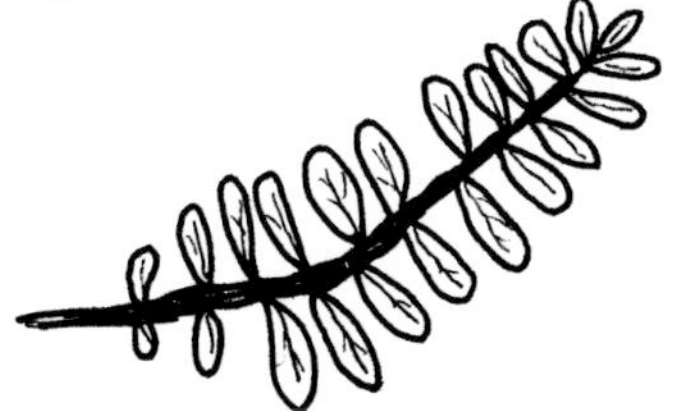

Beautiful Jacob's Ladder
(Tok, AK)

TALL JACOB'S LADDER

Polemonium acutiflorum

Family: Phlox / Polemoniaceae

Habitat: Fields, wet meadows and near streams throughout the area.

Blooming Time: July and August

Description: A tall perennial plant, 10 to 36" (30 to 90cm), with sticky, hairy stems. The pinnately divided leaves are smooth and have 7 to 11 sharply pointed leaflets. Flowers are 3/4 to 1" (2 to 2.5cm) across, have 5 sharply pointed violet-blue petals joined at the base with white centers and hairy, sticky sepals.

Comments: Very variable in size due to habitat and elevation. Color varies from blue to lavender, and, occasionally, white.

Tall Jacob's Ladder
(Pink Mt., BC)

Field Mint, Wild Mint
(Liard Hot Springs, BC)

FIELD MINT, WILD MINT

Mentha arvensis

Family: Mint / Lamiaceae

Habitat: Moist woods, margins of lakes and streams throughout the area.

Blooming Time: July and August

Description: Square stems mostly unbranched stiff and upright up to 30" (75cm). The aromatic leaves are opposite tapering to a long point. They are hairy, broadly lanceolate and toothed along the margins. The very small, lavender, flared, tubular flowers are in tight whorls around the stems just above the leaves.

Comments: Leaves may be used for jellies, teas or flavoring.

Show me Mountains, Lakes and Streams,
Let me feel the summer showers.
Refresh my soul and memories,
Precious time spent with the flowers!

V.E.P.

Wild Blue Flax
(Tok, AK)

WILD BLUE FLAX

Linum perenne

Family: Flax / Linaceae

Habitat: Very dry, sandy soil at lower elevations throughout the area.

Blooming Time: Late June and July.

Description: A wispy plant 15 to 20" (35 to 50cm) tall with narrow, glabrous, blue-green leaves. The 1" blue flowers have 5 rounded, overlapping petals and 5 stamens and are scattered on the branches. Seeds are in a conical hard shell.

Comments: The fibers of this plant have been used to weave into yard goods (linens), and it is a source for linseed oil.

STICKSEED, BLUE BUR

Lappula myosotis

Family: Borage / Boraginaceae

Habitat: Dry roadsides throughout the area.

Blooming Time: June and July

Description: A stiff hairy plant, 10 to 20" (25 to 50cm) tall with light green, hairy, simple leaves. The tiny flowers have 5 pale blue petals, are curled in bud and look very much like a very small forget-me-not. Nutlets have 2 distinct rows of fine prickles. This plant is not native to the area but well established.

Comments: A similar plant, *Lappula occidentalis*, is a slightly smaller plant and the nutlets have 1 row of prickles. The seeds of these plants which stick to socks and animal hair are particularly troublesome with long-haired dogs. Other greatly branched, taller introduced species may be found around Dawson Creek near the canola fields. The Alpine Forget-Me-Not, *Myosotis alpestris,* is the Alaska State Flower. It is a similar, more showy plant found in alpine meadows in parts of AK. See front cover.

Stickseed
(Champagne, YT)

ARCTIC LUPINE

Lupinus arcticus

Family: Pea / Fabaceae

Habitat: Dry slopes, fields, and roadsides throughout most of the area.

Blooming Time: June and early July

Description: A perennial plant, 10 to 16" (25 to 40cm) tall, with many large, full flower stalks. The distinctive palmate leaves consisting of several oval, pointed leaflets and have long stems. The stout flower stalks look wooly in bud due to the hairy calyx lobes. The flowers are blue to dark-blue and very showy and have a pleasant aroma.

Comments: Lupines are very poisonous plants, especially the seeds. DO NOT EAT.

Arctic Lupine
(Whitehorse, YT)

Yukon Beardtongue
(Haines Junction, AK)

Scorpion Weed
(Whitehorse,YT)

Marsh Skullcap
(Liard Hot Springs, BC)

YUKON BEARDTONGUE

Penstemon gormanii

Family: Figwort / Scrophulariaceae

Habitat: Very dry, sandy areas in YT and AK.

Blooming Time: Mid-June and July

Description: A perennial plant with a loose clump of glabrous to slightly hairy leaves. The large rosy lavender flowers are on 8 to 12" (20 to 30cm) stems and make an impressive sight. The flower has 5 joined petals looking much like a snapdragon. They are 1 to 1.5" (2.5 to 3cm) long.

Comments: This is a plant that is endemic to the Yukon River and is seldom seen very distant from it. A similar smaller plant in dry sub-alpine grasslands is Slender Beardtongue, *Penstemon procerus.* See page 1. It has whorls of tiny bluish-purple flowers, becoming a tight cluster near the end of the 6 to 12" (15 to 30cm) stems. The long-stemmed basal leaves are broad at the base and taper to a point. Stem leaves are narrow. Two members of the Waterleaf or Hydrophyllaceae family may be seen in dry areas of AK and YT. 1) Scorpion Weed, *Phaecelia mollis,* is a very small species with stamens longer than the petals. 2) Franklin's Scorpion Weed, *Phaecelia franklinni,* is a taller variety with stamens and petals of nearly the same length.

MARSH SKULLCAP

Scutellaria galericulata

Family: Mint / Labiaceae

Habitat: Wet areas, meadows and margins of lakes.

Blooming Time: July to mid-August

Description: This 8 to 16" (20 to 40cm) plant is usually simple but occasionally branched. The opposite leaves are smooth, broad, taper to a point and are slightly wavy on the edges. The small violet-blue, hooded flowers are few and arise from the junction of the leaves and stem.

BOG VIOLET, BUTTERWORT

Pinguicula vulgaris ssp.*vulgaris*

Family: Bladderwort / Lentibulariaceae

Habitat: Very wet meadows and bogs. Mostly seen in northern BC especially in the mountains.

Blooming Time: June to early July

Description: This insectivorous plant has a rosette of sticky yellowish leaves with rolled-up edges. The 2 to 4"(5 to 10cm) hairy stem is also somewhat sticky and has 1 rosy purple 5-petaled "Violet-like" spurred flower 1/2 to 3/4" (1 to 2cm) wide.

Comments: The sticky leaves trap insects and absorb their nutrients. These plants also absorb nutrients from the soil. *Pinguicula villosa*, a very small variety with hairy stems and calyx may also be seen in bogs or damp areas around lakes. The small rounded leaves and lower portion of stems are hairy.

Bog Violet
(Summit Lake, BC)

Most bog plants are pollinated by gnats or mosquitoes.

BROOK LOBELIA, KALM'S LOBELIA

Lobelia kalmii

Family: Bellflower / Campanulaceae

Habitat: Streams, wet places, especially at mineral springs. Seen only at Liard Hot Springs, BC.

Blooming Time: Late June to mid-August

Description: A small, upright frail plant. Basal leaves are small and somewhat spatulate. Stem leaves are long and narrow. The 10 to 12" (25 to 30cm) stems have small blue flowers.

Brook Lobelia
(Liard Hot Springs, BC)

Four-parted Gentian
(Pink Mt., BC)

FOUR-PARTED GENTIAN

Gentiana propinqua

Family: Gentian / Gentianaceae

Habitat: Fields, woods and dry mountain sides throughout most of the area.

Blooming Time: July and August

Description: A stiff, but slender, branching annual that grows 12 to 20" (30 to 50cm) tall with narrow opposite leaves that are frequently purplish on the edges. Flowers are lavender, usually 4-lobed, tubular, slightly flaring, opening fully only in bright sunshine. The plant branches freely from the base.

Comments: Other common Gentian species are: 1) Northern Gentian, *Gentiana amarella,* a similar, more leafy plant, up to 16" (40cm) with more numerous purplish broader leaves. Flowers are lavender, usually 5-lobed. It is found throughout the area. 2) Glaucous Gentian, *Gentiana glauca,* (photo on next page) a short, up to 4" (10cm) stiff plant found in tundra or alpine slopes throughout the area. Leaves are thick, rounded, close together and often yellowish-green. The tubular flowers are variable and can be light green to dark blue. 3) *Gentiana barbata*, a very tall slender plant, 12 to 20" (30 to 50cm), found in dry fields or open woodlands. Flowers, which open in sunlight, are bright blue and bloom in mid-June to late-July. A common roadside plant from Haines Junction to Tok.

Gentiana barbata
(Tok, AK)

Northern Gentian
(Watson Lake, BC)

MARSH FELSWORT

Lomatogonium rotatum

Family: Gentian / Gentianaceae

Habitat: Meadows, marshy areas and roadside ditches in southern parts of AK, BC and YT.

Blooming Time: July and August

Description: An erect, frail-looking, branched annual, 8 to 12" (20 to 30cm), with light blue tubular flowers that open into a star. Leaves are light-green, opposite and narrow (nearly linear).

MOSS GENTIAN

Gentiana prostata

Family: Gentian / Gentianaceae

Habitat: Damp margins of ponds and moist alpine slopes and tundra throughout most of the area.

Blooming Time: July and August

Description: A very small, low, sprawling plant branching from the base with small, light green, smooth, opposite entire leaves. The small tubular flowers have 5 bright blue petals and open only in sunlight to a pretty star shape. Sometimes a shadow passing over them may cause them to close, making them a real challenge for photographers.

Marsh Felswort
(Tetlin Junction, AK)

Glaucous Gentian
(Summit Lake, BC)

Moss Gentian
(Summit Lake, B.C.)

Showy Oxytrope
(Buckinghorse River, BC)

SHOWY LOCOWEED

Oxytropis splendens

Family: Pea / Fabaceae

Habitat: Dry slopes, fields and roadsides throughout most of the area.

Blooming Time: Late June and July

Description: The entire plant, which is 8 to 12" (20 to 30cm) tall is grayish from dense, silky hairs. The somewhat twisted leaf blades are composed of 40 to 70 oval, pointed leaflets and are quite erect. Flowers can be light pink to deep purplish-pink or lavender, 1/2 to 3/4" (1 to 2cm) long and in dense spikes of many flowers. Color is varied, see page viii.

Comments: Sticky Oxytrope, *Oxytropis viscida,* is a similar, quite common plant found throughout the area. It has flowers ranging in color from white to bluish-lavender. The stiff leaf blades, composed of 20 to 40 leaflets, are very erect and slightly sticky feeling. The calyx is very sticky from glandular hairs. Seed pods are covered with blackish hairs.

Sticky Oxytrope
(Buckinghorse River, BC)

SMALL-FLOWERED OXYTROPE

Oxytropis deflexa ssp. *sericea*

Family: Pea / Fabaceae

Habitat: Dry areas in YT, southern BC, and southern part of central AK.

Blooming Time: June to mid-July

Description: A very common, slightly hairy plant. Leaf blades are very stiff and erect and have 15 to 40 leaflets. Flower stalks are short, extending to 12" (30cm) in seed. The very small flowers are whitish mixed with lavender or pink. Seed pods hang downwards on the stalk. See page 110 for white-flowered variety.

Small-flowered Oxytrope
(Tok, AK)

ALPINE MILK VETCH

Astragalus alpinus

Family: Pea / Fabaceae

Habitat: Roadsides, fields, dry open woodlands, and alpine slopes throughout most of the area.

Blooming Time: June and July.

Description: A low, creeping, matted plant with weak stems. The pinnately divided leaves have many small, somewhat acute tipped, oval leaflets. The small pea-shaped flowers are white near the base and blue to lavender at the tip, often times almost all white. They are clustered in a short raceme at the end of the 4 to 8" (10 to 20cm) stems.

Comments: Other similar, taller members of the pea family that you may encounter are: A native species, American Vetchling, *Vicia americana,* a weak, sprawling plant that climbs with tendrils, found in woodlands in BC. It has magenta to purple flowers. Introduced species commonly seen along the highways are Cow Vetch, *Vicia cracca,* see page viii, with numerous small bluish to purple flowers, that sprawls over other plants smothering them out; and another genera, Alfalfa, *Medicago sativa,* which grows 20 to 28" (50 to 70cm) tall with short ball-shaped heads of very small blue to purple flowers.

Alpine Milk Vetch
(Haines Junction, AK)

American Vetch
(Bucking Horse River, BC)

BLADDER CAMPION

Melandrium apetalum

Family: Pink / Caryophyllaceae

Habitat: Dry, rocky or grassy mountain slopes throughout the area.

Blooming Time: Late June and July

Description: A small plant, up to 5" (13cm), with sticky hairs. The long narrow leaves are opposite on the stems. Flowers have 5 very small white to lavender petals and hang downward. The calyx is swollen and striped with pink to purple lines. The stem is erect in seed.

Comments: Two tall white species might be seen in dry places. *Melandrium taylorae,* found in AK and YT has long narrow leaves and 2 or 3 flowers. *Melandrium taimyrense*, found in AK, YT and northern BC has broader more spatulate leaves and 2 to 5 flowers.

Bladder Campion
(Summit Lake, BC)

Dog Violet
(Liard Hot Springs, BC)

WESTERN DOG VIOLET
EARLY BLUE VIOLET

Viola adunca

Family: Violet / Violaceae

Habitat: Dry meadows and woods in BC and the YT.

Blooming Time: May and early June

Description: The dark green, numerous, somewhat heart-shaped leaves have fine teeth along the margins and are frequently spotted with brown. The numerous flowers are bluish-violet colored and 3/4" (2cm) across. The 2 side petals are white-bearded and the spur is slender. This is a very low, compact plant in the Spring. Stems elongate later in the season.

Comments: Other violet species are: 1) Marsh Violet, *Viola epipsila,* which grows in wet areas at low elevations. Having smaller, light lavender flowers and blooming in May. 2) Selkirk's Violet, *Viola selkirkii*, is a loose, delicate plant. It has rosy violet flowers. The light green, toothed, heart-shaped leaves have a deep, often overlapping, sinus. It is not widespread, but has been found between Dawson Creek and Fort Nelson in moist humusy woodlands. 3) Northern Bog Violet, *Viola nephrophylla*, is a slightly taller variety, 4 to 5" (10 to 12.5cm), having very few leaves and flowers and found growing in very wet areas. Found only at Liard Hot Springs, BC it is a late violet blooming in July.

Marsh Violet
(Fairbanks, AK)

Selkirk's Violet
(Charley Lake, BC)

Northern Bog Violet
(Liard Hot Springs, BC)

WILD CHIVES

Allium schoenoprasum

Family: Lily / Liliaceae

Habitat: Scattered throughout the area in alpine meadows and at hot springs.

Blooming Time: July

Description: Many rose to lavender flowers on a dense, nearly round, umbel just above the clump of long hollow grass-like leaves.

Comments: Bulbs and leaves are eaten like onions. Do not confuse with the flat leaves of Death Camas, see page 83 in White Section, which also grows from an onion-like bulb.

Wild Chives
(Liard Hot Springs, BC)

Pasque Flower
(Tok, AK)

PASQUE FLOWER, SPRING CROCUS

Pulsatilla patens ssp. *multifida*

Family: Buttercup or Crowfoot / Ranunculaceae

Habitat: Dry or sandy soil in AK, the YT and northern BC.

Blooming Time: May to very early June.

Description: A very silky, hairy plant that is quite varied throughout the season. Spring version is covered with silky hairs topped by a short-stemmed large, cup-shaped flower with 5 to 8 slightly pointed, lavender to violet sepals which are very silky on the underside. As the flower matures, the stem elongates up to 14" (35cm) and the flower droops downward. In seed, it is a spectacular sight. See also page 193 for photo.

Comments: Seed heads may be picked and dried. Possibly confusing plants in AK and YT are Alaska Blue Anemone, *Anemone multiceps,* which looks like a miniature, dark, bluish-purple Pasque Flower; and, *Anemone drummondii* whose flowers are more like a miniature Windflower, *Anemone parviflora*, see page 90 in White Section.

Pasque Flower
(Tok, AK)

American Brook Lime
(Buckinghorse River, BC)

AMERICAN BROOK LIME

Veronica americana

Family: Figwort / Scrophulariaceae

Habitat: Moist areas and along streams throughout the area.

Blooming Time: July to early August

Description: A weakly branched sprawling plant with somewhat succulent ovate to lanceolate toothed leaves. Flowering stems arise from the junction of the leaves and main stem. Flowers are light blue and have 4 petals, the uppermost being very broad.

Comments: *Veronica scutellata* is a very weak similar plant with very narrow leaves. Alpine varieties such as *Veronica wormskjoldii* may be seen by those hiking in the high meadows. This is an upright plant up to 8" (20cm) tall with narrow hairy leaves. The small bluish lavender 4-petalled flowers are in a tight cluster at the end of the stem. These are sometimes mistaken for forget-me-nots which have 5 blue petals and a yellow or white center.

Alpine Veronica
(Summit Lake, BC)

The term "officinalis" (The Official Plant), when used as a species name, generally indicates that the plant was once used medicinally.

Blackish Oxytrope
(Summit Lake, BC)

BLACKISH OXYTROPE, PURPLE OXYTROPE

Oxytropis nigrescens

Family: Pea / Fabaceae

Habitat: Dry rocky alpine ridges scattered throughout the area.

Blooming Time: June

Description: A very low sprawling plant with very small bluish-green, pinnately divided leaves. The small purplish flowers usually bloom in pairs. The calyx is covered with gray to blackish hairs which are also evident on the large heavy seed pod.

PINK-FLOWERED PLANTS

Sunny Areas
Stone Mt. Provincial Park, BC
Philadelphia Daisy

Hemp Nettle
(Pink Mt., BC)

HEMP NETTLE

Galeopsis tetrahit

Family: Mint / Lamiaceae

Habitat: Roadsides and pull-offs in BC and YT. An introduced plant.

Blooming Time: Late June to early August

Description: A perennial plant 12 to 24" (30 to 60cm) tall having coarse-looking, opposite leaves that are triangular, hairy and toothed. The tiny, inconspicuous, flaring tubular flowers are in dense clusters at the end of the square branches. Flowers are Light pink to lavender, and often spotted.

There is a roadside beautification program in the United States instituted by Lady Bird Johnson (wife of President Lyndon B. Johnson) to encourage reseeding with wildflowers.

Pink Pyrola
(Whitehorse, YT)

PINK PYROLA, WINTERGREEN

Pyrola asarifolia

Family: Wintergreen / Pyrolaceae

Habitat: Moist woodlands and meadows throughout the area.

Blooming Time: June to early July

Description: An evergreen plant having a rosette of 1 to 1-1/2" (2.5 to 3.5cm), round, smooth, thick, shiny leaves and an 8 to 12" (20 to 30cm) heavy (slightly pinkish) spike of many 5-petaled, slightly nodding, 1/2" to 5/8" (up to 1.5cm) pink flowers with distinctive long protruding styles and obvious, rounded, heavy seed capsules.

Comments: Small-flowered Pyrola, *Pyrola minor*, is similar but a very small, about 5" (13cm) alpine plant with a few 1/4 to 3/8" (up to 1cm) flowers that remain nearly closed. It grows on the tundra and alpine slopes, and occasionally in woods at low elevation. The leaves are much smaller, 1/2 to 3/4" (less than 2cm), than *P. asarifolia* and usually close to the ground.

Small-flowered Pyrola
(Destruction Bay, YT)

FAIRY SLIPPER, CALYPSO ORCHID, VENUS SLIPPER

Calypso bulbosa

Family: Orchid / Orchidaceae

Habitat: Moist, mossy woods in the Fairbanks, AK area and in BC, and southern YT.

Blooming Time: Early May to mid-June.

Description: The 4 to 6" (10 to 15cm) plant is probably semi-parasitic and has a thick, fleshy pinkish stem arising from a fleshy bulb with one basal leaf with linear veins. The leaf, which looks pleated, dies after the plant blooms. A new leaf appears in August. There is one pinkish-lavender flower consisting of 3 pointed sepals, 2 pointed petals and a large lower petal which is sac-like. A very aromatic flower. See page v for white variety.

Comments: This orchid does not transplant. Many orchids are semi-parasitic or at least reliant upon plants or nutrients around them for survival so should not be moved. Certain types die if the flower stalk is picked. Orchids that transplant well have been over-collected and are becoming rare, so that their very existence in the wild is endangered. Please refrain from disturbing them.

Fairy Slipper
(Liard Hot Springs, BC)

TWIN FLOWER

Linnaea borealis ssp. *americana*

Family: Honeysuckle / Caprifoliaceae

Habitat: Woods and dry slopes in the mountains throughout the area.

Blooming Time: Mid-June to early August.

Description: A trailing shrub with thin branches and small, rounded, light green, evergreen leaves placed opposite on the stems, and having a few teeth near the tip. The flowering stems have 1 to 2 sets of leaves and usually 2 pinkish-white, bell-shaped flowers, borne on 3 to 4" (7.5 to 10cm) stems.

Twin Flower
(Whitehorse, YT)

Marsh Willow Herb
(North Pole, AK)

MARSH WILLOW HERB

Epilobium hornemanii

Family: Evening Primrose / Onagraceae

Habitat: Damp areas and near streams from Dawson Creek, BC to Whitehorse, YT and in the Fairbanks, AK area.

Blooming Time: Mid-June through mid-August.

Description: A stiff upright stalk, 5 to 10" (12 to 24cm) with short-stemmed, broad pointed leaves having wavy edges. Leaves are opposite on the lower stem, alternate above. Flowers small, usually pink. Petals slightly indented drooping when young, erect in seed. Seed pods are slightly hairy at first, later glabrous.

Comments: There are many species of Willow Herbs, including: 1) *Epilobium anagallidifolium*, a small alpine plant, 4 to 5" (10 to 12cm) tall. Leaves have short stems, are elliptical, and usually opposite. Flowers droop, often lying on the ground, are very small and bright pink. 2) Tall Willow Herb,*Epilobium adenocaulon*, a very tall, up to 2 feet (60cm), leafy, branched species found in fields and disturbed areas. White Willow Herbs in the area are: 1) *Epilobium lactiflorum* having broader leaves with slightly wavy edges. The lower leaves have stems. 2) *Epilobium davuricum* has very few quite narrow leaves and a basal rosette.

Tall Willow Herb
(Watson Lake, YT)

Epilobium anagallidifolium
(Summit Lake, BC)

COMMON FIREWEED, GREAT WILLOW HERB, BLOOMING SALLY

Epilobium angustifolium, ssp. *angustifolium*

Family: Evening Primrose / Onagraceae

Habitat: Meadows and woods throughout the area.

Blooming Time: Late June to August.

Description: A tall plant, 2-1/2 to 6 feet (up to 2m), growing from deep horizontal roots. Leaves are long, broad at the base and taper to a point. They are placed alternately on the stem which is usually simple, or occasionally branched. The bright pink flowers have 2 large, rounded petals at the base and 2 slightly smaller rounded petals above. The 4 sepals are long, narrow, pointed and purplish. See page viii for light pink variation. The flowers on the long graceful raceme are 1 to 1-1/4" (2.5 to 3cm) across. The lowest flowers on the stems bloom first. Its common name is derived from its ability to revegetate quickly after a fire (due to its deep roots that escape damage). Note page 189. The leaves are bright-colored (orange-red to purplish) in the fall. See page 176 for seed pods.

Comments: The flowers are used to make honey and jelly. The leaves are edible, especially the new (red) shoots in the spring. The inner stem is soft, pithy and very nutritious. Varieties with white or pale pink flowers are sometimes seen, especially along the Klondike Loop Highway which connects Whitehorse to the the Dempster Highway and Dawson City, YT. This is the provincial flower of the Yukon Territory.

Common Fireweed
(North Pole, AK)

Fireweed

BICKNELL GERANIUM

Geranium bicknellii

Family: Geranium / Geraniaceae

Habitat: Roadsides, waste areas throughout BC and some sections of the YT.

Blooming Time: July and August

Description: A low, generally branched, annual or biennial plant up to 15" (38cm) tall. The hairy leaves have 5 deeply toothed lobes and prominent veins. The basal leaves have long stems. The main stems often appear reddish. The flowers are pale pink, usually in twos and 3/8 to 5/8" (1 to 1.5cm) in size.

Bicknell Geranium
(Pink Mt., BC)

Dwarf Fireweed
(Kluane Lake, YT)

DWARF FIREWEED, RIVER BEAUTY

Epilobium latifolium

Family: Evening Primrose / Onagraceae

Habitat: Along streams or river bars and on scree slopes in the mountains throughout the area.

Blooming Time: July and August.

Description: Stems somewhat sprawling up to 20" (50cm) tall. The 4 sepals are pointed and purplish, and the 4 bright pink petals are oval , pointed and all equal size giving it a very symmetrical appearance. Rarely white or light pink.

Comments: Could be confused with Wild Sweet Pea from a distance when growing on river banks due to similarities in size, color and growth form and habitat. See page 190.

Few-flowered Shooting Star
(Tok, AK)

FEW-FLOWERED SHOOTING STAR

Dodecatheon pulchellum ssp. *pauciflorum*

Family: Primrose / Primulaceae

Habitat: Open woods and meadows in AK and BC.

Blooming Time: Late May to early July

Description: A perennial plant up to 12" (30cm) tall with spatulate shaped light green basal leaves, and 3 to 5 pink to magenta flowers in an umbel. The 5 petals are reflexed exposing a yellow and white band and long stamens that look like a bird's beak.

Comments: A similar species, Frigid Shooting Star, *Dodecatheon frigidum,* which is found in alpine meadows is slightly shorter with spade-shaped leaves. Flowers are darker and have no yellow band.

Frigid Shooting Star
(Summit Lake, BC)

Few-flowered
Shooting Star

Frigid
Shooting Star

NAGOONBERRY

Rubus arcticus, ssp. *acaulis*

Family: Rose / Rosaceae

Habitat: Stream banks, moist fields, lake margins, tundra and alpine slopes throughout most of the area.

Blooming Time: June and July

Description: A low plant with long-stemmed, 3-parted, coarsely veined, leaves (much like strawberries) that spread rapidly by underground rhizomes. The 1" (2.5cm) short-stemmed flowers have 5 to 8 long narrow pink petals. In late July or August they bear small, red, very tasty (raspberry-like) berries, but, generally do not produce well except in very wet areas.

Comments: Similar species are: 1) Ssp. *arcticus* which has flowers well above the leaves and broader petals is found in AK. 2) Ssp. *stellatus* which has leaves that are lobed, not divided to the mid-vein and is found in YT.

Nagoonberry
(Muncho Lake, BC)

Spreading Dogbane
(Taylor, BC)

SPREADING DOGBANE

Apocynum androsaemifolium

Family: Dogbane / Apocynaceae

Habitat: Dry fields, woodlands. Common on lower section of the Highway and at hot springs farther north.

Description: A branched plant up to 24" (60cm) with slender stems that contain a white juice. Leaves are opposite on the stems, bright green above, slightly lighter colored and hairy beneath, and during warm weather they droop. They are somewhat egg-shaped and have a sharp spine-like point. The sweet-scented flowers are clustered at the ends of the branches. They have 5 petals that are white to pale pink with darker pink lines (nectaries). They are bell-shaped with the petals slightly reflexed. In late summer, they are replaced by long, 5" (12cm) red seed pods.

Comments: The strong fibers from the stems of this plant were once used to weave into fishing nets. **Poisonous, affecting the cardiovascular system. DO NOT EAT!**

Spreading Dogbane seed pods
(Taylor, BC)

Bog Rosemary
(Destruction Bay, YT)

BOG ROSEMARY

Andromeda polifolia

Family: Heath / Ericaceae

Habitat: Bogs and moist depressions in the mountains throughout most of the area.

Blooming Time: Late May thru June

Description: Dwarf evergreen shrub, up to 8" (20cm) tall, having thick, long, narrow leaves that are grayish-green above and silvery-white beneath with edges rolled under. The light pink, urn-shaped flowers are clustered at the end of the branches. The flower stems are also pink.

Comments: This is a very poisonous plant causing rapid lowering of blood pressure if eaten. (It was once used medicinally, but with great caution). DO NOT EAT!

Bog Cranberry
(Marsh Lake, YT)

BOG CRANBERRY

Oxycoccus microcarpus

Family: Heath / Ericaceae

Habitat: Bogs and wet tundra throughout the area.

Blooming Time: June

Description: A small trailing sub-shrub with very small, about 1/6" (4 to 5mm), ovate, hard evergreen leaves which are broader at the base and alternate on the slender stems. Young stems are smooth. Flowers are produced singularly on a 1 to 2" (2.5 to 5cm) curved stem. The tiny flowers have 5 narrow, light pink, recurved petals exposing long stamens giving it the appearance of a bird's bill. These flowers look like miniature Shooting Stars and produce very tasty, tart, firm, oval, maroon berries in September. The berries lie on the moss because they are too heavy for the stems to support.

Comments: *Oxycoccus palustris* which is present in the southern portion of the area has hairy young stems. The leaves are not broader at the base. The flowers and berries are slightly larger.

Bog Cranberry berries
(Marsh Lake, YT)

BOG BLUEBERRY

Vaccinium uliginosum

Family: Heath / Ericaceae

Habitat: Bogs, woods, tundra and alpine throughout most of the area.

Blooming Time: Late-May to mid-June

Description: A low shrub, 6 to 20" (15 to 50cm), with thinly angled branches and small oval leaves up to 3/4" (2cm). The pinkish bell-shaped flowers produce oval berries from mid-July through August.

Comments: Other species in the area are: 1) Dwarf Blueberry, *Vaccinium caespitosum*, a smaller shrub with round branches and very small, finely toothed leaves. The berries are round with a whitish bloom. Found in BC and southern YT. 2) Canada Blueberry, *Vaccinium myrtilloides*, is a low shrub, up to 18" (45cm), of bogs and shady woods. Young twigs have fine hairs. The shiny thick leaves are 1-1/2 to 2" (3 to 5cm), sharply pointed lanceolate and entire. Flowers are greenish white to pink. Berries, which are sweet and tasty, are blue to bluish-black with a whitish bloom. Grows along the lower section of the Highway. 3) Early Blueberry, *Vaccinium ovalifolium*, a shrub up to 4' (1.5m), grows in moist woods up into the mountains. Young twigs are reddish. Leaves are thin ovate, acute and finely toothed. The flowers are usually pink and somewhat-urn shaped. The tasty berries are blue. Found in moist woods up into the mountains in BC.

Bog Blueberry
(Tetlin, AK)

Bog Blueberry
(Tetlin Junction, AK)

Canada Blueberry
(Pink Mt., BC)

Early Blueberry
(Liard Hot Springs, BC)

Pink Pussytoes
(Tok, AK)

PINK PUSSYTOES, PINK EVERLASTING

Antennaria rosea

Family: Aster / Asteraceae

Habitat: Dry fields and open woods from Steamboat, BC north.

Blooming Time: June to early July

Description: A low matting plant with stolons terminating in rosettes of small acute spoon-shaped leaves that are light silvery gray from from fine hairs. The flowering stems are 5 to 10" (12 to 25cm) tall, hairy and have small modified leaves that somewhat clasp the stems. The white bracts are surrounded by pink bracts.

Comments: The flowers can be dried and used as straw flowers.*Antennaria alborosea* is a similar species with slightly broader leaves that are not hairy on the top side.

WILD SWEET PEA

Hedysarum mackenzii

Family: Pea / Fabaceae

Habitat: Rocky slopes and river bars throughout most of the area.

Blooming Time: June and July

Description: A stout, upright plant, 18 to 24" (40 to 60cm) tall, having pinnately divided leaves with 7 to 15 ovate leaflets with an obvious mid-vein. The bright pink, very aromatic, pea-shaped flowers are 1/4 to 3/8" (6 to 9mm) wide, and 3/4" (18mm) long. They are clustered at the top of the stem, making it a short, broad raceme. Seed pods have transverse veins, see below.

Comments: **Caution: the root is supposedly poisonous.** This plant could be confused with Eskimo Potato which has smaller flowers, longer spikes, and prominent veins on the leaflets. (See Eskimo Potato, next page).

Wild Sweet Pea
(Kluane Lake, YT)

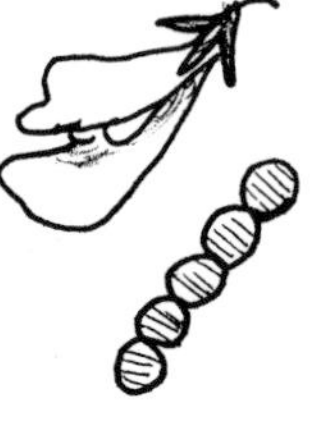

Wild Sweet Pea

Eskimo Potato

FRINGED FLEABANE

Erigeron glabellus ssp. *pubescens*

Family: Aster / Asteraceae

Habitat: Dry places throughout most of the area.

Blooming Time: July to mid-August

Description: A 10 to 18" (25 to 45cm) plant with a cluster of leaves that are slightly wavy along the margin and have short hairs at the base. The branched flowering stem may be erect or slightly curved at the base. Flowers are 1 to 2" (2.5 to 5cm). Ray flowers may be pale pink, lavender or whitish, numerous, and very narrow.

Comments: Other varieties possible to encounter are: Ssp. *yukonensis* -- with narrower leaves and longer hairs, and Ssp. *glabellus* -- no hairs. See page 21 and 168 for Philadelphia Daisy, *Erigeron philadelphicus.*

Fringed Fleabane
(Whirlpool Canyon, BC)

ESKIMO POTATO

Hedysarum alpinum

Family: Pea / Fabaceae

Habitat: Rocky alpine slopes, roadsides and open forests throughout the area.

Blooming Time: June and July

Description: A tall,up to 2' (60cm), (smaller in alpine areas), branched, sprawling plant that grows from a horizontal root. Leaves are pinnately divided with 15-20 ovate leaflets about 1/2 to 1" (1 to 2.5cm) long with obvious middle and branching veins on the under side. Flower stalks are long with many small, narrow light pink to purple, pea-shaped flowers which are up to 1/4" (6mm) wide and 5/8" (15mm) long. The flowers are crowded together and often appear to flow down one side of the stems. Seed pods have net veins.

Comments: The root is eaten by native people either raw or cooked. Alpine Eskimo Potato, *Hedysarum hedysaroides*, is a similar smaller species found in alpine areas. For confusing species, including drawings, see Wild Sweet Pea on previous page.

Eskimo Potato
(Haines Junction, AK)

Tufted Fleabane
(Munson Slough, AK)

TUFTED FLEABANE

Erigeron caespitosus

Family: Aster / Asteraceae

Habitat: Dry places and rocky slopes at low elevations in the lowlands of AK, YT and in the Rocky Mountains.

Blooming Time: June and July

Description: A low plant 6 to 10" (15 to 25cm) freely branching at the base, with many hairy narrow leaves. Flowers are 1 to 1-1/2" (2.5 to 3.5cm), pink, lavender or white. Very variable. This could easily be placed in the White Section.

Hawks Nursery
(North Pole, AK)

Pale Corydalis
(Steamboat, BC)

PALE CORYDALIS, ROCK HARLEQUIN

Corydalis sempervirens

Family: Earth Smoke / Fumariaceae

Habitat: Broken and disturbed ground scattered throughout most of the area.

Blooming Time: Late June to mid-August

Description: A tall, up to 30" (75cm), delicate plant with gracefully arching stems. The bluish-gray smooth leaves are pinnately divided and lobed. Stems are somewhat succulent. Flowers are tubular, pink with a yellow tip and a rounded spur. The seed capsules are upright and very long. This plant prefers soft soil and sunlight, and can be either an annual or biennial.

ALPINE ASTER

Aster alpinus ssp. *vierhapperi*

Family: Aster / Asteraceae

Habitat: Dry grassy areas and alpine tundra mostly in AK and YT.

Blooming Time: July

Description: Plant 5 to 10" (12.5 to 24cm). Basal leaves blunt lanceolate with short stems arising from a stout rootstock. Stem leaves gradually becoming smaller and more narrow. Entire plant having coarse hairs. Flowers are usually solitary 1 to 1-1/2" (2.5 to 4cm). Ray flowers are quite narrow and can be pink to white.

Comments: Coastal Fleabane, *Erigeron peregrinus*, a taller plant, up to 14" (35cm), with single pink, daisy-like flowers might be seen in alpine meadows or at Liard Hot Springs, BC.

Alpine Aster
(Champagne, YT)

BEE BALM, WILD BERGAMOT, HORSE MINT

Monarda fistulosa, var. *menthaefolia*

Family: Mint / Lamiaceae

Habitat: Dry, open areas along the lower section of the highway.

Blooming Time: June to August

Description: An erect plant 12" to 28" (30 to 70cm) tall having a square stem and opposite leaves. The toothed, aromatic, leaves are grayish-green, broad at the base and tapering to a long point. Each stem is topped with a cluster of rosy lavender flowers that are a favorite of bees and hummingbirds. Color can vary and be more lavender.

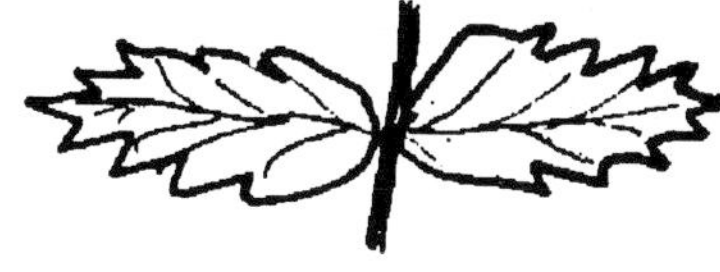

Bee Balm leaves

Bee Balm
(Taylor, BC)

Wooly Lousewort
(Summit Lake, BC)

WOOLY LOUSEWORT

Pedicularis kanei ssp. *kanei*

Family: Figwort / Scrophulariaceae

Habitat: Dry, rocky alpine slopes and tundra throughout most of the area.

Blooming Time: Late May to mid-June

Description: Pinnately divided, toothed, long-stemmed basal leaves surround a thick, wooly flower stalk arising from a long fibrous root. The upper stem leaves are reduced in size. The plant is very short and wooly in bud, elongating in seed up to 10" (25cm). Flowers are many and pink. A very showy plant with 1 to 3 stalks.

Comments: The common name is derived from olden times when sheepherders thought that the wooly plant harbored lice and infected their sheep. "Wort" means "plant"; thus, "Louse plant". The long root is a good source of starch and is used by the native people. 1) Whorled Lousewort, *Pedicularis verticillata,* found in similar areas in AK and the YT, is a less densely flowered, pinkish-lavender species that has leaves in a whorl around its stems. 2) *Pedicularis sudetica* ssp. *interior* is a taller up to 24" (60cm), variety found in the tundra and also in open deciduous woodlands throughout the area. The long stemmed leaves are scattered along the horizontal rhizome. The flowers which are clustered near the top of the stems are purplish-pink.

Pedicularis sudetica ssp. *interior*
(Muncho Lake, BC)

Whorled Lousewort
(Summit Lake, BC)

INDIAN PAINTBRUSH

Castilleja miniata

Family: Figwort / Scrophulariaceae

Habitat: Open meadows and fields in BC.

Blooming Time: Late-June to mid-August

Description: An impressive colorful plant, ranging in size from 6 to 14" (15 to 35cm). Each plant can have many unbranched stems topped with colorful bracts hiding the tiny inconspicuous flowers. Color varies depending on locality. Leaves are long and narrow with a long tapering point. Very obvious from Fort St. John northward.

Comments: Paintbrushes are partially parasitic obtaining some nutrients from plants around them. Color variations are common in this area. Most are salmon pink to magenta, but can be yellowish, rose-colored, or scarlet. See cover photo for color variation.

Indian Paintbrush
(Summit Lake, BC)

Indian Paintbrush Flower

CUT-LEAF ANEMONE

Anemone multifida

Family: Buttercup / Ranunculaceae

Habitat: Dry fields, woods and low-elevation slopes throughout the area.

Blooming Time: May and June

Description: A loose clumping plant, 12 to 18" (30 to 45cm) tall, with long-stemmed, hairy basal leaves. Leaves are divided into 3 sections which are dissected into very narrow segments. Stem leaves have shorter stems and are much smaller. Flowers usually have 5 colorful sepals and no petals. Color is variable, see page 90 in White Section. Seed head is globular and fluffy when mature.

Cutleaf Anemone
(Champagne, YT)

Cuckoo Flower
(Pine Lake, YT)

CUCKOO FLOWER

Cardamine pratensis

Family: Mustard / Brassicaceae

Habitat: Wet places, lake margins and near streams in northern BC, YT and AK.

Blooming Time: June

Description: A slender plant 6 to 10" (15 to 25cm) tall with glabrous stems and leaves. Basal leaves are rounded and have long petioles usually withering before blooming time. Stem leaves are pinnately divided, the leaflets being somewhat rounded. Flowers have 4 pale pink to white petals with darker veins and are 1/2 to 3/4" (12 to 18mm)in size. Seed capsule is long and narrow.

Comments: A species with a similar flower is *Parrya nudicaulis*, a plant of alpine meadows in AK and the YT. Flowers are slightly larger, lavender, pink or white in color and occur in a dense cluster. Leaves are simple with wavy edges.

SANDFAIN

Onobrychis viciaefolia

Family: Pea / Fabaceae

Habitat: Roadsides from Watson Lake to just north of Whitehorse.

Blooming Time: June to August

Description: Large freely branching perennial plant up to 2 feet (60cm) tall. Leaves are pinnately divided (vetch-like) with 20 to 30 leaflets. The light pink flowers have bright pink to purple stripes and are in a tightly packed spike of up to 50 flowers.

Comments: This plant has traditionally been used as a feed plant for animals. Not native to the area. Introduced, probably through road construction.

Sandfain
(Whitehorse, YT)

Sandfain flower

PRICKLY ROSE

Rosa acicularis

Family: Rose / Rosaceae

Habitat: Open woods, clearings, meadows throughout the area.

Blooming Time: June to early July.

Description: A very prickly shrub, 1-1/2 to 6' (up to 2m) tall, generally with toothed 5-parted serrated compound leaves with distinct stipules. See page 187. Leaves are frequently hairy beneath. The large, showy flowers, 2 to 3" (50 to 75cm) have 5 rounded (sometimes notched) pink, soft, velvet-like petals. Sepals are glandular. Twigs are very red in the winter and the leaves turn reddish in the fall.

Comments: Wood Rose, *Rosa woodsii*, is a smaller shrub found mostly in BC. It has 5 to 9 leaflets frequently under 1" (2.5cm) that are glabrous on both sides. Stems are frequently pinkish, have only a few prickles and the light pink flowers are usually under 1-1/2" (4cm). Sepals are slightly hairy. This is a very variable shrub. The "hips" are usually round.The petals of roses are used to make jelly or tea and the "hip" or fruit, which is orange to red, is used for jellies, jams, teas and in baked goods; and is very high in Vitamin C. Do not eat the seeds as they have 2 prongs that might lodge in your intestines and cause considerable irritation.

Prickly Rose
(North Pole, AK)

Rose Hips
(Taylor, BC)

PURPLE MOUNTAIN SAXIFRAGE, FRENCH KNOT PLANT

Saxifraga oppositifolia ssp. *oppositifolia*

Family: Saxifrage / Saxifragaceae

Habitat: Wet, gravelly slopes, ridges and rock crevices in the mountains from the Rocky Mountains northward.

Blooming Time: Very early May to early June

Description: A small, usually loosely matted plant with many trailing branches of tiny, dark green rosettes of leaves; Hence "French Knot Plant". Flowers are magenta to purple with 5 flaring petals with a very narrow base.

Purple Mountain Saxifrage
(Summit Lake, BC)

Low-bush Cranberry
(Tok, AK)

LOW-BUSH CRANBERRY, LINGONBERRY, MOUNTAIN CRANBERRY

Vaccinium vitis-idaea

Family: Heath / Ericaceae

Habitat: Acidic soil, hummocks in bogs, woods and alpine slopes to about 3500 foot elevation, throughout most of the area.

Blooming Time: June and early July

Description: A low evergreen shrub arising from creeping horizontal roots with 3 to 8" (8 to 20cm) upright branches with many shiny, oval, hard, evergreen leaves with rolled-over edges. The pink and white (color is very variable) small bell-shaped flowers are clustered at the end of the branches and produce tasty, firm, round, maroon berries that are used for jelly and baked goods. Usually ripe in early September, the flavor is best after a frost.

Comments: Bog Cranberry, *Oxycoccus microcarpus*, is a trailing, evergreen common in boggy areas. For confusing plants, see Kinnikinnick on opposite page.

Low-bush Cranberry
(Tok, AK)

Moss Campion
(Summit Lake, BC)

MOSS CAMPION

Silene acaulis

Family: Pink / Caryophyllaceae

Habitat: Dry, rocky alpine areas throughout the area.

Blooming Time: June and July

Description: A low "cushion" plant forming tight "moss-like" mats of narrow, short, flat leaves. They are covered with small 1/2" (13mm), light pink, very aromatic (like lilac), 5-petaled, salverform flowers which have very short stems.

KINNIKINNICK

Arctostaphylos uva-ursi

Family: Heath / Ericaceae

Habitat: Dry woods and dry, open, exposed sites throughout the area.

Blooming Time: May to mid-June

Description: A sprawling evergreen shrub, with a main tap root, forming large mats with rounded spatulate leaves that are smooth and leathery above, and rough and lighter colored beneath. Flowers are small, pinkish-white and urn-shaped. Berries are reddish-orange, dry, mealy, and not used for food. Their taste and texture is often compared to a mouthful of lint.

Comments: Sometimes confused with Lowbush Cranberry, *Vaccinium vitis-idaea*, see facing page.

Kinnikinnick
(Munson Slough, AK)

Kinnikinnick
(Munson Slough, AK)

LAPLAND ROSEBAY

Rhododendron lapponicum

Family: Heath / Ericaceae

Habitat: Subalpine woods, moist depressions, and alpine slopes in AK, YT and Rocky Mountains area of BC.

Blooming Time: Late May to mid-June

Description: An evergreen shrub, 6 to 18" (15 to 45cm) tall, with small, oval, hard, dark green leaves with rusty undersides (similar to Labrador Tea). Leaves appear to be arranged in whorls at the ends of the stems. The 5-petaled, 5/8" (1.5cm) open, funnel-shaped, magenta flowers bloom in dense clusters at the end of the branches.

Lapland Rosebay
(Summit Lake, BC)

Lapland Rosebay
(Summit Lake, BC)

Longleaf Mealy Primrose
(Gerstle River, AK)

MEALY PRIMROSE

Primula stricta

Family: Primrose / Primulaceae

Habitat: Moist places (usually saline soil) in YT.

Blooming Time: July

Description: A perennial plant with a small rosette of broad, light green leaves with a slightly wavy margin. Flower stems are leafless, 3 to 12" (7 to 30cm). Flowers are small, 1/4 to 3/8" (5 to 9mm), pinkish lavender, each one is on a short stem and clustered at the ends of the main stem. Stems are farinose (covered with a white powdery substance).

Comments: Similar species are: 1) Long-leaf Mealy Primrose,*P. incana*, found in YT and BC in similar areas, which is slightly taller, has smaller flowers and long pointed leaves with short stems. 2)Greenland Primrose, *P. egaliksensis,* found in similar areas has a loose rosette of very small leaves and very small lavender flowers (stems not farinose). 3) Bird's Eye Primrose, *P. mistassinica,* found usually in alpine meadows has petiolate, broad lanceolate, slightly toothed leaves and pink flowers 3/8 to 3/4" (1 to 2cm) with yellow centers.

Birdseye Primrose Lynn Catlin

Mealy Primrose
(Champagne, YT)

YELLOW-FLOWERED PLANTS

Sub-Alpine slope, Bear Creek Summit, BC
Coastal Paintbrush

Yellow Monkeyflower
(Liard Hot Springs, BC)

YELLOW MONKEYFLOWER, WILD SNAPDRAGON

Mimulus guttatus

Family: Figwort / Scrophulariaceae

Habitat: Edges of streams, lakes and wet rocky slopes throughout the area.

Blooming Time: July and August

Description: A sprawling plant with upright blooming branches that are 8 to 16" (20 to 40cm) tall. The stem leaves are round to oblong, toothed along the edges, dark green, and opposite. The light green calyx is inflated and holds a 5-petaled irregular-shaped tubed flower with flaring petals (much like a snapdragon). The petals are bright yellow with reddish spots in the throat. Flowers bloom a few at a time and are bright and showy.

Comments: The leaves are edible, both raw and cooked.

Butter and Eggs
(Tok, AK)

BUTTER AND EGGS, TOADFLAX

Linaria vulgaris

Family: Figwort / Scrophulariaceae

Habitat: Roadsides and waste places throughout the area.

Blooming Time: July and August

Description: An aggressive upright plant, 10 to 16" (25 to 40cm), with long narrow bluish-green leaves and spikes of many fairly small (snapdragon like) flowers that are light yellow and orange and have a very long narrow spur.

Comments: This plant is not native, but has become naturalized due to deep roots and extreme hardiness. Another introduced species, Dalmatian Toadflax, *Linaria dalmatica*, can be found in dry areas of southern BC. There are many bright yellow flowers on the stiff stem which can be up to 2' (60cm) tall. The light green, oval, pointed leaves are somewhat cupped, quite rigid and clasp the stems.

Dalmatian Toadflax
(Taylor, BC)

YELLOW PAINTBRUSH

Castilleja caudata

Family: Figwort / Scrophulariaceae

Habitat: Roadsides, fields and dry hillsides in AK and YT.

Blooming Time: July and August

Description: A medium 8 to 12" (20 to 30cm) plant with long, pointed, somewhat hairy leaves with 3 ribs. The flowers are minute and nearly hidden by the light yellowish bracts that cluster close to the ends of the stems. Stems are frequently reddish.

Comments: Paintbrushes are semi-parasitic plants that live off nutrients produced by other plants (probably nitrogen). Similar species are: 1)*Castilleja unalaskensis* that may be seen in alpine areas of YT is a taller plant, the stems are never reddish. See page 41. 2) *C. hyperborea* which is a shorter plant with divided leaves may also be seen around Bear Creek Summit in YT.

Yellow Paintbrush
(Tok, AK)

LABRADOR LOUSEWORT

Pedicularis labradorica

Family: Figwort / Scrophulariaceae

Habitat: Bogs, woodlands, tundra and low alpine slopes throughout most of the area.

Blooming Time: June and July

Description: A greatly branched plant 8 to 16" (20 to 40cm) tall. Leaves are narrow, pinnately divided and shallowly toothed. The irregular shaped flowers, which are borne singularly, are yellow (often tinged with orange or red). The whole plant is reddish early in the season. A very common plant and very distinct in seed.

Comments: Oeder's Lousewort, *Pedicularis oederi*, is an alpine plant with a stout stalk and a dense cluster of bright yellow flowers.

Labrador Lousewort
(Marsh Lake, YT)

Oeder's Lousewort
(Summit Lake, BC)

Rattlebox
(Buckinghorse River, BC)

RATTLEBOX

Rhinanthus minor

Family: Figwort / Scrophulariaceae

Habitat: Open fields and meadows throughout most of the area.

Blooming Time: July and August

Description: An annual plant 12 to 20" (30 to 50cm) tall, usually branched. Leaves are opposite, broad at the base, long and narrow with teeth along the edges. The flowers are small, inconspicuous, and protrude slightly from the calyx. The somewhat hairy calyx forms an urn-like structure that rattles when seeds within the ovary are mature. See below.

Comments: These plants may be semi-parasitic and gain some nutrients from the plants around them.

Dandelion sp.
(Tok, AK)

DANDELION

Taraxacum sp.

Family: Aster / Asteraceae

Habitat: Dry, open, sunny places throughout the area.

Blooming Time: June through August

Description: An introduced, deeply rooted perennial plant with a rosette of deeply toothed dark green leaves. The hollow stems contain a bitter milky juice.

Comments: The large tap root can be roasted and used as a coffee substitute. The leaves and flower buds are edible raw or cooked (bitter except when young). The flowers may be cooked or made into wine. The flowers are beautiful and impressive, but despised by most people as they spread rapidly and crowd out other plants. Native dandelions in the area are very small and are usually alpine plants; such as, *Taraxacum alaskanum*.

Taraxacum alaskanum
(Summit Lake, BC)

BLACK TWIN-BERRY, BRACTED HONEYSUCKLE

Lonicera involucrata

Family: Honeysuckle / Caprifoliaceae

Habitat: Moist woodlands along the lower section of the Highway.

Blooming Time: June to August

Description: A shrub, 3 to 6' (1 to 2m) tall, with large, up to 5" (12.5cm) opposite, lance-shaped leaves, the underside of which are coarsely veined. The small, tubular flowers are in pairs, dull yellow and sit on top of 2 green-ish yellow bracts. These bracts reflex backward towards the stem and turn red when the black berries appear in August or September.

Comments: Birds and animals seem to enjoy the disagreeable tasting berries.

Black Twin Berry
(Squanga Lake, BC)

Black Twin Berry (berries)
(Wonowon, BC)

TWINING HONEYSUCKLE

Lonicera dioica, var. glaucescens

Family: Honeysuckle / Caprifoliaceae

Habitat: Wooded areas in BC and YT.

Blooming Time: June and early July

Description: A shrub with long, vine-like branches, and opposite leaves. Leaves are broad at the base with a pointed tip. The clusters of trumpet-shaped, light yellowish flowers are cupped by the small leaves at the ends of the branches. Flower color changes to orange or red as the season progresses and they produce red berries in the fall.

Comments: These flowers fill the woods with their pleasant aroma.

Twining Honeysuckle
(Muncho Lake, BC)

Twining Honeysuckle
(Muncho Lake, BC)

Capitate Lousewort
(Summit Lake, BC)

CAPITATE LOUSEWORT

Pedicularis capitata

Family: Figwort / Scrophulariaceae

Habitat: Rocky alpine slopes and tundra throughout most of the area.

Blooming Time: June to early July

Description: A small, 3 to 5" (7.5 to 12.5cm), plant with flowering stalk often appearing to be separated from the individual pinnately-divided leaves that are toothed in outline. The few-flowered terminal cluster has large hooded flowers that are pale yellow, the top becoming pink and then rusty in age.

Silverberry
(Tanacross, AK)

Silverberry flower
(Fireside, BC)

SILVERBERRY, WOLF WILLOW

Elaeagnus commutata

Family: Oleaster / Elaeagnaceae

Habitat: Dry slopes and gravel bars along rivers—especially glacial——in AK, BC and YT.

Blooming Time: Late May to mid-June

Description: A shrub, 2 to 9' (up to 3m) with alternate, oblong, slightly pointed, silvery leaves. Both sides of the leaves are rough and scaly like sandpaper. The young twigs are brownish and scaly (older ones dark reddish-brown to black). The yellow, tubular, salviform flowers have 4 silvery sepals turned out flat exposing the yellow interior and 4 stamens. The small, fragrant flowers are in a tight cluster at the base of the leaves. They produce a dry, mealy, scaly, silver berry which is edible but quite tasteless.

Comments: Often confused with Willows which have only 1 bud scale and leaves that are smooth or hairy (not scaly), and flowers in a dense spike following a hairy catkin. The aromatic flowers smell somewhat like jasmine.

YELLOW SEDUM, COMMON STONECROP

Sedum lanceolatum

Family: Stonecrop / Crassulaceae

Habitat: Dry or rocky places from Haines Junction, YT south.

Blooming Time: June and July

Description: A succulent 3 to 5" (7.5 to 12.5cm) plant, singular or clustered, from shallow trailing root stock. The thick leaves are narrow, smooth and light green. A cluster of 4 or 5-petaled yellow star-like flowers top the 2 to 4" (5 to 10cm) fleshy stem.

Common Stonecrop
(Wolf Creek, YT)

SOAPBERRY, BUFFALO BERRY

Shepherdia canadensis

Family: Oleaster / Elaeagnaceae

Habitat: Dry, sandy, sunny areas or open woodlands throughout most of the area.

Blooming Time: May

Description: A deciduous shrub up to 3' (1m) tall, having distinctive, scurfy, brownish scales (like sandpaper) on young twigs, undersides of leaves and sepals. This causes the new buds in spring to look copper colored. The leaves, which start appearing with the early blooms, are ovate, green above and whitish beneath, with brown scales. Flowers are salverform, yellowish, very small, have 4 sepals and are sessile. They produce small, edible, oval, red, bitter, translucent berries in August. Male and female flowers are borne on separate bushes.

Comments: Indians used the sweetened, whipped berries as a dessert topping, and the berries are a favorite food of bears.

Soapberry flowers
(Champagne, YT)

Soapberry berries
(Champagne, YT)

Golden Saxifrage
(Summit Lake, BC)

Yellow-spotted Saxifrage
(Summit Lake, BC)

Spider Saxifrage
(Summit Lake, BC)

GOLDEN SAXIFRAGE, YELLOW MT. SAXIFRAGE

Saxifraga aiziodes

Family: Saxifrage/ Saxifragaceae

Habitat: Moist, gravelly or sandy areas from Steamboat, BC to just north of Whitehorse, YT.

Blooming Time: Late June to mid-August

Description: A low, up to 5" (12.5cm), shallow rooted, delicate plant with very small, narrow, almost succulent, light green leaves alternating up its stems. Each stem has a few short-stemmed, small, about 1/2" (1.25cm), yellow flowers with 5 narrow, pointed petals. The petals are usually orange-spotted.

Comments: Other yellow saxifrages that you might encounter are: 1) Bog Saxifrage, *Saxifraga hirculus*, a bog or wet tundra plant, tufted with small narrow leaves. The 3 to 6" (7 to 15cm) slightly hairy stems have one to three 1/2 to 3/4" (1 to 2cm) flowers with pointed petals. Sepals have hairs along their edges and reflex soon after the flowers open. 2) Yellow Spotted Saxifrage, *S. bronchialis* ssp. *funstoni*, which forms loose clumps in moist rocky places throughout most of the area. The small oval, pointed leaves are in sausage-like clusters and have hairs along the edges. The small flowers, although mostly cream colored, appear yellow due to the bright spots on them. They are in terminal clusters atop a 3 to 6" (7 to 15cm) stem with several small narrow leaves. See page 79 in White Section for a confusing species. 3) Spider Saxifrage, *S. flagellaris*, which might be seen on stony scree slopes such as at Summit Lake, BC. The leaves are in a dense rosette with indistinct jagged edges. The red runners are its most distinct feature.

Bog Saxifrage
(Tetlin Junction, AK)

MOUNTAIN BUTTERCUP, ESCHSCHOLTZ BUTTERCUP

Ranunculus eschscholtzii

Family: Buttercup / Ranunculaceae

Habitat: Alpine meadows along creeks in the BC and YT.

Blooming Time: Late May and June

Description: This is a very variable plant in regards to plant and flower size, and shape of leaves. Although not very tall, 3 to 6" (7.5 to 15cm), it is branched and has many flowers which have 5 shiny rounded petals and 5 yellowish sepals sometimes with yellow hairs. Stems and basal leaves are glabrous and come from a common rootstock.

Comments: Similar species are: 1) Snow Buttercup, *Ranunculus nivalis*, which usually has only a few flowers and leaves, and has black hairs on the sepals. It may be seen in alpine meadows in AK, northern BC, and YT. 2) Dwarf Buttercup, *R. pygmaeus*, is a very small variety that may also be seen in alpine meadows and snow beds right after the snow leaves. **ALL BUTTERCUPS ARE POISONOUS. DO NOT EAT.**

Mountain Buttercup
(Summit Lake, BC)

Dwarf Buttercup
(Summit Lake, BC)

SHORE BUTTERCUP, SPADE-LEAF BUTTERCUP

Ranunculus cymbalaria

Family: Buttercup / Ranunculaceae

Habitat: Damp places at low elevations. Usually saline soil throughout most of the area.

Blooming Time: June

Description: Leaves are on long stems and are rounded to spade-shaped with rounded teeth along the margins. They arise from a central caudex that produces runners that root at nodes. Flowers are yellow and usually have 5 small rounded petals and 5 glabrous sepals about the same length. Seed head is oval and pointed. Seeds have a short beak (hooked end).

Shore Buttercup
(Whitehorse, YT)

Cursed Crowfoot
(Bougie Creek, BC)

Macoun's Buttercup
(Near Watson Lake, YT)

Creeping Crowfoot
(Buckinghorse River, BC)

CURSED CROWFOOT

Ranunculus sceleratus

Family: Buttercup / Ranunculaceae

Habitat: Moist places throughout the area.

Blooming Time: July and August

Description: A weak annual plant, upright at first, later sprawling, 6 to 12" (15 to 30cm) tall. Leaves are light green, 3-parted and deeply divided. Flowers are very small and pale. Fruiting head is a very long oval. This plant contains a large quantity of protoanemonin which causes irritation if the leaves come in contact with your skin.

Comments: Other species are: 1) *Ranunculus abortivus*, a taller sprawling variety with notched, somewhat heart-shaped basal leaves and rounded fruiting head. 2) Macoun's Buttercup, *R. macounii*, a tall hairy variety with large, deeply toothed, 3-parted leaves. Sepals are reflexed. 3) *R. pedatifidus* is a tall, weak plant. The basal leaves are deeply lobed. Stem leaves divided into narrow linear segments. **ALL RANUNCULUS ARE POISONOUS!**

CREEPING CROWFOOT

Ranunculus gmelini

Family: Buttercup / Ranunculaceae

Habitat: Wet places at low elevations throughout most of the area.

Blooming Time: June to mid-July

Description: A low small-flowered creeping plant with deeply dissected 3 to 5-lobed leaves. It may be found growing in shallow water or mud around the edges of lakes or streams.

Comments: Dwarf Creeping Buttercup, *Ranunculus hyperboreus*, is similar but has 3 to 5-lobed leaves and is found around ponds and in wet meadows and tundra throughout the area. Seeds are in a tight oval pointed cluster and each seed has a curved hook at the end. Lapland Buttercup, *R. lapponicus*, may be found in bogs. See drawing below. This plant creeps on horizontal runners producing single long-stemmed leaves and very small flowers on long stems.

MARSH MARIGOLD, COW SLIP

Caltha palustris

Family: Buttercup / Ranunculaceae

Habitat: Marshes, streams, and margins of lakes in low to mid-elevations in AK and YT.

Blooming Time: Late May to mid-June

Description: A water plant with hollow stems. Leaves are large, 2 to 4" (5 to 10cm), round to somewhat kidney-shaped or heart-shaped and finely toothed on the edges. Flowers are large, 1 to 1-1/2" (2.5 to 3.5cm) and have 5 to 7 bright yellow slightly rounded sepals with a greenish cast to the underside.

Comments: This plant is an excellent vegetable when cooked. **It contains a poison when raw**. *Caltha natans* is a smaller variety that creeps along in muddy areas and might be seen in BC.

Marsh Marigold
(Burwash Landing, YT)

YELLOW ANEMONE, RICHARDSON'S ANEMONE

Anemone richardsonii

Family: Crowfoot / Ranunculaceae

Habitat: Moist woods near streams and alpine meadows throughout most of the area.

Blooming Time: Late May to mid-July

Description: A plant 4" to 7" (10 to 17.5cm) tall. The basal leaves have long stems, are yellowish-green, 3-parted, notched, and arise from horizontal roots. The flower stem arises from the center of a modified leaf. The flowers have 5 to 8 bright yellow, pointed sepals that are brownish on the underside.

Comments: Often mistaken for buttercups, but buttercups have both petals and sepals, the petals are rounded and the stem leaf is positioned to one side of the stem. **ALL ANEMONES ARE VERY POISONOUS PLANTS! DO NOT EAT!**

Yellow Anemone
(Liard Hot Springs, BC)

Hooker's Potentilla
(Wolf Creek, YT)

Norwegian Cinquefoil
(Tok, AK)

Mt. Meadow Cinquefoil
(Summit Lake, BC)

HOOKER'S POTENTILLA (CINQUEFOIL)

Potentilla hookeriana

Family: Rose / Rosaceae

Habitat: Dry, open or rocky slopes and roadsides in AK, northern BC, YT, and the Rocky Mountains.

Blooming Time: Late May to late June

Description: A small plant, 4 to 12" (20 to 25cm), with basal leaves that have 3 distinctly toothed leaflets, the end tooth being longer than the others. Leaflets are dark green, hairy above and densely hairy beneath. Petioles have long straight hairs. Stems are branched, leaves are reduced and modified. Flowers are small, 1/2 to 3/4" (1 to 2cm) and have 5 petals.

Comments: Many taller species of small-flowered potentillas are frequently found introduced along roadsides and growing naturally in some alpine areas. The following are some species that you might encounter: 1) Norwegian Cinquefoil, *Potentilla norvegica,* is commonly seen in fields in July and August. It is 12 to 18" (30 to 45cm) tall, the flowers are about 1/2" (1.25cm), and the leaves have 3 leaflets. 2) Mt. Meadow Cinquefoil, *P. diversifolia,* grows up to 18" (45cm) tall and may be seen in alpine meadows (seldom below treeline) throughout the area. Basal leaves are digitate, have 5 to 7 bluish-green leaflets that are wedge-shaped at their junction and toothed at the ends (sometimes hairy). The flowers are about 3/4" (2cm) in size. 3) *P. gracilis,* an introduced species found along roadsides, also has digitate leaves with 5 to 7 leaflets (toothed along entire margin) that are dark green, glossy, glabrous on the top sides and densely hairy beneath. 4) *P. pennsylvanica,* a tall mid-elevation plant having pinnate leaves with 7 to 15 toothed leaflets that are dark green above and densely hairy beneath.

Potentilla gracilis

Pennsylvania
Cinquefoil

ONE-FLOWERED CINQUEFOIL

Potentilla uniflora

Family: Rose / Rosaceae

Habitat: Rocky, exposed slopes and ridges throughout most of the area.

Blooming Time: Mid-May to mid-June

Description: A low, 4 to 8" (10 to 20cm), tufted plant from a stout, course stem with many old dried stipules. The coarsely toothed leaves, which are divided into 3 leaflets, are densely hairy beneath (like a blanket) and dark green with a few hairs on the upper surface. The bright yellow flowers, 3/4 to 1" (1.5 to 2.5cm), have 5 petals with an orange spot at the base, and a slight notch at the tip. Potentilla petals have a soft velvety look, not shiny like a buttercup.

Comments: *P. hyparctica* is a slightly smaller plant with slightly smaller flowers. The hairs on the underside of the leaves are longer and not as dense (more shaggy looking). *P. biflora* is an alpine plant with 5-parted leaves having very narrow segments.

One-flowered Cinquefoil
(Summit Lake, BC)

A narrow road (4-wheel drive only) just before Summit Lake leads to the top of the mountain behind the lakes.

Potentilla biflora
(Summit Lake, BC)

POTENTILLA MULTIFIDA

Potentilla multifida

Family: Rose / Rosaceae

Habitat: Dry, gravelly sunny slopes and river bars in AK and YT.

Blooming Time: June and July

Description: A perennial plant from a heavy taproot, with pinnately divided leaves having 5 to 7 narrow (nearly linear) divisions. The under side tomentose (wooly like a blanket). The calyx has long white hairs. Flowers are very small and on 5 to 10" (12 to 25cm) branched stems, frequently sprawling in a circle on the ground.

Comments: *Potentilla virgulata* is a similar taller, upright species found in open fields and clearings. The calyx has only a few hairs.

Potentilla multifida
(Whitehorse, YT)

Shrubby Cinquefoil
(North Pole, AK)

SHRUBBY CINQUEFOIL, TUNDRA ROSE

Potentilla fruticosa

Family: Rose / Rosaceae

Habitat: Bogs, tundra, and occasionally, alpine slopes throughout most of the area.

Blooming Time: Late June, July and August

Description: A shrub 1 to 3' (30 to 90cm) tall. The stems are reddish-brown and have shedding bark. The leaves are thick, bluish-gray green above and 5-parted. The flowers are large, 1 to 1-1/2" (2.5 to 3.5cm), and the petals rounded. A common shrub throughout most of the area.

Comments: Bracteoles (modified leaves below the calyx, see below) are persistent on potentillas and fold up over the seed pod, a distinct characteristic of these species.

Potentilla egedii
(Whitehorse, YT)

SILVERWEED

Potentilla egedii ssp. *yukonensis*

Family: Rose / Rosaceae

Habitat: Near rivers in northern BC and YT.

Blooming Time: June and July

Description: A plant with dark green, toothed, pinnately divided leaves that are densely hairy below. The solitary 5-petaled, bright yellow flowers are 3/4 to 1" (2 to 2.5cm) across. The runners are glabrous.

Comments: *Potentilla anserina* is a similar introduced plant found in waste areas and along roadsides. Runners and backside of leaves are very hairy. Entire plant has silvery appearance. Large dense patches appear very gray.

One man's weed is another man's flower.

Potentilla anserina
(Champagne, YT)

YELLOW DRYAS

Dryas drummondii

Family: Rose / Rosaceae

Habitat: Dry gravelly areas, river bars and flood plains throughout the area north of Ft. Nelson, BC.

Blooming Time: Late May into July

Description: A sprawling sub-shrub with coarse-looking oval basal leaves that sometimes have rolled edges. The leaf veins are very prominent and leaf edges wavy. They are greenish-brown above to whitish from hairs beneath. The 3 to 4" (7 to 10cm) high flower stem is leafless and often whitish looking. The calyx has blackish-brown hairs and the flowers are nodding and only partially open. The seed head is in a spiral (see page 85 for twisted seed head of similar species) opening fully to a tannish fluffy head. It may be seen in profusion in some areas. This plant is a pioneer of gravelly flood plains. The stems extend to 8" (20cm) or more when the plants go to seed (late July and August) and is especially noticeable at this time. This is a pioneer plant of flood plains where it frequently forms large round mats.

Yellow Dryas
(Jake's Corner, YT)

Yellow Dryas seed head
(Toad River, YT)

SIBBALDIA PROCUMBENS

Sibbaldia procumbens

Family: Rose / Rosaceae

Habitat: Fields, meadows and grasslands from lowlands to alpine throughout the area.

Blooming Time: July and August

Description: A low plant with 3 foliate leaves. The hairy, bluish-green leaflets are broad and 3-toothed at the ends tapering to the base. The coarse woody base is shaggy from old stipules. The 5 yellow petals are very small, the sepals being more noticeable. The flowers have only 5 stamens which is uncommon for this family, which usually has many.

Sibbaldia procumbens
(Summit Lake, BC)

Northern Oxytrope
(Tok, AK)

Maydell's Oxytrope
(Summit Lake, BC)

Pineapple Weed
(Fairbanks, AK)

NORTHERN OXYTROPE

Oxytropis campestris

Family: Pea / Fabaceae

Habitat: Dry stony and sandy slopes and roadsides from sea level to alpine throughout most of the area.

Blooming Time: Late May, June and July

Description: A low plant, 6 to 8" (15 to 20cm), with grayish-green, hairy, pinnately divided leaves with small oval pointed leaflets. The small, light yellow pea-shaped flowers are clustered at the ends of the branches. Old stipules at the base of the plant are light to medium tan in color.

Comments: See page 109 in White Secton for white variety. Maydell's Oxytrope, *Oxytropis maydelliana,* is a confusing alpine species that has reddish-brown old stipules. The yellow flowers are usually smaller and less numerous. Many oxytropes contain a toxin and are commonly called Loco-weed, as grazing cattle are strangely affected by it, causing an uneven gait. **DO NOT EAT OXYTROPES!** Many members of the Pea family are toxic due to the absorbtion of selenium from the soil. This is a variable condition depending on mineral content of the soil.

PINEAPPLE WEED

Matricaria matricarioides

Family: Aster / Asteraceae

Habitat: Waste places throughout the area.

Blooming Time: July and August

Description: A small, feathery, annual plant, 5 to 8" (12.5 to 20cm), with small yellowish heads that look and smell somewhat like pineapple.

Comments: This is an introduced plant that is commonly seen. The aromatic flower heads can be steeped to make a flavorful tea. They may be used fresh or dried. It is sometimes called Wild Camomile.

GOLDEN CORYDALIS

Corydalis aurea

Family: Earthsmoke / Fumariaceae

Habitat: Dry sandy banks, roadsides at low to mid elevations throughout the area.

Blooming Time: June to mid-July

Description: An annual or biennial greatly branched, low, 3 to 8" (7.5 to 20cm), gray-green sprawling plant with pale finely-divided leaves. Flowers are golden yellow, curved and clustered at the ends of branches, later extending as the long curved seed capsules develop.

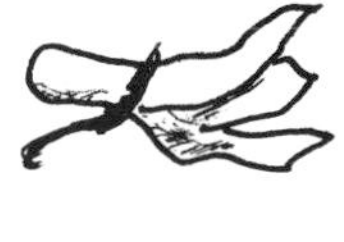

Golden Corydalis
(Toad River, YT)

LARGE LEAF AVENS

Geum macropyllum ssp. *macrophyllum*

Family: Rose / Rosaceae

Habitat: Meadows and woods throughout the area.

Blooming Time: Late June to mid-July

Description: A tall, erect plant, 1-1/2 to 2-1/2' (45 to 75cm), with large pinnately divided leaves. The leaflets are toothed, the terminal one lobed and much larger than the rest. Leaves and stems are covered with stiff hairs. The yellow flowers are small, about 3/8 to 1" (1 to2.5cm), the petals longer than the reflexed sepals. The seedhead looks much like a round bur.

Comments: Similar species are:
1) Ssp. *perincisum* which has a more deeply divided terminal leaflet. Petals are shorter than sepals. It is found throughout the area. 2) *G. aleppicum*, found in woods in southern BC, has leaves that are more pointed and having deeply dissected segments. Petals are longer than sepals.

Large Leaf Avens
(Bougie Creek, BC)

Geum allepicum
(Buckinghorse River)

Western Salsify
(Taylor, BC)

Western Salsify seed heads
(Taylor, BC)

Yellow Sweet Clover
(Watson Lake, YT)

WESTERN SALSIFY, GOATSBEARD, OYSTER PLANT

Tragopogon dubius

Family: Aster / Asteraceae

Habitat: Dry fields and roadsides along the lower section of the Highway.

Blooming Time: June and July

Description: A tall, 2 to 3' (up to 1M), erect plant with long grass-like, light bluish-green leaves. The stem has a milky white juice. The long triangular-shaped buds are deeply grooved and open into a light yellow dandelion-type flower, the bracts extending beyond the flowers. The seed heads are like very large dandelion heads.

Comments: This is an introduced plant.

YELLOW SWEET CLOVER

Melilotus officinalis

Family: Pea / Fabaceae

Habitat: Roadsides and waste places throughout the area.

Blooming Time: Late June to September.

Description: A branched, usually erect, plant up to 3' (1m) tall. Leaves are trifoliate with slightly notched edges. Flowers are many, and very small on a long curved stem.

Comments: It is very sweet smelling. A weed introduced through farming and roadside revegetation. White Sweet Clover, *Melilotus albus,* is frequently seen in the same areas. There are many introduced large yellow, erect, or sprawling members of the Pea Family seen along the roadsides; such as, Luzerne or Alfalfa, *Medicago falcata.* See page x for color variations.

HAWKSBEARD

Crepis capillaris

Family: Aster / Asteraceae

Habitat: Roadsides and waste areas throughout the area.

Blooming Time: June through August

Description: An introduced annual, 6 to 16" (16 to 40cm) with a rosette of dandelion-type leaves at the base, becoming linear up the branched rough stems. Basal leaves may be withered at flowering time. Flowers, much like a small dandelion, are 3/4 to 1" (2 to 2.5cm).

Comments: A similar, taller introduced species is *Crepis tectorum*, which grows up to 3' (1m) tall. Basal leaves are larger, broad, and may be slightly toothed -- soon withering. Stem leaves becoming narrow. Flowers are slightly larger than *C. capillaris*. Perennial Sow-thistle, *Sonchus arvense*, may also be seen. The basal leaves are often reddish. Buds and upper parts of stem are blackish with hairs.

Hawsbeard
(Pink Mt., BC)

ELEGANT HAWKSBEARD

Crepis elegans

Family: Aster / Asteraceae

Habitat: Sandy, gravelly places throughout the area.

Blooming Time: June and July

Description: A glabrous perennial plant, up to 8" (20cm) tall, with branched inflorescences of very small yellow, half-open dandelion-type flowers. The rosette of basal leaves is very distinct. Leaves are petiolate, acute and somewhat spade-shaped with shallow, broad indentations. Stem leaves are small, sessile and narrow.

Comments: Alpine Hawksbeard, *Crepis nana*, is a similar shorter species with a tight rosette of mostly oval leaves, frequently reddish. Flowers are individual and on short stems. Plant forms a tight cushion. *Hieracium gracile* is a similar appearing alpine meadow flower on a tall, up to 12" (30cm), slender hairy stem. The involucral bracts are densely covered with shaggy black hairs.

Elegant Hawksbeard
(Toad River, BC)

Alpine Hawksbeard
(Summit Lake, BC)

Common Groundsel
(Tok, AK)

BLACK-TIPPED GROUNDSEL

Senecio lugens

Family: Aster / Asteraceae

Habitat: Margins of bogs and fields, and in the tundra throughout most of the area.

Blooming Time: Late June to early August

Description: A plant from 12 to 24" (36 to 60cm) tall. Basal leaves are large, lance-shaped, have a pointed end and are shallowly toothed. Stem leaves becoming smaller and narrower. The bracts of the shaggy, daisy-type flowers are edged with black.

Comments: *Senecio pauciflorus* has more deeply toothed stem leaves and quite tight orange-colored flowers. Common Groundsel, *S. vulgaris* is an introduced species with very tight yellow flowers. Black-tipped bracts, rounded basal leaves and deeply toothed stem leaves. There are many short groundsels, up to 8" (20cm), usually with single flowers. Most grow in damp tundra, are quite wooly when young, and bloom very early; such as, *S. atropurpureus* and *S. fuscatus*, see page 166. *S. conterminus* is a branched, low-growing variety found in dry fields and open woodlands in AK, YT and the Rocky Mts. Dwarf Arctic Butterweed, *S. resedifolius,* is a small glabrous plant having reddish stems and seen in gravelly alpine slopes.

Dwarf Arctic Butterweed
(Summit Lake, BC)

Senecio conterminus
(Whitehorse, YT)

Black-tipped Groundsel
(Tetlin Junction, AK)

FEW-FLOWERED GROUNDSEL

Senecio pauperculus

Family: Aster / Asteraceae

Habitat: Moist places in BC and YT.

Blooming Time: July and August

Description: A perennial plant, 12 to 20" (30 to 50cm) tall. Basal leaves are smooth, spatulate, shallowly toothed, and have stems. Stem leaves are sessile, pinnately lobed and with a pointed tip. Ray flowers are short.

Comments: *Senecio cymbalarioides*, a similar plant, is 8 to 15" (20 to 37cm) tall, and has thick, toothed, oblanceolate basal leaves. The pinnately divided stem leaves are sessile and rounded. Triangular-leafed Fleabane, *S. triangularis*, is a taller, very leafy plant found growing near streams and in alpine meadows. The large leaves are coarsely toothed, broadly triangular and are topped by larger, shaggy flowers. Tall Groundsel, *S. jacobaea,* is a very tall plant up to 6' (2m) that is found in disturbed sites or fields and open woodlands. Stem leaves are numerous, pinnatifid and toothed. Senecios differ from most other yellow composites by having 2 or more distinct rows of involucral bracts; and, usually have narrow shaggy ray flowers. Leaves are alternate and may be simple, pinnate or deeply toothed.

Senecio cymbalarioides
(Wonowon, BC)

Few-flowered Groundsel
(Watson Lake, YT)

Tall Groundsel
(Wonowon, BC)

Decumbent Goldenrod
(Whitehorse, YT)

Northern Goldenrod
(Tok, AK)

DECUMBENT GOLDENROD

Solidago decumbens

Family: Aster / Asteraceae

Habitat: Dry fields, roadsides and open woodlands throughout most of the area.

Blooming Time: Mid-June, July and August

Description: A perennial plant, 10 to 16" (25 to 40cm) tall, with alternate leaves on a somewhat curved or decumbent stem which is frequently reddish. Basal leaves are oval to spatulate, rounded at the tip and shallowly toothed. Stems of basal leaves are usually smooth or with a few scattered hairs. Stem leaves are longer and taper to a blunt tip.

Comments: Confusing species are: 1) Northern or Rocky Mt. Goldenrod, *Solidago multiradiata,* of which there are 3 varieties common throughout the area. Hybridization of the 3 varieties causes much confusion. They differ from *S. decumbens* by having slightly pointed leaves, and the stems of basal leaves have hairs along the edges. Goldenrods differ from most other yellow composites by having many clusters of very small heads with very short ray flowers. Leaves are simple and may have shallow teeth.

Tufted Loosestrife
(Liard Hot Springs, BC)

TUFTED LOOSESTRIFE

Lysimachia thyrsiflora

Family: Primrose / Primulaceae

Habitat: Edges of lakes or marshes (in standing water) in scattered locations.

Blooming Time: July

Description: A 12 to 24" (30 to 60cm) tall plant with reddish heavy stems with many long narrow glabrous leaves. The small yellow flowers are in short racemes close to the main stem. Leaves may be alternate but middle and upper ones are opposite. Flowers are very variable-- 5 to 7 petalled on the same stalk. This plant, when not in bloom, could easily be mistaken for a willow herb. However, willow herbs grow in damp areas, and shallow water in streams. They are seldom found in deep standing water.

CANADA GOLDENROD

Solidago canadensis var. *salebrosa*

Family: Aster / Asteraceae

Habitat: Roadsides and fields throughout BC and scattered localities in northwestern YT and central AK.

Blooming Time: Late July and August

Description: Rigid upright stems, 3 to 6' (1 to 2m) tall, from horizontal rootstock. Leaves are numerous and they are up to 6" (15cm) long, broad at the base and tapering to a point. Lower leaves are much larger that the upper ones. Flowers are small and numerous in a broadly triangular raceme.

Canada Goldenrod
(Fireside, BC)

MARSH FLEABANE, MASTODON FLOWER

Senecio congestus

Family: Daisy, Aster or Composite/Asteraceae.

Habitat: Wetlands, marshes and lake margins in AK, YT, and some parts of BC.

Blooming Time: July to early August

Description: A tall, 2-1/2 to 5 feet (60 to 150cm), quite stout plant. Basal leaves are absent. Stem leaves are long and pointed, quite broad at the base, and have deeply cut teeth. Flower clusters are large, dense, wooly and light yellow.

Marsh Fleabane
(Tetlin Junction, AK)

Marsh Fleabane, Mastodon Flower
(Tetlin Junction, AK)

Frigid Arnica
Summit Lake, BC)

FRIGID ARNICA

Arnica frigida

Family: Aster / Asteraceae

Habitat: Gravelly and rocky hillsides and alpine ridges in AK, YT and the Rocky Mts.

Blooming Time: June

Description: An upright plant, up to 1' (30cm) tall, with a cluster of ovate leaves at its base. Leaves are oval and pointed at the tip and have a few teeth. One or two pairs of opposite leaves are on the hairy flowering stem. The bright yellow flowers are large, about 2" (5cm), nodding at first.

Comments: Arnicas are large yellow daisy-type flowers that track the sun to absorb more heat. Other confusing low species are: 1) Alpine Arnica, *Arnica alpina* ssp. *angustifolia*, whose leaves are longer and more pointed. It grows in gravelly areas at low elevations. 2) Lessing's Arnica, *A. lessingii*, has a few leaves at its base. Flowers are solitary, light lemon yellow in color and nodding. The 8 to 10" (20 to 30cm) stems are very hairy, as is the calyx. It may be found on alpine slopes in AK and YT.

Alpine Arnica
(Delta, AK)

Hairy Arnica
(Kluane Lake, YT)

Heart-leaf Arnica
(Charlie Lake, BC)

HORSEWEED

Conyza canadensis

Family: Aster / Asteraceae

Habitat: Waste places in BC.

Blooming Time: July and August

Description: An introduced weed, up to 16" (40cm) tall, very common along roadsides in some areas. Freely branched from a main stem with narrow glabrous leaves and small light yellowish-white fleabane-like flowers with short ray flowers.

Comments: Other introduced plants that might be seen near farm areas are Wild Lettuce, *Lactuca* sp., having sharp teeth. Flowers can be yellow or blue and look more like open Hawksbeard, see page 59.

Horseweed
(Fort St. John, BC)

TALL ARNICA

Arnica alpina ssp. *attenuata*

Family: Aster / Asteraceae

Habitat: Dry areas throughout the area.

Blooming Time: June

Description: A hairy, 15 to 24" (42 to 60cm) plant with 3 to 5 flowers and 3 to 5 pairs of opposite leaves. Flowers are large, 2 to 2-1/2" (5 to 6cm). Basal leaves have long stems.

Comments: There are many tall arnicas within the area. 1) Hairy Arnica, *Arnica alpina* ssp. *tormentosa,* is covered with soft white hairs. 2) Long-leaved Arnica, *A. lonchophylla,* is very similar having long-stemmed stem leaves. 3) Heart-leaf Arnica, *A. cordifolia*, see previous page, has ovate to heart-shaped long-stemmed basal leaves. Stems have 2 to 3 pairs of leaves, the upper ones mostly stemless. Flowers are large, bloom singularly on stems from the junction of leaves and main stem (1 to several per plant). 4) Meadow Arnica, *A. latifolia,* has 2 to 4 pairs of broad stemless leaves. Basal leaves usually wither early. Flowers are smaller than on the plants listed above and are usually singular. 5) Tall Meadow Arnica, *A. chamissonis* ssp. *chamissonis* has short-stemmed, toothed, broad, basal leaves that taper to a long point. Upper leaves are stemless.

Tall Arnica
(Tok, AK)

Long-leaved Arnica
(Toad River, YT)

Yellow Draba
(Liard Hot Springs, BC)

YELLOW DRABA

Draba aurea

Family: Mustard / Brassicaceae

Habitat: Dry, gravelly or rocky slopes throughout the area.

Blooming Time: Late May and June

Description: A very variable plant having from one to many stems arising from rosettes of long oblong, grayish, hairy basal leaves that are usually toothed. Lower leaves are often reddish, especially later in the season. The 6 to 12" (15 to 30cm) stems have many leaves that hug the stem. Flowers are very small and in dense clusters at the top of the stems, and from the axil of stem leaves. Seed pods have hairs and often are twisted.

WINTER CRESS

Barbarea orthoceros

Family: Mustard / Brassicaceae

Habitat: Moist places at low to mid-elevations throughout the area.

Blooming Time: Late June to mid-August

Description: A glabrous perennial plant up to 20" (50cm) with many dandelion-type leaves, the end lobe being ovate. Some of the basal leaves are also oval and pointed. Leaves are reddish very early in the season becoming dark green, then becoming reddish again late in the season or in exceedingly dry spells. Flowers are small and have 4 petals.

Comments: The leaves are tasty and were used as a food source by early settlers. There are many introduced mustards. Most are weedy, have somewhat lyrate leaves, clusters of small flowers and grow in dry disturbed ground.

Winter Cress
(North Pole, AK)

Winter Cress
(North Pole, AK)

YELLOW WALLFLOWER

Erysimum cheiranthoides ssp. *altum*

Family: Mustard / Brassicaceae

Habitat: Grassy slopes throughout most of the area.

Blooming Time: June and July

Description: A tall, up to 20" (50cm), biennial plant. Leaves are long, pointed and have slightly wavy edges. The 4-petalled flowers are small and in a cluster at the end of the stem. The stem elongates in age leaving behind scattered long seed capsules.

Comments: *Erysimum inconspicuum* is an early blooming, similar, much smaller variety. It grows up to 8" (20cm), usually has only 1 stem, and is widely scattered throughout the area.

Yellow Wallflower
(Champagne, YT)

CANOLA

Brassica sp.

Family: Mustard / Brassiciaceae

Habitat: Fields and roadsides in and near Dawson Creek, BC.

Blooming Time: Late June through August

Description: This colorful annual is a horticultural hybrid being grown extensively in the Dawson Creek area, see page 152. It is up to 2' (30cm) tall and has somewhat clasping smooth leaves. Lower leaves are lobed, the upper leaves broad at the base and tapering to a blunt point. Flower clusters are flat-topped. Flowers are up to 1/2" (1cm) across.

Comments: An oil extracted from this plant is marketed as a non-cholesterol cooking oil.

Canola
(Dawson Creek, BC)

Bladder Pod
(Summit Lake, BC)

BLADDER POD

Lesquella arctica

Family: Musard / Brassicaceae

Habitat: Very dry sandy bluffs in AK, the Rocky Mt. area of BC, and YT.

Blooming Time: May to early June

Description: A clumping type of plant, up to 6" (15cm) tall, having coarse looking, spatulate, silvery basal leaves with slightly rounded tips and short stems. Close inspection will reveal some stellate hairs on the leaves. This is an easily recognized plant due to leaf color and the long-stemmed round seed capsules with a protruding style.

Yellow Pond Lily
(Fireside, BC)

YELLOW POND LILY

Nuphar polysepalum

Family: Water Lily / Nymphaeaceae

Habitat: Ponds and slow streams throughout the area.

Blooming Time: July and August

Description: A large plant with small, thin, submerged leaves and large, long-stemmed floating leaves. The large 3 to 4" flowers have 7 to 9 sepals that are green on the underside, and are supported by large, fleshy stems. Petals are very narrow and small.

Comments: This plant has been used as a source of food by many native groups. The thick root, or rhizome, may be boiled and eaten. The root and seeds may be roasted, ground and used as a grain. The seeds may also be popped like popcorn, and served as a cereal or snack.

Bladderwort
(Liard Hot Springs)

BLADDERWORT

Utricularia intermedia

Family: Bladderwort / Lentibulariaceae

Habitat: Shallow marshes or slow-moving water scattered throughout most of the area.

Blooming Time: July and August

Description: A floating plant with very slender stems supporting one or two flowers about 3" (8cm) above the water. Leaves are many and narrow. Stems have inflated bladders that help support the plant and to trap insects.

YELLOW LADY'S SLIPPER

Cypripedium calceolus ssp. *parviflorum*

Family: Orchid / Orchidaceae

Habitat: Wet woodland and depressions in the mountains in BC.

Blooming Time: June

Description: 8 to 16" (20 to 44cm) plant with heavy stalks arising from a stout rootstock. 3 to 5 fairly large oval pointed leaves clasp the stem as they angle upwards. The veins and margins of the leaves are ciliate (have rows of hairs). They have 1 to 3 large flowers with 3 purplish-green sepals and 3 yellowish petals, the upper two twisted (spiralled), the lower one sac-like.

Comments: CAUTION--some varieties of lady slipper contain a toxin in their leaves that can cause an allergic reaction in humans. Many species are rare due to overcollecting, so please treat them with care. A similar orchid is the Spotted Lady Slipper, *Cypripedium guttatum*, 8 to 10" (20 to 25cm) which is cream colored with maroon or brownish flower blotches, and 2 large stem leaves near the base. This species is not common but might be encountered in the YT near the AK border or the Fairbanks area.

Yellow Lady's-Slipper (Brooks Range, AK) Gary Davies

THOROUGHWAX

Bupleurum triradiatum ssp. *arcticum*

Family: Parsley / Apiaceae

Habitat: Open stony ridges in AK, the Rocky Mt. areas of BC and YT.

Blooming Time: Late June to early August

Description: A perennial plant from 4 to 24" (10 to 60cm) with long stiff narrow leaves. Stem leaves are shorter and uppermost somewhat clasping. Flowers are sometimes blotched with purple and are in tight umbels arising from yellow bracts.

Comments: Could be mistaken for the lily family because of the long narrow, clasping leaves.

Thoroughwax (Tok, AK)

Arctic Poppy
(Dot Lake, AK)

ARCTIC POPPY

Papaver lapponicum

Family: Poppy / Papaveraceae

Habitat: Sandy or gravelly soil in AK and near YT border.

Blooming Time: Mid-June to early August

Description: Clumping type plants with hairy long-stemmed, pinnately-divided leaves. The cup-shaped yellow flowers have 4 yellow (rarely white) petals. They nod in bud and become upright - up to 10" (25cm) in full bloom. Stamens are many. The capsules are longer than broad, taper to the base and have 6 or 7 stigmatic rays.

Comments: Other poppies that may be seen in the same area are: 1) Macoun's Poppy, *Papaver macounii.* Its seed capsule is broadest at the mid-point and has 4 or 5 stigmatic rays. 2) Alaska Poppy, *Papaver alaskanum,* which has many old dead leaf stalks. The seed capsule is shorter than broad. 3) Iceland Poppy, *Papaver nudicauli,* which is a taller, non-hairy, introduced species may be seen along roadsides. Color may be yellow, orange, white or pinkish coral. See page x.

Heart-leaved Alexanders
(Dawson Creek, BC)

HEART-LEAVED ALEXANDERS

Zizia aptera

Family: Parsley / Apiaceae

Habitat: Open woods and meadows at low elevations along the lower section of the Highway.

Blooming Time: Late June and July

Description: A perennial plant up to 24" (60cm) tall with branched stems. Basal leaves have stems and are heart-shaped. Stem leaves are divided into narrower (usually 3) segments. The small, bright yellow flowers are in somewhat flat umbels.

Be sure to pick up your "I drove the Alaska Highway" certificate.

WHITE AND CREAM FLOWERED PLANTS

Open Meadow, Turnagain Pass, AK
Cotton Grass

Tall Cotton Grass
(Teslin Lake, YT)

TALL COTTON GRASS

Eriophorum angustifolium

Family: Sedge / Cyperaceae

Habitat: Wet, peaty soil, margins of lakes, shallow water and roadside ditches throughout the area.

Blooming Time: June and July

Description: A stiff, erect plant, 12 to 18" (30 to 45cm) tall with narrow grass-like leaves. The flower stalks have 3 to 5 seed heads on long drooping stems.

Comments: There are many species of Cotton Grass. Most have one seed head and are found in wet meadows, roadside ditches and lakeshores. Other common species throughout the area are: 1) White Cotton Grass, *Eriophorum scheuchzeri*, which grows in slender tufts with one black sheath from horizontal roots. Scales at the base of the glistening white bristles are grayish-black. 2) Alaska Cotton Grass, *E. brachyantherum*, is similar but with two grayish-brown sheaths and yellowish-white bristles with dark scales. 3) Tufted White Cotton Grass, *E. callitrix*, grows in dense tufts and has white bristles. Scales are dark but have a translucent margin. 4) Tufted Cotton Grass, *E. vaginatum* ssp. *vaginatum*, grows in dense mounds and sheaths are light reddish-brown. Bristles are grayish-white, often in a tighter rounded head, and scales are gray. See also pages 71 and 189.

Tufted White Cotton Grass
(Tok, AK)

Tufted Cotton Grass
(Tetlin Junction, AK)

WILD CALLA

Calla palustris

Family: Arum / Araceae

Habitat: Margins of lakes and ponds in AK, southern BC and northern YT.

Blooming Time: July and August

Description: A thick stemmed plant with elongated, thick, shiny, heart-shaped leaves arising from a thick creeping rhizome. The tiny greenish flowers surround a short, thick stem arising from a white spathe (modified leaf). They are followed by light red berries.

Comments: **The whole plant is poisonous, especially the berries.** They contain saponin-like substances and poisonous acids. Although the poisons are neutralized by boiling or drying, it is **not** recommended that they be eaten. An unmistakable plant. Although the actual flowers are not white, it was included in this section because the white spathe looks like a petal.

Wild Calla
(Kenai, AK)

White Water Crowfoot
(Buckinghorse River, BC)

WHITE WATER CROWFOOT

Ranunculus aquatilis

Family: Buttercup / Ranunculaceae

Habitat: Shallow ponds or slow moving water throughout most of the area.

Blooming Time: July

Description: Floating stems with dark green floating 3-lobed leaves. The middle section has 3 teeth, the two side sections divided again, each section having 2 to 3 teeth. Submerged leaves are very finely dissected. Flowers are 1/2 to 3/4" (1.25 to 2cm) and held well above the water.

Comments: Other species are: 1) *Ranunculus confervoides* which does not have any floating leaves. 2) *R. trichophyllus* which is similar to *R. aquatilis* but has smaller flowers that are close to the water.

Ranunculus confervoides
(Tok, AK)

Coltsfoot
(Pink Mt., BC)

COLTSFOOT

Petasites palmatus

Family: Aster / Asteraceae

Habitat: Moist woods and meadows throughout BC and southern YT.

Blooming Time: Late May thru mid-June

Description: A distinctive plant with very large, green, glabrous, palmately divided, slightly wavy edged leaves. The underside of the leaves are covered with soft white hairs. The whitish flowers, which bloom early in the season (often before the leaves appear), are in a wide rounded cluster.

Comments: The mixture from soaked roots of coltsfoot has been used for the treatment of insect bites. Other Coltsfoot species are: 1) Arrowleaf Coltsfoot, *Petasites sagittatus*, having large triangular, wavy edged leaves. The top side is dark green and slightly hairy, the underside densely hairy. Flowers are in a small cluster, atop a 12 to 18" (30 to 45cm) stem. They usually bloom in June over most of the area. 2) Frigid Coltsfoot, *Petasites frigidus*, has large leaves shaped like a horse's hoof with slight indentations, glabrous above, densely hairy beneath. Flowers are pinkish on a 4 to 12" (10 to 30cm) stem and usually bloom before the leaves appear. Blooms late May and early June in AK and YT. 3) Northern Coltsfoot, *P. hyperboreus*, has large broadly triangular leaves, deeply indented, glabrous above and densely hairy beneath. Flowers are white, atop a 6 to 15" (15 to 38cm) stem, usually flowering before the leaves. Found in AK and YT.

Arrowleaf Coltsfoot
(Fairbanks, AK)

Frigid Coltsfoot
(Tok, AK)

Northern Coltsfoot
(Tok, AK)

PUSSY TOES

Antennaria sp.

Family: Aster or Daisy / Asteraceae

Habitat: Dry, open woodlands and rocky areas in AK, northern BC and YT.

Blooming Time: June

Description: A low, mat-forming plant with silvery appearance. Leaves are in rosettes, small, hairy, wide at the base tapering to a point. These plants produce stolons (horizontal stems) that rest on the ground and produce new rosettes. Flowers are on a 4 to 6" (10 to 15cm) silky, hairy stem and consist of several button-like flower heads. Stems of the side heads are longer than stems of the central head. Involucral bracts are whitish.

Comments: Easily recognized by its low mat of silvery rosettes. There are many species which are separated by minor characteristics: 1) *Antennaria media* is similar except stems of heads are about equal. 2) *A. neglecta* has short stolons. Bracts have brownish tips and upper surface of leaves lack hairs. 3) Cat's Paw, *A. monocephala*, is an alpine species having greener, less hairy leaves and white flower heads. 4) Tall Pussy Toes, *A. pulcherrima*, which is scattered throughout the area, may be up to 18" (45cm) tall. It has long narrow grayish-green leaves. Two varieties may be seen, one has hairy leaves and the other is glabrous.

Pussy Toes
(Munson Slough, AK)

Antennaria neglecta Sally Karabelnikoff
(Summit Lake, BC)

Tall Pussy Toes
(Kluane Lake, YT)

Cat's Paw
(Summit Lake, BC)

Long-leaf Fleabane
(Northway Jct., AK)

Northern Yarrow
(Tok, AK)

Siberian Yarrow
(Fairbanks, AK)

LONG-LEAF FLEABANE

Erigeron lonchophyllus

Family: Aster / Asteraceae

Habitat: Bogs and wet meadows throughout most of the area

Blooming Time: July and early August

Description: A slender slightly hairy plant 3 to 10" (7.5 to 30cm) tall with very long narrow, alternate leaves. Basal leaves are few and slightly wider. Flowers are small and inconspicuous.

Comments: *E. elatus* is a very similar plant with broader leaves on the flowering stems.

NORTHERN YARROW

Achillea borealis

Family: Aster / Asteraceae

Habitat: Roadsides, fields, dry open woods and alpine meadows and low alpine slopes throughout most of the area.

Blooming Time: July through August

Description: A very common, weedy sturdy perennial plant up to 24" (60cm) tall with fine, ferny 2 to 3 times pinnately dissected leaves which are variable in length and width. Somewhat reduced in size as they progress up the stem. They have an easily recognized flat-topped cluster of small, white flowers. The flat-topped brown seed heads are used for flower-arranging. The involucral bracts are rounded and have a dark margin.

Comments: Very common along highways. The aromatic leaves are used as a pot herb and to make a soothing, pleasing tea. *Achillea lanulosa* is similar having bracts with light brown to yellowish margins and very short white ray flowers. Common Yarrow, *A. millefolium*, is an introduced weed that is common in BC. The leaves are similar to Northern Yarrow, *A. borealis*. Flower may be white or pink. Siberian Yarrow, *A. sibirica,* has long, narrow leaves with deep serrations and is found more in AK and YT. This genus was named for Achilles, the Greek warrior, whose injured heal was treated with this plant.

Siberian Yarrow

Northern Yarrow

CUT-LEAF FLEABANE

Erigeron compositus var. *glabratus*

Family: Aster / Asteraceae

Habitat: Dry or rocky soils at all elevations. Common from Whitehorse, YT to Port Alcan.

Blooming Time: Late May thru June

Description: A small plant arising from a thick rootstock with many finely cut small leaves that are covered with fine hairs. The white to pinkish flowers are on a 3 to 8" (7 to 20cm) somewhat hairy stem. Flowers have narrow rays and are 3/4 to 1" (2 to 2.5cm) wide. They are often very pink in bud, but usually white when in bloom.

Cut-leaf Fleabane
(Whitehorse, YT)

CUSHION FLEABANE

Erigeron eriocephalus

Family: Aster / Asteraceae

Habitat: Dry, gravelly areas in AK and YT.

Blooming Time: June and July

Description: An attractive, very low growing hairy plant with small spatulate leaves. Flowers are 1/2 to 3/4" (1 to 2cm). Ray flowers are narrow and mostly white. The involucral bracts are purplish with white hairs.

Comments: Hybridization with Mountain Fleabane, *Erigeron humilis,* (usually an alpine plant with one flower per stem) occurs causing purplish hairs. *Erigeron purpuratus*, another similar plant of rocky areas and riverbanks, also has purplish hairs on the involucrum but also has purple pappus (hairs on seeds). Mt. Erigeron, *E. humilus* and *E. eriocephalus* have white hairs. These are difficult species to distinguish from one another without the use of a microscope.

Cushion Fleabane
(Roadside north of Tok, AK)

The common name of Fleabane was derived from former usage of plants of this genus. Bane means poison -- hence, poison for fleas.

Mountain Fleabane
(Summit Lake, BC)

Entire leaf Chrysanthemum
(Summit Lake, BC)

ENTIRE LEAF CHRYSANTHEMUM, NARROW LEAF CHRYSANTHEMUM

Chrysanthemum integrifolium

Family: Aster / Asteraceae

Habitat: Gravelly or rocky alpine slopes in BC.

Blooming Time: July

Description: A small plant, up to 4" (10cm) tall with rosettes of small narrow dark green glabrous leaves. The white daisy-type flowers are 1 to 1-1/4" (2.5 to 3cm) and have long, wide ray flowers.

RUSH ASTER

Aster junciformis

Family: Aster /Asteraceae

Habitat: Wet meadows and bogs

Blooming Time: July and August

Description: A stiff, slightly hairy perennial, 12 to 20" (30 to 50cm) tall, with long, narrow, dark green leaves that are rough feeling along their edges. Involucral bracts are not hairy, are long, pointed and often purple tipped.

Comments: Another tall white daisy-type flower seen at Liard Hot Springs and scattered southern locations is Philadelphia Fleabane, *Erigeron philadelphicus*. Leaves are broad at the base and sometimes toothed. Leaves sometimes clasp the stem. Heads have narrow ray flowers and can be pink or white. See pages 21 and 168 for pink variety.

Philadelphia Fleabane (Liard Hot Springs, BC) Sally Karabelnikoff

Rush Aster
(Liard Hot Springs, BC)

PRICKLY SAXIFRAGE

Saxifraga tricuspidata

Family: Saxifrage / Saxifragaceae

Habitat: Dry, rocky, open sub-alpine and alpine slopes throughout most of the area.

Blooming Time: Late May to mid-June

Description: A low, loosely-matted, evergreen plant with rosettes of small, wedge-shaped, thick, somewhat fleshy leaves having 3 sharply pointed prongs on the ends. During dry seasons, they become very sharp and prickly. During the winter and in early spring, the leaves are very red. The lower part of the stems contain many dried up old leaves. The flower stem, 4 to 6" (10 to 15cm), is quite stout, light in color and has a few small modified leaves. The stems are topped with a cluster of small flowers with protruding ovaries. Each flower has 5 lavender spotted, sharply-pointed, cream-colored petals.

Comments: Sometimes confused with Yellow Spotted Saxifrage, see page 48 in Yellow Section.

Prickly Saxifrage
(Jake's Corner, YT)

MAYWEED

Anthemis cotula

Family: Aster / Asteraceae

Habitat: Waste areas and roadsides throughout the area.

Blooming Time: July thru September

Description: A branched annual with finely dissected, glabrous leaves. A strong scented introduced plant. The white ray flowers frequently reflex in age.

A weed is just a flower out of place.

Mayweed
(Prophet River, BC)

Wild Rhubarb
(North Pole, AK)

WILD RHUBARB

Polygonum alaskanum

Family: Buckwheat / Polygonaceae

Habitat: Roadsides and open woods in AK and YT.

Blooming Time: July and early August

Description: A tall, 2 to 5' (up to 1.5m), perennial with a thick root and a somewhat woody, branched stem. The leaves are smooth, broad at the base and taper to a long point, medium green above and lighter beneath. The tiny flowers are yellowish-white and in a dense branched panicle.

Comments: Young stems and leaves may be eaten, raw or cooked. **Leaves** of common **garden rhubarb** are poisonous due to a higher content of oxalic acid.

Baneberry
(Anchorage, AK)

BANEBERRY, SNAKEBERRY

Actaea rubra

Family: Crowfoot / Ranunculaceae

Habitat: Woodlands throughout most of the area.

Blooming Time: Late May to early June

Description: Erect, perennial plant, 18 to 30" (45 to 75cm), with fairly large compound, 3 to 5-parted, toothed leaves. All leaves have long stems that grow from the main flower stalk. The delicate white flowers are small and in rounded clusters. The red or white, long stemmed clusters of berries are high above the leaves and ripen from mid-July through August. The berries are opaque, have an indentation or crease down one side (like a peach) and a black dot at the end.

Comments: CAUTION—HIGHLY POISONOUS. The ingestion of as few as 6 berries has been known to cause death of a small child.

Baneberry berries
(Charlie Lake, BC)

Baneberry flowers
(Anchorage, AK)

WATER HOREHOUND, NORTHERN BUGLEWEED

Lycopus lucidus ssp. *americanus*

Family: Mint / Lamiaceae

Habitat: Moist areas near springs, streams and lakes.

Blooming Time: July and August

Description: Stiff, upright, square-stemmed plant, 1 to 2' (30 to 60cm) tall. The faintly aromatic leaves are opposite and deeply serrated. The small pinkish-white flowers are in small clusters positioned close to the main stems.

Water Horehound
(Liard Hot Springs, BC)

GRASS OF PARNASSUS, BOG STAR

Parnassia palustris

Family: Saxifrage / Saxifragaceae

Habitat: Wet meadows, roadside ditches and lake margins throughout most of the area.

Blooming Time: July and August

Description: A perennial plant growing in a small clump with small, nearly heart-shaped, yellowish-green leaves at the base. Flower stems are long, 5 to 15" (12 to 37cm), with one smaller modified leaf and one, 3/4 to 1" (up to 2.5cm), 5-petaled flower per stem. The petals are pointed and conspicuously veined. The center and seed capsule are prominently pointed.

Comments: This late blooming flower is not easily confused with any other. Small Grass of Parnassus, *Parnassia kotzebuei*, found in wet alpine areas, is much smaller with small petaled flowers. Fringed Grass of Parnassus, *P. fimbriata,* is a late-blooming alpine variety, 6 to 12" (15 to 30cm) tall, with fine white hair-like fringe on the petals. It has an abundance of long-stemmed kidney-shaped leaves and is found in BC and southern YT.

Grass of Parnassus
(Swift River, YT)

Fringed Grass of Parnassus
(Summit Lake, BC)

Small Grass of Parnassus
(Bear Creek Summit, YT)

Alpine Meadow Bistort
(Summit Lake, BC)

ALPINE MEADOW BISTORT

Polygonum viviparum

Family: Buckwheat / Polygonaceae

Habitat: Dry meadows, heaths and tundra throughout most of the area.

Blooming Time: June and July

Description: A variable plant, 5 to 8" (12 to 20cm), with long, narrow entire leaves arising from a thick, hard rhizome. The top surface of the leaves are dark green and glabrous, the undersides are grayish. The tiny 5-petalled flowers are white to pinkish and are rapidly replaced by bulblets sprouting leaves and roots before they fall from the adult plant.

Comments: The boiled roots are a good starch food source and the leaves and bulblets may be eaten raw or cooked.

Northern Bedstraw
(Prophet River, BC)

NORTHERN BEDSTRAW

Galium boreale

Family: Madder / Rubiaceae

Habitat: Woodlands, fields and meadows throughout most of the area.

Blooming Time: July to early August

Description: An erect, branched perennial, 12 to 20" (30 to 50cm) tall, having square stems with intervals of 4 leaves in whorls around stem. The leaves are long and pointed with 3 linear veins that appear parallel. Flowers are numerous, very small and have 4 white petals.

Comments: The plant was used in early times as mattress stuffing because it is sweet scented and its square stems did not crush easily. There are several bedstraws in the area. The rest are weak, trailing woodland plants with inconspicuous flowers and broader leaves. Sweet-scented Bedstraw, *G. triflorum,* is a common weak stemmed, woodland variety usually having 3 flowers per stem section and 6 leaves in each whorl. Found in BC and southern YT. Small Bedstraw, *G. trifidium,* is a very weak species having 4 small leaves in a whorl and very small flowers. Found in moist places throughout the area.

Sweet-scented Bedstraw
(Wonowon, BC)

DEATH CAMAS, CAMAS WAND LILY

Zygadenus elegans

Family: Lily / Liliaceae

Habitat: Open woods and meadows throughout the area.

Blooming Time: Late June to early August

Description: A bulbous perennial plant, 12 to 18" (30 to 45cm) tall, with narrow,strap-like, slightly bluish-green leaves that appear folded down the center line. The flowers are well spaced on an open raceme on a long stem and are greenish-yellow to cream-colored. Each flower has 6 tepals (3 petals & 3 sepals that look alike). There is a bract or reduced leaf at the base of each flower stem.

Comments: **EXTREME CAUTION! Highly toxic poison** which causes vomiting, lowered temperatures and breathing difficulties.

Death Camas
(Summit Lake, BC)

NODDING ONION

Allium cernuum

Family: Lily / Liliaceae

Habitat: Dry rocky or gravelly areas along the lower section of the Highway.

Blooming Time: June and July

Description: This slender plant grows up to 8" (20cm) tall from a small onion-like bulb. It has 2 to 5 linear leaves that are channelled at first then flattened toward the tip and are shorter than the flower stalk. The pinkish lavender flowers are in a loose nodding head above 2 light pink bracts. The stem is erect in seed.

Comments: This was a favored food of the indigenous people. **Do not confuse with Death Camas which also has a bulb, but no onion odor.**

Nodding Onion
(Taylor, BC)

Sticky False Asphodel
(Marsh Lake, YT)

STICKY FALSE ASPHODEL

Tofieldia glutinosa

Family: Lily / Liliaceae

Habitat: Bogs and lake margins in BC.

Blooming Time: June and early July

Description: Leaves stiff, linear at least half as long as the glandular flowering stem, up to 10" (25cm), with 1 bract. Flowers are very small, cream-colored and in a spike. Seed heads are red.

Comments: *Tofieldia pussila* is a similar, shorter, up to 5" (12cm), alpine species with short flat (Iris-like) leaves. False Asphodel, *T. coccinea* is a small alpine species having 2 or 3 bracts on the flower stem and pinkish anthers.

ROUGH-FRUITED FAIRY BELL

Disporum trachycarpum

Family: Lily / Liliaceae

Habitat: Woodlands in southern BC.

Blooming Time: Late May and June

Description: A leafy plant, 1 to 2' (30 to 60cm) tall, with drooping arched branches. The edges of the broadly oval pointed leaves appear crinkled. The flowers have narrow whitish petals and look like bells in bud, but open wide at maturity. The edible round fruit is orange-red when mature and is covered with bumps.

False Asphodel
(Summit Lake, BC)

Rough-fruited Fairy Bell
(Charlie Lake, BC)

SITKA BURNET

Sanguisorba stipulata

Family: Rose / Rosaceae

Habitat: Bogs and meadows throughout most of the area.

Blooming Time: July and August

Description: A perennial plant having a flowering stem 1 to 2' (30 to 60cm) tall with a few small leaves. The long stemmed basal leaves consist of many glabrous, toothed oval pointed leaflets. It has a spike of many tiny flowers with 5 greenish-white sepals, no petals and many long stamens.

Comments: The maroon colored Burnet, *Sanguisorba officianalis,* which might be seen in wet areas at low elevations in AK has very short stamens. See page 125 in Misc. Section.

Sitka Burnet
(North Pole, AK)

MOUNTAIN AVENS

Dryas octopetala

Family: Rose / Rosaceae

Habitat: Alpine slopes and tundra in AK and YT.

Blooming Time: June

Description: A mat-forming shrub with coarse, oblong leaves with the edges wavy and slightly rolled under. The top side dark green and coarse-looking and the underside lighter. The flowers are large, over 1" (2.5cm), and usually have 6 to 10 petals, the stamens are bright yellow. When the flowers go to seed, they have a characteristic twist (see photo) and then progress into a tan seed head much like a dandelion. See Yellow Dryas on page 55 for similar seed head.

Comments: Entire Leaf Avens, *Dryas integrifolia*, is a very similar species found in throughout the area. It has leaves with smooth edges. Hybridization between the two species is common where their ranges overlap.

Mountain Avens

Entire Leaf Avens

Mountain Avens
(Anchorage, AK)

Mountain Avens seed capsule
(Anchorage,AK)

False Solomon's Seal
(Taylor, BC)

FALSE SOLOMON'S SEAL

Smilacina stellata

Family: Lily / Liliaceae

Habitat: Meadows and sub-alpine slopes throughout the area.

Blooming Time: Late May to late June

Description: A perennial plant, 6 to 24" (15 to 60cm) tall, growing from horizontal rhizomes. Leaves are alternate, long, broad at the base tapering to a point and have parallel veins. They are rigid and usually angle upwards on the stiff upright stem. Flowers are in a short raceme at the ends of the stems, and have 6 pointed, white tepals. Fruit is 3-parted, dark red with 3 large seeds.

Comments: **Poisonous.** Take care not to confuse with the spring shoots of Watermelon Berry (see next page). False Solomon's seal is bitter and has no black hairs on stem. A similar species *Smilacina racemosa* has flowers on an open branched raceme and is found in southern BC. *S. trifolia* which is found in bogs has 2 to 4 large elliptical leaves at its base and a few scattered flowers.

False Solomon's Seal fruit
(Taylor, BC)

New Shoots

Smilacina recemosa
(Squanga Lake, YT)

WATERMELON BERRY, TWISTED STALK, WILD CUCUMBER

Streptopus amplexifolius

Family: Lily / Liliaceae

Habitat: Moist woods and meadows throughout BC and southern YT.

Blooming Time: Mid-June to late July

Description: A tall, 1-1/2 to 4' (up to 1m), branched, perennial plant with many smooth, rather thin, alternate leaves on the crooked (somewhat zigzag) stem. Leaves clasp the stems, have parallel veins, are oval to lance-shaped and have an acute tip. In the spring, the young shoots (see above) can be eaten raw and taste like cucumber. The lower stems are covered with fine, dark hairs. The flowers are on a twisted stem and are attached to the under side of the leaf at its base. The flowers have 6 white to cream-colored tepals that are reflexed. In August, they produce a red, oval berry with many seeds.

Comments: The sweet, juicy berries are used for jellies and syrups. The new shoots, younger leaves and flower buds are tasty additions to salads. The zigzag stem, twisted flower stalk, and characteristic hairs on the lower stems help to differentiate it from the toxic False Solomon's Seal (see preceding page).

FALSE LILY OF THE VALLEY

Maianthemum dilatatum

Family: Lily / Liliaceae

Habitat: Moist woods in southern BC and at hot springs.

Blooming Time: June and July

Description: Plant with a creeping rhizome sending up 8 to 10" (20 to 30cm) stems with 2 large long-stemmed leaves. They are shiny, palmately veined, heart-shaped and have a long tapering point. The tiny flowers are not characteristic for the family, having only 2 sepals, 2 petals (that are reflexed), 4 stamens and a 2-parted ovary. The raceme of flowers produces brownish berries that eventually turn red.

Comments: POISONOUS! This plant contains glycosides that affect the heart.

Watermelon Berry
(Squanga Lake, YT)

Watermelon Berry
(Squanga Lake, YT)

Wild Lily of the Valley
(Charlie Lake, BC)
Sally Karabelnikoff

Northern White Lady's Slipper (Muncho Lake, BC)

NORTHERN WHITE LADY'S SLIPPER, SPARROW'S EGG LADY SLIPPER, FRANKLIN'S LADY SLIPPER

Cypripedium passerinum

Family: Orchid / Orchidaceae

Habitat: Woods and bogs throughout the area.

Blooming Time: Early June to mid-July

Description: A perennial plant, from a creeping rootstalk, that has one flower per stem. The stems are 10 to 16" (25 to 44cm) tall and have 2 to 4 slightly sticky, hairy leaves. The sepals are greenish, the petals white, the lower forming a pouch and having purplish spots inside. See cover photos.

RATTLESNAKE PLANTAIN

Goodyera repens

Family: Orchid / Orchidaceae

Habitat: Moist mossy woodlands throughout the area.

Blooming Time: July and early August

Description: A perennial plant with a rosette of variegated leaves. The dark green veins are bordered with pale tissue that lacks chlorophyll. The alternate leaves are 1/2 to 3/4" (up to 2cm) and slightly hairy on the top side. The tiny creamy-white tubular flowers bloom down one side of the 4 to 8" (10 to 20cm) stem.

Comments: *Goodyera oblongifolia* has longer and broader leaves that are medium green with a lighter green stripe down the mid-vein. Flowers are small and greenish-white. It may be seen in southern BC.

Rattlesnake Plantain (Iron Creek, BC) Flower close-up

Goodyera oblongifolia

ENCHANTER'S NIGHTSHADE

Circaea alpina

Family: Evening Primrose / Onagraceae

Habitat: Woods in BC and the Fairbanks area of AK.

Blooming Time: July

Description: A glabrous plant up to 6" (15cm) tall with thin, somewhat heart-shaped leaves that are shallowly toothed. Flowers are pinkish-white, very small, and have 2 sepals and 2 notched petals.

Enchanter's Nightshade
(Liard Hot Springs, BC)

HOODED LADIES' TRESSES

Spiranthes romanzofiana

Family: Orchid / Orchidaceae

Habitat: Margins of lakes and in wet meadows throughout the area.

Blooming Time: Late June and July

Description: An 8 to 12" (20 to 30cm) plant with a few basal leaves and a few reduced stem leaves. The small, somewhat tubular, white flowers are arranged in vertical rows that spiral around the heavy light green stalk.

Comments: Bog Candle, *Platanthera dilatata*, is a 10 to 18" (25 to 45cm) orchid of similar habitats with more open, very aromatic flowers on a heavy stalk of many flowers.

Hooded Ladies' Tresses
(Marsh Lake, YT)

Bog Candle
(Teslin Lake, YT)

Narcissus-flowered Anemone
(Haines Junction, YT)

NARCISSUS-FLOWERED ANEMONE

Anemone narcissiflora

Family: Buttercup / Ranunculaceae

Habitat: Alpine meadows and slopes, and slightly subalpine open woodlands in AK and YT.

Blooming Time: June through mid-August

Description: A somewhat hairy, clumping perennial plant, 8 to 14" (20 to 35cm) tall having deeply dissected, 3 to 5-lobed, hairy leaves on long stems arising from the base of plants. The showy, 1 to 2" (2.5 to 5cm) flowers are on stems above the leaves and are variable. They have 4 to 10 white, somewhat acute sepals usually with a slight bluish cast on the underside. The modified leaf on the stem below the flowers completely surrounds the stem; a characteristic of Anemones.

Comments: Few-flowered Anemone, or Windflower, *Anemone parviflora,* has more rounded glabrous leaves, blooms very early and almost always has 5 rounded, white sepals that are quite bluish on the underside. It blooms soon after the snow leaves and is found in moist woodlands, alpine meadows and snow flushes. A large-flowered, over 1" (2.5cm), variety, Ssp. *grandiflora*, is common in AK. Cut-leaf Anemone, *Anemone multifida*, has more finely and deeply cut, hairy leaves and smaller flowers, 3/4 to 1" (up to 2.5cm), that are creamy inside and rosy or lavender underneath. Flowers are occasionally bright pink or yellow inside and out. It grows in dry fields, open woods and hillsides. See pages viii and 35 for color variations.

Cut-leaf Anemone
(Champagne, YT)

Windflower
(Muncho Lake, BC)

ALDER LEAF SERVICEBERRY, JUNEBERRY

Amelanchier alnifolia

Family: Rose / Rosaceae

Habitat: Woods, rocky areas and sub-alpine slopes throughout most of the area.

Blooming Time: Late May to mid June

Description: A shrub up to 12' (4m) tall, shorter in exposed, dry sites. Leaves are 1-1/2 to 2-1/2" (3.75 to 6.25cm) broad and oval with teeth around the slightly pointed tip and having a distinct crease along the center. Flowers have 5 narrow petals in terminal racemes. The sweet edible berries, which look a bit like a small apple, are dark purplish-blue when ripe and have a pronounced "blossom end". The seeds are large and triangular which limits their use. The berries may be dried like raisins, and made into jellies or pies. They taste like a sweet blueberry with almond flavoring. They ripen in early September and remain on the shrub until dry.

Comments: Occasionally confused with Blueberries or Huckleberries, which usually have small untoothed leaves and are lacking the pronounced "blossom end" to the berry. See page 29.

Serviceberry
(Taylor, BC)

Serviceberry
(Taylor, BC)

RASPBERRY

Rubus idaeus

Family: Rose / Rosaceae

Habitat: Fields and borders of woods throughout the area.

Blooming Time: Mid-June to early August

Description: A biennial plant producing berries on the 2 year old, prickly canes that die after bearing fruit. The coarse-looking 3 to 5 foliate leaves have serrated edges, are sharply pointed, and are whitish beneath. The fruit is red and has an excellent flavor.

Raspberry flower

Raspberry
(Contact Creek, BC)

Cloudberry
(Tetlin Junction, AK)

CLOUDBERRY, BAKED APPLEBERRY, SALMONBERRY

Rubus chamemorous

Family: Rose / Rosaceae

Habitat: Bogs and tundra throughout the area.

Blooming Time: Late May and June

Description: A low, herbaceous plant having coarse veined, long stemmed, leaves with 5 lobes and 1" (2.5cm) flowers with 5 (sometimes 4) rounded white petals (much like an apple blossom). The tasty, orange, raspberry-like berries, which ripen in mid-July to early August, are usually not found in abundance, and are often deformed. They look much like a cluster of salmon eggs and taste a bit like a baked apple. The plants are unisexual, having male and female flowers on separate plants.

Cloudberry berries
(North Pole, AK)

WILD STRAWBERRY

Fragaria virginiana

Family: Rose / Rosaceae

Habitat: Dry fields and roadsides throughout much of the area.

Blooming Time: June through early August

Description: A low herbaceous plant with reddish runners producing new plants. The 3-foliate, sharply toothed leaves have long stems. The plants produce small, tasty red fruit in August and September - a delight to the traveler.

Wild Strawberry fruit
(Summit Lake, BC)

Wild Strawberry
(Jake's Corner, YT)

STAR FLOWER

Trientalis europea ssp. *arctica*

Family: Primrose / Primulaceae

Habitat: Woodlands and low alpine slopes throughout most of the area.

Blooming Time: June to early July

Description: A low perennial with reddish runners. The oval pointed (often reddish) leaves are in a whorl around the stem. The flowers usually have 7 pointed white (sometimes pinkish) petals and the seed is a small silvery ball.

Comments: An easily recognized plant. Another sub-species, *europaea*, has fewer leaves that are narrower and more pointed.

Starflower
(Bear Creek Summit, YT)

RED BEARBERRY

Arctostaphylos rubra

Family: Heath / Ericaceae

Habitat: Tundra, bogs and moist subalpine slopes throughout the area.

Blooming Time: Mid May to early June

Description: A very low, up to 4" (20cm), deciduous, branched shrub forming large mats with spatulate-shaped leaves. Flowers are creamy-white, urn-shaped and bloom as the leaves are opening; occasionally before. The red, juicy, shiny berries are edible, but not widely used.

Comment: Alpine Bearberry, *Arctostaphylos alpina*, has coarse leaves, hairs along the margins and grows in the mountains above treeline, and on the tundra in AK and parts of YT. It has creamy-white flowers, black berries and red leaves in the fall.

Red Bearberry
(Marsh Lake, YT)

Red Bearberry
(Marsh Lake, YT)

Alpine Bearberry
(Summit Lake, BC)

Ripe Alpine Bearberry

Large-flowered Wintergreen
(Gardiner Creek, AK)

LARGE-FLOWERED WINTERGREEN

Pyrola grandiflora

Family: Wintergreen / Pyrolaceae

Habitat: Woodlands and dry places on the tundra, and in the mountains throughout most of the area.

Blooming Time: June and early July

Description: An evergreen plant of rich humus soil. The long-stemmed, large, basal leaves are round to kidney-shaped, thick and glossy. The 5-petalled white flowers are 1/2 to 3/4" (up to 2cm), have pinkish veins, and are clustered at the top of 5 to 10" (12.5 to 25cm) tall thick pinkish stems. Typical of pyrolas, they have a pronounced style that curves at maturity. The seed capsule is round and has 5 sections with a protruding style (see below).

Dwarf Dogwood
(Charlie Creek, BC)

Dwarf Dogwood berries
(Summit Lake, BC)

DWARF DOGWOOD, BUNCHBERRY, CANADIAN DWARF CORNEL

Cornus canadensis

Family: Dogwood / Cornaceae

Habitat: Woods, tundra, and low alpine slopes throughout the area.

Blooming Time: Woodlands-June, Alpine-July

Description: A low herbaceous shrub. Stems are 4 to 8" (10 to 20cm) tall, with one small pair of leaves near the base and a whorl of leaves at the top having prominent arched veins. The flowers are in a cluster set off by 4 white, unequal, pointed bracts, each flower having 4 greenish sepals. A bunch of soft orange or reddish berries are seen in August and September. Leaves turn red or orange in the fall. See page 180.

Edibility: Questionable, but not dangerous. The Pilgrims made a pudding out of the berries, but some people complained of stomach upsets after eating large quantities. Recipes are still seen occasionally in wild berry books.

SINGLE DELIGHT, SHY MAIDEN

Moneses uniflora

Family: Wintergreen / Pyrolaceae

Habitat: Moist woods throughout most of the area.

Blooming Time: June and July

Description: A small plant with a rosette of small, light green, roundish leaves about 1/2" (1.25cm) with shallow teeth. The flower is on a leafless stem 2-1/2 to 4" (6 to 10cm) high and has 5 pointed, waxy petals. It has a protruding ovary and faces downward. The capsule is round with protruding stigma (see below).

Comments: A distinctive plant frequently found with other pyrolas—very fragrant.

Single Delight
(Squanga Lake, YT)

Take time to enjoy
The fresh open air.
Bend down and discover
Perfumed flowers there.

V.E.P.

WESTERN CANADA VIOLET

Viola canadensis

Family: Violet / Violaceae

Habitat: Moist woods along the lower section of the Highway and at Liard Hot Springs.

Blooming Time: May and June to mid-July

Description: Plant up to 12" (30cm) with long stemmed, very large, heart- shaped basal leaves. Smaller heart-shaped leaves extending upwards, flowering at the ends. Flowers are white with lavender tint, purple veins and a yellow center.

Comments: White Wood Violet, *Viola renifolia*, has very small flowers that are white with lavender spots. Leaves are round to kidney-shaped when fully developed and wavy along the edges. Might be seen in BC or southern YT. Blooms in May or early June.

Western Canada Violet Sally Karabelnikoff
(Charlie Lake, BC)

White Wood Violet
(Liard Hot Springs, BC)

Trailing Red Blackberry
(Wonowon, BC)

TRAILING (RED) BLACKBERRY

Rubus pubescens

Family: Rose / Rosaceae

Habitat: Open, moist woods along the lower section of the Highway and at Liard Hot Springs, BC.

Blooming Time: June

Description: A trailing, thornless plant having leaves with 3 toothed leaflets. Plants up to 1 foot (30cm) tall. Leaves approximately 3" (7.5cm) across. The white flowers have 5 petals and produce tasty dark red berries in August.

Mountain Ash berries are a favored food of Bohemian Waxwings as they migrate through these areas.

Greene Mt. Ash
(Destruction Bay, YT)

GREENE MOUNTAIN ASH

Sorbus scopulina

Family: Rose / Rosaceae

Habitat: Woods and sub-alpine areas throughout most of the area.

Blooming Time: June

Description: A shrubby tree up to 12' (4m) tall with reddish bark. Winter buds are sticky looking. The leaves are arranged alternately on the stems and are pinnately divided into 11 to 13 notched pointed leaflets, which are glabrous above and sparsely hairy beneath. The small flowers are 5-petaled and in rounded, rather flat clusters at the ends of branches. Large, round, reddish-orange shiny berries are obvious in the fall and are a favorite food of the Bohemian Waxwings.

Comments: The berries of Mt. Ash can be used as food, but are bitter until frozen and thawed a few times. This happens naturally on the tree. They may be stewed and sweetened for a tasty winter fruit.

Greene Mt. Ash
(Hatcher Pass. AK)

BIRCH-LEAFED SPIRAEA

Spiraea betulifolia

Family: Rose / Rosaceae

Habitat: Moist woods and meadows in BC.

Blooming Time: Late June through early August

Description: A glabrous shrub, 1 to 3' (up to 1m) tall, with rather broad, flat, spreading clusters of tiny white flowers. Leaves are mostly broad, oval, pointed, coarsely toothed with obvious veins and short petioles. The mildly aromatic flowers are followed by brown seed heads that may remain on the shrub for 1 or more years.

Comments: Alaska Spiraea, *Spiraea beauverdiana*, is common in AK and upper YT, and grows in bogs, woodlands and alpine areas. Height 1 to 1-1/2' (30 to 45cm). Branches are thin with shedding bark. Leaves are broadly oval and toothed near the ends. Flower clusters are smaller and tighter than Birch-leafed Spiraea.

Birch leafed Spiraea
(Charlie Lake, BC)

Alaska Spiraea
(Northway, AK)

Birch-leafed Spiraea

Alaska Spiraea

CHOKE CHERRY

Prunus virginiana

Family: Rose / Rosaceae

Habitat: Open woods and hillsides in southern BC.

Blooming Time: Late May and June

Description: A small, up to 10' (3m), shrubby tree with oval, pointed leaves that are shallowly toothed and shiny on the top surface. Flowers are 5-petalled, small and white. Fruit is red to purplish when ripe.

Choke Cherry
(Taylor, BC)

Northern Jasmine
(Champagne, YT)

NORTHERN JASMINE

Androsace septentrionalis

Family: Primrose / Primulaceae

Habitat: Dry, rocky places throughout the area.

Blooming Time: May and June

Description: A small plant consisting of a rosette of small, lanceolate, slightly toothed leaves that frequently turn reddish when the plant is in seed. The tiny 5-petaled flowers are in an umbel atop the 3 to 8" (7 to 20cm) stems.

Comments: *Androsace chamejasme* is a shorter, larger flowered, member of this genus that is found in AK and YT, The runners lie on the ground and produce tight hairy rosettes of leaves. The hairy 2 to 4" (5 to 10cm) stems have an umbel of three to several 1/4" (6 to 8mm) white flowers with bright yellow centers.

Northern Jasmine
(Champagne, YT)

SNOW BERRY

Symphoricarpus albus

Family: Honeysuckle / Caprifoliaceae

Habitat: Lower section of the Highway.

Blooming Time: June and July

Description: A shrub 3 to 6' (up to 2m) tall with opposite branches. Leaves are entire, broad, oval and pointed, and have a few hairs on the underside. The pink to white flowers are bell-shaped. Fruit is a soft white berry.

Comments: POISONOUS! DO NOT EAT!

Snow Berry
(Charlie Lake, BC)

Snow Berry berries
(Charlie Lake, BC)

HIGH-BUSH CRANBERRY

Viburnum edule

Family: Honeysuckle / Caprifoliaceae

Habitat: Woods and alpine areas up to at least 2500 feet, throughout the area.

Blooming Time: June to early July

Description: Usually an upright shrub up to 8' (2.5m) tall with smooth branches. Leaves are opposite on the stems, varied in shape, and have very coarse veins. Upper leaves are elliptical, the lower 3-lobed much like a maple leaf. All are toothed and turn red to maroon in the fall. The small 5-petaled, white to pinkish flowers are tubular, flare out at the end and are in clusters above the leaves. The soft, translucent, red berries ripen in August and have an unusual musky odor. Leaf buds are very red in the winter and spring.

Comments: The sour berry with a long flat seed makes good jelly, syrup and catsup. Berries are frequently confused with red currants. Berries of the currants hang down in chains, leaves are all maple-leaf shape and are alternate on the stems. See page 138 in Miscellaneous Section.

High Bush Cranberry
(Anchorage, AK)

High Bush Cranberry berries
(Muncho Lake, BC)

PALE COMANDRA, BASTARD TOADFLAX

Commandra umbellata ssp. *pallida*

Family: Sandlewood / Santalaceae

Habitat: Dry sandy grasslands along the southern portion of the Highway.

Blooming Time: Late June and July

Description: A perennial, 4 to 12" (10 to 30cm) tall, with numerous small, about 1" (2.5cm), narrow bluish-green alternate leaves. The small greenish-white flowers are in a flat-topped cluster and they produce an olive green fruit. This is probably a root parasite plant.

Pale Comandra
(Taylor, BC)

Field Chickweed
(Summit Lake, BC)

FIELD CHICKWEED, MOUSE EAR CHICKWEED

Cerastrium arvense

Family: Pink / Caryophyllaceae

Habitat: Dry, rocky hillsides.

Blooming Time: June and July

Description: A low, mat-forming, 5 to 8" (12 to 20cm) plant with opposite, narrow, hairy, silvery leaves. Flowers are 3/4" (2cm) across and have 5 rounded and notched white petals that are 2 to 3 times longer than the sepals. This plant has obvious sterile side shoots (non-flowering branches) at the junction of the leaves and main stem.

Comments: A similar species, Bering Sea Chickweed, *Cerastrium beeringianum* var. *beeringianum*, does not have sterile side shoots, is less leafy and its petals are only twice as long as sepals.

Bering Sea Chickweed
(Tok, AK)

TALL SANDWORT

Arenaria Capillaris

Family: Pink / Caryophyllaceae

Habitat: Dry, rocky places at mid-elevations in AK and YT.

Blooming Time: Late June and July

Description: A clump plant up to 6" (15cm) tall with long narrow grass-like leaves, usually bluish-green. It has two to three 5-petalled 5/8" (1.5cm) flowers per stem, with anthers frequently reddish.

Comments: A similar looking flower is Arctic Sandwort, *Minuartia arctica,* a cushion type alpine plant with very narrow, short leaves and covered with short-stemmed flowers.

Tall Sandwort
(Whitehorse, YT)

Arctic Sandwort
(Kluane, YT)

LONG STALK STARWORT, STELLARIA

Stellaria longipes

Family: Pink / Caryophyllaceae

Habitat: Fields and rocky places from low elevations up into the alpine throughout the area.

Blooming Time: June to early August

Description: A plant with underground rhizomes producing many stiff silvery leaves. The small flowers have 5 small, narrow petals that are divided and look like 10 petals. They have prominent reddish anthers.

Comments: There are many Stellarias in the area. Some are weak sprawling plants of wet places; such as, Northern Starwort, *Stellaria calycantha*, with light green glabrous leaves and small flowers. *Stellaria longifolia* grows in wet stoney places and also has broader glabrous leaves.

Long Stalk Starwort
(Steamboat, BC)

GROVE SANDWORT

Moehringia lateriflora

Family: Pink / Caryophyllaceae

Habitat: Very common in woodlands and alpine slopes throughout most of the area.

Blooming Time: Late May and June

Description: A small, rather delicate, upright plant, 4 to 7" (10 to 17cm) tall with small, opposite, oval leaves. The small flowers have 5 white petals.

Comments: This plant is easily mistaken for a Chickweed (*Stellaria*) which has 5 petals, each split, appearing to be 10, see below.

Grove Sandwort
(Tok, AK)

Stellaria longifolia
(Northway, AK)

Draba hirta
(Rocky Mountains, BC)

DRABA HIRTA

Draba hirta

Family: Mustard / Brassicaceae

Habitat: Dry, stony places throughout the area.

Blooming Time: June to early July

Description: Basal leaves in a rosette. Oblong with coarse teeth and stellate or branched hairs. Flowers on an elongated stem up to 8" (20cm). Flower stems (which are mostly glabrous) are about as long as the seed capsules.

Comments: There are many small white Drabas from 2 to 8" (5 to 20cm) tall in the area. Most have a rosette of hairy, oblong to oblanceolate leaves. They grow in dry, gravelly or rocky areas and bloom early. *Draba longipes* is one of the many small varieties. It differs in having hairy flower stems that are longer than the seed capsules.

SHEPHERD'S PURSE

Capsella bursa-pastoris

Family: Mustard / Brassicaceae

Habitat: Waste areas throughout the area.

Blooming Time: July and early August

Description: An introduced weed having a rosette of toothed (dandelion-type) leaves. Stem leaves vary from toothed to entire. Flowers have 4 petals and are very small, blooming from the bottom up on the 10 to 16" (4 to 7cm) stem. Fruits are somewhat heart-shaped and on a stem.

Comments: There are many introduced mustard plants. Most have round seed capsules. One similar plant with toothed stem leaves is Pepper Grass, *Lepidium* sp.

Pepper Grass

Shepherd's Purse
(Whitehorse, YT)

LYRE-LEAF ROCKCRESS

Arabis lyrata

Family: Mustard / Brassicaceae

Habitat: Dry, open woodlands at low to mid-elevations throughout most of the area.
Blooming Time: Late May thru June

Description: A low plant, 6 to 9" (15 to 22.5cm) tall with a long taproot (typical of mustard family). Lower basal leaves are lyrate similar to a dandelion. Upper and stem leaves are entire in margin. The small white flowers have 4 petals and 6 stamens.

Comments: Edible leaves. Several species of *Arabis* are found growing in dry places throughout the area. Most have a rosette of hairy leaves and small white to pinkish flowers on stems far above the rosette. Holboell's Rockcress, *Arabis holboelli,* is very common on dry slopes. It has lavender to white, bell-shaped flowers on a 6 to 24" tall stem arising from a rosette of hairy leaves. Stem leaves are narrow and angle upwards. The long narrow seed capsules droop downward. Drummond's Rockress, *A. drummondii,* has broad siliques that angle upward. Hairy Rockcress, *A. divaricarpa* has seed capsules that spread out at different angles. *A. hirsuta* has broader, toothed leaves and seed capsules that angle upwards.

Arabis hirsuta
(Tok, AK)

Lyre-leaf Rockcress
(Tok, AK)

Hairy Rockcress
(Tok, AK)

Bell Heather
(Summit Lake, BC)

BELL HEATHER, LAPLAND CASSIOPE

Cassiope tetragona ssp. *tetragona*

Family: Heath / Ericaceae

Habitat: Mountain slopes (frequently the north side) throughout the area.

Blooming Time: June and July

Description: A matted dwarf evergreen shrub, 6 to 10" (15 to 25cm) tall with small thick leaves in 4 rows stacked on top of each other (in columns). A distinctive plant. Branches look much like a Phillips screwdriver. Leaves are grooved on the back. The campanulate flowers which are composed of 5 joined, slightly flared, white petals hanging downward on curved stems.

Comments: Heather has an overpowering aroma; pleasant at a distance. Ssp. *saximontana* is a similar variety found throughout the area. It has very short flower stems. *C. mertensiana* is a matted dwarf shrub seen on mountain slopes. It has narrower stems and leaves and smaller flowers that are white to pinkish and have reddish sepals. Leaves are <u>not</u> grooved on the back.

Buckbean
(Watson Lake, YT)

BUCKBEAN, BOGBEAN

Menyanthes trifoliata

Family: Buckbean / Menyanthaceae

Habitat: Swamps, bogs and margins of lakes throughout the area.

Blooming Time: Late May and June

Description: Glabrous plant arising from a creeping rootstock. The dark green leaves have 3 ovate leaflets. The fragrant flowers are in a raceme at the top of a 6 to 12" (15 to 30cm) flower stem. They have 5 fringed white petals (that are occasionally pink tinged).

Buckbean
(Watson Lake, YT)

LABRADOR TEA

Ledum palustre ssp. *groenlandicum*

Family: Heath / Ericaceae

Habitat: Heaths, bogs, woods and alpine slopes throughout the area.

Blooming Time: June

Description: Low to medium height evergreen shrub, 10 to 30" (25 to 75cm), with a rusty pubescence on young twigs and under side of leaves. Leaves are green, long, oblong with edges rolled under. Leaves are brownish and leathery in the winter. The small flowers have 5 flaring petals and usually 10 stamens.

Comments: Distinctive plant because of rusty hairs on stems and aromatic odor. Narrow-leaf Labrador Tea, *Ledum palustre* ssp. *decumbens* is somewhat smaller, has very narrow leaves, sometimes pinkish flowers, and is found in bogs and alpine heaths in AK and YT. The ledum genus contains "ledol", a poison causing cramps and acting as a diuretic. A tasty tea is made of the leaves, but should be taken sparingly at first, until the system adjusts to its effects. Leatherleaf, *Chamaedaphne calyculata,* is a shrub with a similar appearance, having rusty scales on its leaves. The white urn-shaped flowers hang under the branches and bloom in May. The leaves are elongated, oval and evergreen. They are brown and leathery in the winter and spring, greenish in the Summer. It is common in AK and parts of YT.

Labrador Tea
(Tetlin Jct., AK)

Leatherleaf
(Anchorage, AK)

MENZIESI'S CAMPION

Silene menziesii ssp.*williamsii*

Family: pink / Caryophyllaceae

Habitat: Gravelly, well drained areas in AK and YT.

Blooming Time: Late June to early August

Description: A weak stemmed, low, greatly branched light yellowish-green plant. The narrow leaves are opposite and sharply pointed. The small White Flowers are at the ends of the branches and emerge from a swollen calyx.

Comments: A similar variety is ssp. *menziesii* which has broader leaves and grows in damper areas in BC and YT.

Menziesi's Campion
(Salcha Bluffs, AK)

Water Hemlock
(Liard Hot Springs, BC)

WATER HEMLOCK

Cicuta douglasii

Family: Parsley / Apiaceae

Habitat: Marshes and edges of lakes in BC.

Blooming Time: July and August

Description: Plant with 2-1/2 to 4' (75 to 120cm) tall hollow stems. Leaves are compound, divided into 3 to 5 broad, pointed, toothed leaflets. The veins of leaflets end in notches, while in most other members of this family they end at points. Leaf stems have a clasping base. Flowers are small, have 5 white petals and are arranged in double umbels.

Comments: The roots contain Cicutotoxin and are **VERY POISONOUS**! This is the plant that was used to kill Socrates. The roots have hollow transverse chambers (see photo) unlike other genera in this family. This plant is sometimes confused with Angelica or Wild Celery, which is edible, see next page. *C. mackenzieana* is a similar plant with very narrow leaflets that might be seen in AK or the upper YT.

Water HemlockRoot

WHITE CLOVER

Trifolium repens

Family: Pea / Fabaceae

Habitat: Roadsides and waste areas throughout the area.

Blooming Time: June through August

Description: A low, creeping plant with 3-parted leaves. The white to pinkish flowers are in rounded heads. An aromatic plant introduced through farming and roadside revegetation.

White Clover

COW PARSNIP

Heracleum lanatum

Family: Parsley / Apiaceae

Habitat: Moist fields, woodlands, and alpine meadows throughout most of the area.

Blooming Time: July to mid-August

Description: A tall, 5 to 8' (up to 2.5m), plant with large hollow stems and very large, somewhat palmate, leaves that are deeply divided into threes with deep extra incisions. Leaf stems connect to the main stalk with a clasping sheath. The leaves and stems have conspicuous hairs. The small flowers have 5 petals, are frequently covered with flying insects and are in large, up to 8" (20cm), double umbels. The seed heads are used for flower-arranging. The seeds are flat and are divided into 2 sections.

Cow Parsnip
(Liard Hot Springs, BC)

Comments: Very distinctive plant because of plant and flower head size. The hairs on the leaves and stems are very irritating to some people's skin causing itching and rash. It may cause the skin to become overly sensitive to the sun (photo-sensitivity) causing severe sunburn with blisters which are very slow to heal. The peeled raw stems and the cooked roots are eaten by some people, and are said to be tasty. Wild Celery, *Angelica lucida*, is a closely related plant which might be seen near streams or lakes in AK. It is a stout plant, 18 to 36" (up to 1m) tall. Leaves have inflated, almost translucent, stems where they clasp the main stem. They are trifoliate, divided into 3 to several toothed leaflets. This is a strongly flavored but edible plant with greenish-white flowers in rounded double umbels up to 5" (12cm) across.

Cow Parsnip being pollinated by flies
(Anchorage, AK)

Wild Celery
(Delta, AK)

Cnidium cnidiifolium
(Tok, AK)

CNIDIUM CNIDIIFOLIUM

Cnidium cnidiifolium

Family: Parsley / Apiaceae

Habitat: Meadows and fields in AK and YT.

Blooming Time: Late June to August

Description: A perennial plant, 18 to 30" (45 to 75cm) tall, with long-stemmed basal leaves which are divided into 4 major sections. These sections are further divided 1 or 2 times into finely dissected segments. The small white flowers are in double umbels at the top of the stems.

Comments: Might be confused with Queen Anne's Lace, *Daucus carota*, which is an introduced plant that may occasionally be found along the southern portion of the Highway. Most of its leaves are basal and carrot-like.

Chamaerhodo
(Champagne, YT)

CHAMAERHODO

Chamaerhodos erecta

Family: Rose / Rosaceae

Habitat: Dry, sandy places especially in YT.

Blooming Time: Mid-June to early July

Description: A hairy, strongly branched plant up to 12" (30cm) tall with a rosette of deeply divided leaflets. Flowers are very small and at the end of the branches. Petals are indented. This plant has only 5 stamens which is uncommon for the Rose family.

Comments: Note photo showing young rosette next to mature plant.

WHITE CINQUEFOIL

Potentilla arguta ssp. *convallaria*

Family: Rose / Rosaceae

Habitat: Dry grasslands at low elevations in AK, BC south of the Rocky Mountains, and YT.

Blooming Time: June to early August

Description: A perennial plant, 12 to 22" (30 to 55cm) tall, with pinnately divided hairy basal leaves having stipules and 7 to 9 toothed, oval, often pointed, coarse leaflets. Stem leaves are smaller and have fewer leaflets. The 5-petalled creamy-white flowers are 5/8 to 3/4" (1.5 to 2cm) across and are in flat-topped inflorescenses.

Comments: All other Potentillas in the area are distinctly yellow.

White Cinquefoil
(Dawson Creek, BC)

Because they absorb extra selenium from the soil, many members of the Pea family become toxic in areas where this mineral is in great abundance.

WHITE NORTHERN OXYTROPE

Oxytropis campestris

Family: Pea / Fabaceae

Habitat: Dry stony and sandy slopes and roadsides from sea level to low alpine throughout most of the area.

Blooming Time: Late May into July

Description: A low plant, 8 to 15" (20 to 37cm) tall, with grayish-green, hairy, pinnately divided leaves with small oval pointed leaflets. The small clusters of pea-shaped flowers are close at first and later elongated. Old stipules at the base of the plant are light to medium tan in color.

Comments: See page 56 for yellow variety. Another white oxytrope that you may see is Small-flowered Oxytrope, *Oxytropis deflexa,* see next page. Its leaves are very stiff and the blade looks quite flat. The flowers are very small and the seed pods hang downward. See page 16 for color variations.

White Northern Oxytrope
(Delta, AK)

American Milk Vetch
(North Pole, AK)

AMERICAN MILK VETCH

Astragalus americanus

Family: Pea / Fabaceae

Habitat: Fields and open woods in damp areas throughout most of the area.

Blooming Time: July and early August

Description: A mostly glabrous, bushy-looking, greatly branched plant, 16 to 24" (40 to 60cm) tall. Leaves are pinnately divided into 11 to 15 leaflets which extend beyond the racemes of creamy white flowers.

Comments: Other similar varieties are: 1) Canadian Milk Vetch, *Astragalus canadensis*, with long racemes of flowers. It may be seen in open areas along the southern portion of the Highway. 2) White Pea Vine, *Lathrus ochroleucus*, a weak plant with tendrils and a raceme of several flowers. It is found in moist woods along the lower portion of the Highway. 3) *Astragalus adsurgens* has a tight flower head. It may be upright or sprawling. Variable depending on habitat.

White Pea Vine
(Charlie Lake, BC)

Astragalus adsurgens
(Summit Lake, BC)

Small-flowered Oxytrope
(Haines Jct., AK)

RED TWIG DOGWOOD, AMERICAN DOGWOOD

Cornus stolonifera

Family: Dogwood / Cornaceae

Habitat: Moist woods throughout the area.

Blooming Time: June to early July

Description: A shrub, 6 to 15' (up to 5m) tall, having opposite branches that are reddish-brown. Leaves are ovate with arcuate veins, dark green above, lighter green and somewhat hairy beneath. It has flat-topped clusters of very small white flowers producing white berries in the late summer and fall. Leaves turn yellowish to copper-colored in the fall.

Red Twig Dogwood
(Liard Hot Springs, BC)

Dogwood berries
(Liard Hot Springs, BC)

NORTHERN BLACK CURRANT

Ribes hudsonianum

Family: Gooseberry / Grossulariaceae

Habitat: Moist woods throughout the area.

Blooming Time: June

Description: An erect shrub, up to 3' (1m) tall, with tan, rather smooth branches. Leaves alternate, toothed and 3 to 5-lobed. The small white flowers are in a short erect raceme. The ovary has stalkless glands. Fruit is a dull black with dried petals still attached. It is edible but bitter. Leaves have a strong odor and turn yellow in the fall.

Black Currant fruit
(Pine Lake, YT)

Northern Black Currant
(Tetlin, AK)

Round Leaf Sundew
(Liard Hot Springs, BC)

Long Leaf Sundew
(Liard Hot Springs, BC)

Eyebright
(Buckinghorse River, BC)

ROUND LEAF SUNDEW

Drosera rotundifolia

Family: Sundew / Droseraceae

Habitat: Bogs and margins of lakes throughout the area

Blooming Time: June

Description: A very small insectivorous plant with a rosette of round succulent leaves that are covered with soft sticky reddish hairs. The small white 5-petalled flowers bloom only for a short time and are seldom seen. A plant of nitrogen poor soils.

Comments: A similar variety is Long Leaf Sundew, *Drosera anglica,* which has long leaves and grows in similar areas. These plants also obtain nutrients from the soil.

EYE BRIGHT

Euphrasia disjuncta

Family: Figwort / Scrophulariaceae

Habitat: Moist open areas throughout most of the area.

Blooming Time: July to early August

Description: A weak annual, usually with one glandular, hairy stem. Leaves are hairy, small, broadly oval and with rounded teeth. The leaves are widely spaced along the lower part of the stem, becoming very close at the top, with very small irregular flowers with lavender markings.

Eyebright
(Buckinghorse River, BC)

CORAL ROOT ORCHID

Corallorrhiza trifida

Family: Orchid / Orchidaceae

Habitat: Moist woods throughout the area.

Blooming Time: Early Spring

Description: Flowering stem yellowish with very small flowers. Plant is parasitic lacking leaves and chlorophyll. Rhizome looks like coral.

Comments: Red Coral Root Orchid, *Corallorrhiza maculata* ssp. *mertensiana*, is a similar reddish plant having white flowers and purplish spots is present in moist woods in southern BC. See also Striped Coral Root Orchid, *Corallorrhizaq maculata* ssp. maculata on page 156.

Coral Root Orchid
(Pine Lake, YT)

Seed head

Coral Root rhizome

ROUND-LEAF ORCHID
FLY-SPECKED ORCHID

Amerorchis rotundifolia

Family: Orchid / Orchidaceae

Habitat: Moist woods and boggy tundra in the Rockies and in scattered areas near the AK/YT border.

Blooming Time: Mid-June to mid-July

Description: A perennial plant, 5 to 8" (12.5 to 20cm), with thick roots and one rounded leaf at the base. Flower stems are pinkish and leafless. Flowers are small, 3/8 to 3/4" (1 to 2cm) and in small terminal racemes. Sepals and upper petals are pink and white, the lower lip white speckled with pink & maroon.

Round Leaf Orchid
(Destruction Bay, YT)

Capitate Valerian
(Northway Jct., AK)

CAPITATE VALERIAN

Valeriana capitata

Family: Valerian / Valerianaceae

Habitat: Moist woods, heaths and tundra in AK and YT.

Blooming Time: June and July

Description: A mostly glabrous plant, 5" to 12" (12 to 30cm) tall, with dark green leaves. Basal leaves are oval and pointed. The stem leaves are wavy, the lower ones divided into 3 leaflets (the middle one being long and pointed). Upper stem leaves are entire and nearly linear. Bracts in flower heads are glabrous. The tight, round flower head is maroon in bud, turning pink to pinkish-white, then white in full bloom.

Comments: Wild Heliotrope or Sitka Valerian, *Valeriana sitchensis*, is a tall plant, 18 to 24" (45 to 60cm), with a few rounded, pinnate basal leaves found in alpine areas of AK and YT. Stem leaves are pointed and pinnately divided. Bracts in the flower head are slightly hairy. The basal leaves of *Valeriana dioica* are mostly oval and long petiolate. Stem leaves are pinnate with 9 to 15 leaflets with entire margins. It may be seen in BC and YT.

Black Snake-root
(Liard Hot Springs, BC)

BLACK SNAKE-ROOT

Sanicula marilandica

Family: Parsley / Apiaceae

Habitat: Deep wet woods. Seen only at Liard Hot Springs, BC.

Blooming Time: Late June and July

Description: A tall plant commonly up to 24" (60cm) with one long-stemmed basal leaf up to 10" (25cm) across. These consist of several smooth dark-green toothed leaflets in a whorl. Stem leaves are in smaller groups. The very small greenish-white flowers are in tight (nearly round) umbels. Perfect flowers (those containing both stamens and ovaries) have short stems. Male flowers have no stems appearing shorter. The seed capsules are oval, about 3" (7.5cm) long, bristly and have a persistent style appearing like a long hook.

MISCELLANEOUS PLANTS AND TREES

Moist Woodlands, Charlie Lake, BC
Wild Sarsaparilla berries

Wild Sarsaparilla
(Liard Hot Springs, BC)

WILD SARSAPARILLA

Aralia nudicaulis

Family: Ginseng / Araliaceae

Habitat: Damp shaded woods along the lower section of the Highway and at Liard Hot Springs, BC.

Blooming Time: June and early July

Description: A 12 to 20" (30 to 50cm) plant of the forest floor with one large, spreading, triple-compound leaf with fine teeth. The flower stem is much shorter and has many small green flowers, followed in August or September by purplish-black berries. See page 115.

Comments: The aromatic root, that spreads just below the surface of the ground, was once used to make a cooling drink.

Timberberry berries
(Whitehorse, YT)

TIMBERBERRY, NORTHERN COMANDRA, PUMPKIN BERRY

Geocaulon lividum

Family: Sandlewood / Santalaceae

Habitat: Dry places, usually open woods throughout most of the area.

Blooming Time: Very early. Mid to late May

Description: An upright plant with alternate, oval leaves on a 3 to 6" (7.5 to 15cm) stem, arising from a horizontal root. The tiny green flowers with 5 sepals produce orange to brown berries in the fall.

Timberberry
(Whitehorse, YT)

Comments: This plant is considered to be semi-parasitic, and often the leaves are mottled with yellowish-brown. The berries are edible, but not very tasty.

MARSH CINQUEFOIL, MARSH FIVEFINGER

Potentilla palustris

Family: Rose / Rosaceae

Habitat: Very wet meadows, marshes, in shallow water, and along streams throughout the area.

Blooming Time: July

Description: A sprawling plant, up to 2' (60cm), which has a somewhat woody, creeping rootstock. The toothed leaves are somewhat palmate, have 5 to 7 separate leaflets and stipules. The purplish-brown, 3/4" (up to 2cm), 5-petaled, pointed flowers are distinctive. After blooming, the sepals fold up over the ovary; a characteristic of potentillas.

Marsh Cinquefoil
(Watson Lake, YT)

BISHOP'S CAP

Mitella nuda

Family: Saxifrage / Saxifragaceae

Habitat: Wet places along streams, in very moist woods.

Blooming Time: Late June and July

Description: Flowering stem, 6 to 12" (15 to 30cm) tall, mostly leafless with a few very small, 5-petaled, finely divided flowers with 10 stamens. Leaves are round to kidney-shaped with a deep sinus, shallow rounded teeth and a few scattered hairs.

Comments: Alpine Mitrewort, *Mitella pentandra*, has shallowly lobed, toothed, oval and somewhat pointed hairy leaves. Flowering stems are mostly leafless with very small flowers having only 5 stamens.

Alpine Mitrewort
(Summit Lake, BC)

Bishop's Cap Lynn Catlin

Bishop's Cap in seed
(Bougie Creek, BC)

Sweet Cicely
(Liard Hot Springs, BC)

SWEET CICELY

Osmorhiza depauperata

Family: Parsley / Apiaceae

Habitat: Woodlands in BC.

Blooming Time: July

Description: A 15 to 24" (42 to 60cm) tall plant with long stemmed basal leaves divided into 3 deeply lobed and toothed leaflets. Flowers are very small, greenish-white, on stems well above the leaves. Fruits are widely spread out on stems tapering at stem end. The green seeds tastes like licorice.

WESTERN MEADOW RUE

Thalictrum occidentale

Family: Buttercup / Ranunculaceae

Habitat: Open moist shady areas along the southern portion of the Highway.

BloomingTime: July

Description: A tall plant, growing up to 4' (120cm), with delicately divided, 3-parted leaves. These plants are dioecious (male and female flowers on separate plants). The small flowers have greenish sepals and no petals.

Comments: Few-flowered Meadow Rue, *Thalictrum sparsiflorum,* also occurs along the Highway. It is a slightly smaller plant with smaller leaves and the plants have perfect flowers (male and female components together).

Western Meadow Rue with seed capsules
(Squanga Lake, YT)

Western Meadow Rue, male flowers
(Charlie Lake, BC)

STRAWBERRY SPINACH, STRAWBERRY BLITE

Chenopodium capitatum

Family: Goosefoot / Chenopodiaceae

Habitat: Dry soil, waste places and roadsides throughout the area.

Blooming Time: July, fruiting in July and August

Description: An upright (sometimes decumbent in fruit) annual. The triangular, glabrous leaves with wavy edges look somewhat like spinach leaves. The flowers are very tiny and inconspicuous, but followed by showy, bunched, round, reddish fruits.

Comments: The sweet, edible fruit may be eaten raw or used for jelly and syrup. The tasty leaves are very similar to its close relative, spinach.

Strawberry Spinach
(Champagne, YT)

WESTERN COLUMBINE

Aquilegia formosa

Family: Buttercup / Ranunculaceae

Habitat: Wooded mountain slopes and meadows in a few scattered localities in YT and southern BC.

Blooming Time: Mid-June through July

Description: A branched perennial plant up to 30" (75cm) tall. The basal leaves are twice divided into 3 parts with rounded shallow lobes. Stem leaves are divided once. Leaves are dark green above and grayish-green below. Flowers are large, 1 to 1-1/2" (2.5 to 4cm), have 5 red sepals with spurs and yellow tubular petals with protruding stamens.

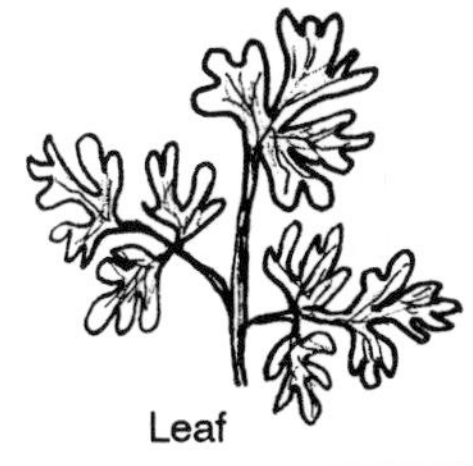

Leaf

Seed capsules

Western Columbine
(Tetlin Jct., AK)

Common Wormwood
(North Pole, AK)

COMMON WORMWOOD

Artemisia tilesii ssp. *elator*

Family: Aster / Asteraceae

Habitat: Open woodlands in low elevations and sandy places in low mountainous areas throughout the area.

Blooming Time: July and August

Description: A tall plant, 2 to 5' (60 to 150cm), with many branched flower spikes with nodding greenish-yellow flowers that look like the center of a daisy. The leafy plant has sharply-pointed, deeply cut 3-5 lobed leaves that are smooth and green on top and silvery and hairy beneath.

Comments: Ssp. *Tilesii* is a smaller alpine variety with larger flower heads. Artemisias are used in dried flowers arrangements and also added to salves and bath water, as they are very aromatic.

Prairie Sagebrush
(Whitehorse, YT)

PRAIRIE SAGEBRUSH, FRIGID WORMWOOD

Artemisia frigida

Family: Aster / Asteraceae

Habitat: Dry, rocky, open, well-drained slopes throughout the area.

Blooming Time: June and July

Description: A low plant, 6 to 14" (15 to 35cm), having a woody base with finely divided, silvery, and silky leaves that are 2 to 3 times divided and strongly aromatic (like sage). The flowers which are on upright stems, are inconspicuous, nodding and look like the center of a daisy.

Comments: Another common, low-growing, silky-looking variety is Alaska Wormwood, *Artemisia alaskana*. Leaflets are more blunt and although aromatic, do not smell like sage. Northern Wormwood, *A. borealis,* is another hairy variety. Basal leaves are 3 to 5-parted. Stem leaves are long and narrow. Involucral bracts are quite broad and have a thin transparent margin. Flowering stems are stiff, erect and very silvery. See page 121.

ARCTIC WORMWOOD

Artemisia arctica

Family: Aster / Asteraceae

Habitat: Alpine meadows and slopes throughout the area.

Blooming Time: Late June and July

Description: Sharply dissected, pinnately divided, dark green leaves. The nodding long-stemmed flower heads are yellowish. Stems and flowers are grayish from hairs..

Comments: This species is distinct because of the dark green leaves. *Artemisia laciniata* has similar looking leaves but more dissected and slightly more hairy. It is found in dry woodlands in YT. Canada Wormwood, *A. canadensis,* an introduced species found along roadsides has yellowish-green leaves with mostly linear segments and very few hairs. Stems are often reddish. Flower heads are nearly erect on short, stout stems. Stem leaves are longer than flower heads. Involucral bracts are rounded and nearly transparent in margin. *A. dracunculus* is an introduced species with reddish flower heads. See page x.

Arctic Wormwood
(Tok, AK)

A. Laciniata
(Whitehorse, YT)

Northern Sagebrush
(Kluane Lake, YT)

Canada Sagebrush
(Whitehorse, YT)

Northern Green Bog Orchid
(Summit Lake, BC)

NORTHERN GREEN BOG ORCHID

Platanthera hyperborea

Family: Orchid / Orchidaceae

Habitat: Wet meadows, bogs, ditches, and along streams from sea level to treeline throughout the area.

Blooming Time: Late June into August

Description: Upright, heavy, fleshy stems, 8 to 14" (20 to 35cm), with long, narrow, light green leaves with linear veins. The small, yellowish-green, sweet scented flowers with 3 petals and 3 sepals cover most of the heavy stems. The whole plant becomes dwarfed in heavy, non-fertile soils. They become very yellowish in adverse conditions and after pollination.

Comments: These plants hybridize easily with Bog Candle, *Platanthera dilatata,* see page 89 in White Section. Small Northern Bog Orchid or One-leaf Rein Orchid, *P. obtusata*, is much shorter and has one leaf at the base. The 4 to 6" (10 to 15cm) stem is few-flowered and grows in moist, mossy woodlands. *Malaxis monophyla* has one very small leaf and a spike of very tiny yellowish-green flowers. It is found in very wet areas at Liard Hot Springs, BC. Round-leaf Rein Orchid, *P. orbiculata*, has 2 large round leaves at its base and an 8 to 10" (20 to 25cm) spike of greenish-white flowers.

Round-leaf Rein Orchid
(Charlie Lake, BC)

One-leaf Rein Orchid
(Marsh Lake, YT)

FROG ORCHID

Coeloglossum viride

Family: Orchid / Orchidaceae

Habitat: Meadows and moist woods in BC.

Blooming Time: June and early July

Description: A thick stemmed plant 5 to 14" (12 to 35cm) tall with 3 to 6 alternate leaves that are ovate to oblong, blunt and glossy. Many small green flowers. The lower bracts which look like narrowed pointed leaves are 2 to 6 times longer than the flowers.

Frog Orchid
(Summit Lake, BC)

HEART-LEAVED TWAYBLADE, HEART-LEAVED TWYBLADE

Listera cordata

Family: Orchid / Orchidaceae

Habitat: Moist, mossy woods and meadows in BC and southern YT.

Blooming Time: July and early August

Description: A slender plant with 2 opposite, somewhat heart-shaped, leaves about half-way up the 5 to 9" (12 to 22cm) stem. Flowers are very small, either green or purplish-brown. The lower lip is divided into 2 long, pointed lobes.

Comments: A distinct plant, Northern Twayblade, *Listera borealis*, has green to greenish-yellow flowers and rounded, oval leaves. Lower lip has 2 broad lobes. *L. convallariodes* has 2 broad pointed leaves. The lower lip is barely indented and has hairs along the edges. It may be found in southern BC.

Heart-leaved Twayblade
(Iron Creek, BC)

After fertilization

Northern Twayblade
(Liard Hot Springs, BC)

Northern Water Carpet
(Summit Lake, BC)

NORTHERN WATER CARPET

Chrysosplenium tetrandrum

Family: Saxifrage / Saxifragaceae

Habitat: Wet places throughout the area, usually below treeline.

Blooming Time: Early June to mid-July

Description: Low, spreading, glabrous plants. Leaves are light green, round to kidney-shaped, have stems and wavy to lobed edges. Flowers consist of green sepals cupped in bracts, 4 stamens and smooth red fruits that become the seeds.

GREEN PYROLA

Pyrola chlorantha

Family: Wintergreen / Pyrolaceae

Habitat: Woods throughout the area.

Blooming Time: Late June and July

Description: Evergreen plant with a rosette of small, roundish, yellowish-green, shiny, petiolate leaves. Flower stem is 5 to 8" (12 to 20cm) tall with few to several flowers. Flowers face downward and have a slightly protruding style.

Comments: Another green flowering pyrola that is common throughout the area is Sidebells Pyrola, *Pyrola secunda* ssp. *secunda*. It is a low evergreen plant with yellowish-green, shiny, oval, pointed leaves. The small green bell-shaped flowers usually hang on one side of the slightly curved 3 to 5" (7.5 to 12.5cm) stems. They have a protruding style and the seed heads are distinctive. Ssp. *obtusata* has leaves with a blunt tip.

Green Pyrola
(Marsh Lake, YT)

Sidebells Pyrola
(Marsh Lake, YT)

RED BURNET

Sanguisorba officinalis

Family: Rose / Rosaceae

Habitat: Damp areas at low elevations in AK.

Blooming Time: July

Description: A perennial plant with pinnately divided, long-stemmed basal leaves with 7 to 11 toothed, coarse-looking, oval leaflets. Stem leaves have shorter stems and less leaflets. The maroon colored flower spikes are oval and at the ends of the 18 to 30" (45 to 75cm) stems.

Red Burnet
(Big Delta, AK)

The section of road from Dot Lake to Fairbanks is old and bumpy, but most roadside vegetation (including Red Burnet) is natural and undisturbed.

PRAIRIE SMOKE, PURPLE AVENS, THREE-FLOWERED AVENS, OLD MAN'S WHISKERS

Geum triflorum

Family: Rose / Rosaceae

Habitat: Moist to dry areas, usually along the edge of prairies in southern BC.

Blooming Time: June

Description: A perennial plant, up to 15" (38cm) tall, with pinnately divided basal leaves. Stem leaves are divided into 3 parts. The small petals are yellow with a purplish cast and are overshadowed by the large, showy rosy-purple sepals. Flowers are usually in threes and have many protruding stamens. Seed heads are fluffy and whitish.

Prairie Smoke
(Taylor, BC)

Ostrich Fern
(Liard Hot Springs, BC)

Moonwort
(Champagne, YT)

Rattlesnake Fern
(Liard Hot Springs, BC)

OSTRICH FERN

Matteuccia struthiopteris

Family: Lady Fern / Athyriaceae

Habitat: Very wet woods (at low elevations) especially along streams in the Fairbanks, AK area and scattered places in BC.

Blooming Time: No blooms. This plant produces spores on a separate "leaflike" fertile frond.

Description: A clump fern with fronds, 1-1/2 to 3' (up to 1m) tall, growing in a funnel-like form. Leaflets start small near the base, become long in the middle, then narrowing to a point at the tip. The short leaf-like fertile frond of this large fern helps in identification.

Comments: The lack of scales on the fiddleheads of this fern make it a tasty vegetable, cooked briefly like asparagus. When gathering ferns, pick only a few from each plant, since picking all of the fiddleheads will kill the plant. Ferns are also tasty raw, but should be eaten in moderation because they contain chemicals that may cause stomach upsets.

MOONWORT

Botrychium lunaria

Family: Adder's Tongue / Ophioglossaceae

Habitat: Grassy spots throughout the area.

Blooming Time: No bloom, spore-bearing on a separate fertile frond.

Description: This is a small plant with one light-green leaf blade with 7 to 11 wider-than-long, rounded, wavy edged segments that lack a mid-vein, the end one being lobed. This leaf in Spring is somewhat wrapped around the spore-bearing stem which elongates at maturity.

Comments: *Botrychium boreale* has more deeply lobed leaf segments that have a distinct mid-vein. The whole leaf is somewhat triangular. *B. lanceolatum* has a broadly triangular leaf (individual leaflets longer than wide) with distinct mid-veins. Rattlesnake Fern, *B. virginianum,* has a large, spreading leaf with many dissected leaflets, the fertile blade connected at the mid-point of the stem and the solitary leaf held high above it. These are all very interesting plants and are edible in the young stages.

WOOD FERN

Dryopteris dilatata

Family: Shield Fern / Aspidaceae

Habitat: Moist woods and meadows in AK north of Tok, BC, and southern YT.

Blooming Time: There are no "blooms". Spores are visible on the underside of leaves by mid-summer.

Description: A tall fern, up to 2' (60cm), arising from a stout, coarse rootstock covered with bases of old stipes. Stipes are covered with coarse brown scales. Leaflets start about halfway up the stipe; starting broad and tapering to a point at the end.

Comments: The curled fronds ("fiddleheads", the early spring growth form) are edible; but, best if the brown scales are rubbed off. This should be done when they are dry. A similar looking fern is Lady Fern, *Athyrium filix-femina*, which grows 2 to 5' (60 to 140cm) tall. Leaflets start small near the base of the stipe, are longer in the middle, and then taper to a point at the end. Spores are produced on the under sides of the leaves. This fern might be seen in damp woods or meadows along the southern portion of the Highway and in the Fairbanks area of AK.

Wood Fern
(Liard Hot Springs, BC)

It takes about 3 years for spore-bearing plants to be recognizable.

Lady Fern
(Liard Hot Springs, BC)

FRAGILE FERN

Cystopteris fragilis ssp. *fragilis*

Family: Lady Fern / Athyriaceae

Habitat: Moist, rocky places in woods and clearings throughout the area.

Blooming Time: No "blooms". Spore bearing on the underside of leaves.

Description: A small, up to 7" (17cm), delicate fern in small groupings, spreading by underground rhizomes.

Fragile Fern
(Summit Lake, BC)

Rusty Woodsia
(Liard Hot Springs, BC)

Woodsia glabella
(Summit Lake, BC)

Roseroot
(Summit Lake, BC)

RUSTY WOODSIA

Woodsia ilvensis

Family: Ladyfern / Athyriaceae

Habitat: Dry, rocky areas scattered throughout the area.

Blooming Time: No bloom. It is spore-bearing.

Description: A small, up to 6" (15cm), clump fern with old, broken stipes at the base. The mature plant has a reddish-brown appearance. Leaves are dull green, segments longer than broad, having scales and hairs on the underside. Fronds are silvery early in the season due to the abundance of small hairs.

Comments: Other species are: 1)*Woodsia scopulina* which is a more loose-looking plant found on alpine slopes on the southern part of the Highway. Leaf segments are longer than broad, but lack scales. 2) *W. alpina* which does not have hairs on the upper surface of the shallowly-toothed, triangular leaves. 3) *W. glabella* which has no hairs nor scalaes on either surface of the lobed somewhat triangular leaves.

ROSEROOT, ROSEWORT, KING'S CROWN

Sedum rosea

Family: Stonecrop, Crassulaceae

Habitat: Rocky places and alpine slopes throughout the area.

Blooming Time: June

Description: A fleshy 4 to 12" (10 to 30cm) plant with slightly toothed, crowded, flat, glabrous, bluish-green leaves on heavy stems. The stems are topped by a rounded cluster of small dark reddish (occasionally yellow) 4 or 5-petalled flowers. The heavy root, when cut, smells somewhat like roses.

Comments: The young plants may be eaten raw or cooked. This plant is very variable in size and density depending upon elevation and habitat.

FRAGRANT FERN

Dryopteris fragrans

Family: Shield Fern / Aspidiaceae

Habitat: Rocky slopes in AK, northern BC and YT.

Blooming Time: No bloom. It is spore-bearing.

Description: A 5 to 10" (12 to 25cm) clump type fern with many dried up, old fronds. Fronds are stiff and coarse looking. Margins of fronds are rolled under.

Fragrant Fern
(Liard Hot Springs, BC)

OAK FERN

Gymnocarpium dryopteris

Family: Shield Fern / Aspidiaceae

Habitat: Woods and sub-alpine meadows throughout the area.

Blooming Time: No bloom. It is spore-bearing on under sides of leaves.

Description: Creeping rhizome sending up individual blades, each having 3 distinct, triangular segments. Each segment is about the same length. Blades, which are light green, frequently open flat about 8 to 12" (20 to 30cm) above the forest floor.

Comments: *Gymnocarpium robertianum* is similar, but side leaflets are smaller than terminal ones. Hybridization occurs. *Thelypteris phegopteris* is a fern similar in size. It has one triangular leaf blade that comes to a narrow point. The lower 2 pinnae (leaflets) are angled downward towards the stem. It can be found in interior AK, or BC along the southern portion of the Highway.

Oak Fern
(Liard Hot Springs, BC)

Thelypteris phegopteris
(North Pole, AK)

Field Horsetail
(Wolfe Creek, YT)

Vegetative stem

FIELD HORSETAIL

Equisetum arvense

Family: Horsetail / Equisetaceae

Habitat: A variety of different habitats, elevations and soil conditions throughout the area.

Blooming Time: No blooms, spore bearing..

Description: Hollow stems with vertical ridges. Very narrow, rough feeling, stems in whorls at joints on the main stems. Spreads rapidly by horizontal roots, frequently forming lacy (somewhat ferny) carpets in moist woodlands. The spore-bearing spring phase dies down after production, and is replaced by the vegetative or leafy phase. The leaf-like stems generally face upwards.

Comments: The plant can be used as an abrasive cleaner for pots and pans as it contains silica. The peeled inner portion of the "Spring Phase" is tasty. There are several varieties of horsetail in the area. Some produce a spore-bearing portion at the end of the vegetative stem. In some varieties, the leaves are so short, that they appear almost non-existent. *Equisetum pratense* is a similar woodland variety that produces its spores atop the main stem early in Spring, and then leafs out in whorls of straggly branches. *E. sylvaticum* has whorls of finely branched and dissected leaves. Spores are produced above the leaves in mid-June. *E. scirpoides* is a small woodland variety with 3 very small leaves at joints on the stems.

Equisetum pratense
(North Pole, AK)

Equisetum sylvaticum
(North Pole, AK)

Equisetum scirpoides
(Tok, AK)

EQUISETUM FLUVATILE

Equisetum fluvatile

Family: Horsetail / Equisetaceae

Habitat: Shallow water or marshy places throughout the area.

Blooming Time: No bloom. Spore bearing at the end of the stem.

Description: May or may not have side branches in a whorl. Central cavity of stem is wide, the vertical grooves are very shallow.

Comments: *E. palustre* of similar habitat is similar in appearance, but stems are not as numerous and not in a whorl. Main stem is not as stout. *E. variegatum* is found in woodlands, it does not have side branches. It has flat-topped ridges on the main stems and spores atop the main stem. *E. hyemale* looks similar to *variegatum* but is evergreen and is frequently found growing in water.

Equisetum fluvatile
(Watson Lake, YT)

MARE'S TAIL

Hippuris vulgaris

Family: Water Milfoil / Haloragaceae

Habitat: Shallow water throughout the area.

Blooming Time: June to July

Description: Stiff erect stems extending up to 1' (30cm) above the water. The long, narrow, glabrous leaves are in a whorl of 6 to 12. Flowers are very small and below the water level.

Comments: This plant looks like miniature spruce trees growing in water.

Mare's Tail
(Squanga Lake, YT)

Equisetum palustre
(Watson Lake, YT)

Squirrel Tail Grass
(Tok, AK)

SQUIRRELTAIL GRASS

Hordeum jubatum

Family: Grass / Gramineaceae

Habitat: Sandy or gravelly soil throughout most of the area.

Blooming Time: July and August

Description: A distinctive, showy, annual grass seen introduced along many roadsides. It is 10 to 16" (25 to 40cm) tall, and has large rose to purple flowering spikes.

Comments: Although beautiful, this grass bears caution if you have pets, as the spiked seeds can lodge in their throats requiring medical attention for the animal.

Common Juniper
(Tetlin Jct., AK)

COMMON JUNIPER

Juniperus communis

Family: Cypress / Cupressaceae

Habitat: Dry, rocky places up to 4500 feet (1500m) throughout the area.

Blooming Time: Requires 2 years to produce cones ("juniper berries").

Description: A low, prostrate shrub with prickly evergreen leaves, very variable in color and form.

The oval cones are green at first and blue to black when mature (2 to 3 years).

Comments: Creeping Savin or Horizontal Juniper, *Juniperus horizontalis*, is a prostrate shrub. Leaves are flat and scale-like, not prickly. Northern specimens are bluish-green but color is variable. It grows in dry, sandy or rocky areas in BC and YT. Rocky Mt. Juniper, *Juniperus scopulorum*, has many short blunt stems and may be seen from the Rocky Mts. north to Whitehorse.

Creeping Savin
(Whitehorse, YT)

Rocky Mt. Juniper
(Rocky Mt. Lodge, BC)

STIFF CLUB MOSS

Lycopodium annotinum

Family: Club Moss / Lycopodiaceae

Habitat: Woodlands and low alpine slopes throughout most of the area.

Blooming Time: No blooms. It is a spore-producing plant.

Description: A low, 4 to 7" (10 to 21cm), creeping, evergreen plant with stiff needle-like yellowish-green leaves bearing spikes of fine spores.

Comments: The spores readily ignite and were used as the flashpowder of early day photographers. There are several varieties of club moss in the area and they are common in woodlands. Most have spike-like branches; except for Ground Pine or Tree Club Moss, *L. obscurum*, which looks like miniature pine trees; and, Creeping Jenny or Christmas Greens, *L. complanatum*, which has branched flat (cedar-like) leaves. This variety has been commonly used like a rope to bind together other evergreens for Christmas wreaths. Fir Club Moss, *L. selago*, has branched stems and is yellowish-green in color. Alpine Club Moss, *L. alpinum*, is a low, spreading species, usually bluish-green in color. *L. clavatum* has creeping runners with soft fir-looking branches.

Stiff Club Moss
(Deadman Lake, AK)

Fir Club Moss
(Tanacross, AK)

Alpine Club Moss
(Summit Lake, BC)

Creeping Jenny or Christmas Greens
(Tetlin Jct., AK)

Hairy Plantain
(Salcha Bluffs, AK)

Common Plantain
(Delta, AK)

Arrow Grass
(Liard Hot Springs, BC)

HAIRY PLANTAIN

Plantago canescens

Family: Plantain / Plantaginaceae

Habitat: Dry, grassy slopes and sandy riverbanks throughout the area.

Blooming Time: Late May to early June

Description: A low, clump-type plant with hairy, lanceolate basal leaves with veins that appear to be linear. Flower stalk is 4 to 7" (10 to 17cm) tall.

Comments: *Plantago eriopoda* might be seen around saline ponds. Leaves are longer and fleshy. Common Plantain, *P. major* is an introduced variety found in waste areas and roadsides. It has large oval pointed leaves with palmate veins. This plant was used medicinally because the juice extracted by crushing the leaves will stop bleeding. The Native Americans called it "White Mans' Foot", because it came over from Europe with the settlers and soon appeared wherever the white man walked.

ARROW GRASS

Triglochin maritimum

Family: Arrow Grass / Juncaginaceae

Habitat: Bogs and marshes including saline water.

Blooming Time: July

Description: Heavy rootstock with long, narrow, thick leaves. Dense flower spike up to 30" (75cm) with tiny, inconspicuous flowers. Seed capsule has 6 compartments.

Comments: *Triglochin palustris* is a similar variety with much narrower leaves. Stems are thin and seed capsule has 3 compartments..

Horticulture spots to visit:

Yukon Gardens
Whitehorse, YT
A nice display of native and non-native plants.

Hawks Nursery
On the west side of the Highway just south of North Pole, AK
Showy, photogenic grounds

ARCTIC DOCK

Rumex arcticus

Family: Buckwheat / Polygonaceae

Habitat: Wet places throughout most of the area.

Blooming Time: July and August

Description: A large, up to 4' (120cm) tall, heavy-stalked plant with large, glabrous, leaves that are broad at the base and taper to a point. Most leaves are on the flowering stalk, clumping near the base, and are reduced in size and number as the stalk extends upwards. The tiny flowers, which have no petals, have large, colorful red or green bracts beneath them on the branched colorful stalk.

Comments: *Rumex fenestratus* has broad lower leaves with a cordate base. Mountain Sorrel, *Oxyria digyna* has kidney-shaped, shiny, very sour tasting leaves. The flowering stem is 6 to 10" (15 to 25cm). Flowers and seeds of this alpine plant are reddish. Sheep Sorrel, *R. acetosella,* an introduced plant, grows in waste areas and has small spade-shaped leaves. Leaves of all varieties are sour and edible. The flower stalks may be dried for use in floral arrangements.

Arctic Dock
(Northway Jct., AK)

Sheep Sorrel
(Tok, AK)

Mountain Sorrel
(Summit Lake, BC)

Alum Root
(Dawson Creek, BC)

ALUM ROOT

Heuchera richardsonii

Family: Saxifrage / Saxifragaceae

Habitat: Moist meadows, fields and woods along the southern most portion of the Highway.

Blooming Time: June to early July

Description: A perennial plant with a clump of basal leaves and a flowering stem 10 to 20" (25 to 50cm) tall. Leaves are 2 to 3" (5 to 7cm) across, somewhat rounded to heart-shaped, lobed and toothed. Flower color is pink to purplish (sometimes brown), but the flowers are nearly hidden by the large green calyx.

Stinging Nettle
(Liard Hot Springs, BC)

Lyall's nettle
(Liard Hot Springs, BC)

STINGING NETTLE

Urtica gracilis

Family: Nettle / Urticaceae

Habitat: Moist fields, stream banks and edges of wooded areas in AK and BC.

Blooming Time: Late June through July

Description: A tall rigid plant up to 40" (1m) with slender square stems. The toothed, strongly veined, coarse-looking leaves have short stems and are placed opposite on the stems. They are long and narrow, broader at the base and have stinging hairs. The numerous tiny green flowers are on long drooping chains arising from the junction of the leaves and stem.

Comments: A similar species is Lyall's Nettle, *Urtica lyallii*, which has leaves that are much broader at the base.

CROWBERRY, MOSSBERRY

Empetrum nigrum

Family: Crowberry / Empetraceae

Habitat: Woods, heaths, bogs, and alpine slopes (especially north-facing) throughout the area.

Blooming Time: May and early June

Description: A low, mat-forming, evergreen shrub with small, narrow, needle-like leaves. The shrub looks wine or maroon colored early in the season. The leaves of many evergreen plants have ways to protect them from the cold. The leaves darken to absorb more heat and the edges curl under to avoid dehydration from the pores.The early blooming (often as the snow melts) flowers are small, maroon colored, 3-parted, inconspicuous. They are followed by firm, round, black, juicy (but seedy), edible berries.

Comments: The berries are also called blackberry by some natives. The berries may be used for jelly or pies. They are easy to pick, and they keep well.

Crowberry, Mossberry
(Anchorage, AK)

Crowberry, Mossberry berries
(Tetlin Jct., AK)

MUSK ROOT, MOSCHATEL

Adoxa moschatellina

Family: Moschatel / Adoxaceae

Habitat: Moist woods throughout the area.

Blooming Time: Early spring. Late April to late May

Description: A delicate, glabrous, very small plant, up to 4" (10cm), arising from a creeping white root. The long-stemmed light yellowish-green, toothed, basal leaves are divided into 3 leaflets (could be mistaken for a buttercup) which are again divided into 3 segments. Flowering stems have one or two smaller leaves and a tight cluster of green flowers. The top flower has 4 sepals and 8 stamens. Side flowers have 5 sepals and 10 stamens.

Musk Root
(Liard Hot Springs, BC)

Northern Red Currant
(Tok, AK)

NORTHERN RED CURRANT

Ribes triste

Family: Gooseberry / Grossulariaceae

Habitat: Moist woods and meadows up to timberline throughout the area.

Blooming Time: Mid-May to mid-June

Description: A shrub with shredding bark usually upright; but, occasionally, sprawling, 2 to 3' (up to 1m) tall. Leaves are toothed and 3 to 5-lobed (maple shaped). They are arranged alternately on the branches and turn red in the fall. The small, brick red flowers are on weak, drooping stems hanging under the leaves. The tasty berries which ripen in July are red and translucent.

Comments: Other similar plants are: 1) Skunk Currant, *Ribes glandulosum,* which is quite decumbent and has leaves with 5 lobes and serrations. Flowers are green to pink. Berries are red and hairy. 2) Trailing Black Currant, *R. laxiflorum*, which has pink to purplish flowers, 5-lobed, serrated leaves and purplish-black berries with hairs. See also 3) Black Currant on Page 111. Gooseberries might also be encountered. They have smaller leaves. 4) Swamp Gooseberry, *R. lacustre,* has very prickly stems and shiny black berries with hairs. 5) Purple Gooseberry, *R. oxyacanthoides* has scattered prickles and smooth purplish berries.

Northern Red Currant
(Tok, AK)

Trailing Black Currant
(Liard Hot Springs, BC)

Purple Gooseberry
(Liard Hot Springs, BC)

DUCK WEED

Lemna minor

Family: Duck Weed / Lemnaceae

Habitat: Margins of ponds at low elevations throughout much of the area.

Blooming Time: Late June to August

Description: A very small floating plant with fine roots. The thick, round leaf has one short root. They cluster together in shallow, rather still water. The flowers are very small and inconspicuous and rarely bloom in cold climates.

Comments: *Lemna trisulca* is a similar plant with slightly longer, more pointed, submerged leaves that are connected by horizontal stems.

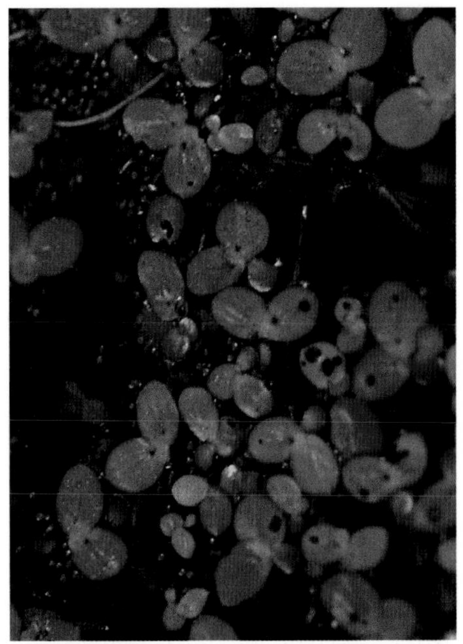

Duckweed
(Squanga Lake, YT)

CATTAIL

Typha latifolia

Family: Cattail / Typhaceae

Habitat: Marshes and shallow water in AK and BC.

Blooming Time: July

Description: A stout perennial up to 60" (1.75m) tall with long, flat, wide, iris-like leaves. The flowers are on the top on the thick round stalks; the pistillate on a thick brown spike, the staminate narrower but about the same length and above the pistillate.

Comments: This is a very distinctive plant seen in roadside ditches and lake margins. The young stems are a tasty food source, as are the flower buds which are a bit like immature corn. Most obvious near Fort Nelson, BC. **Be sure not to confuse the young stems with iris which is poisonous.** Cattails usually grow in water or in areas under water most of the year, while Iris usually grow in damp areas.

Cat Tail
(Ft. Nelson, BC)

Mt. Alder bark and leaves
(North Pole, AK)

Mt. Alder male flower / cone spikes
(North Pole, AK)

Broom Rape
(Tetlin Jct., AK)

MOUNTAIN ALDER

Alnus crispa

Family: Birch / Betulaceae

Habitat: Open areas in woods and subalpine throughout the area.

Blooming Time: May to early June

Description: Branches grayish with whitish markings. Up to 9' (3m). Leaves broadly oval and pointed with fine, sharp teeth, dark green and glabrous above, hairs on veins below. A fast-growing shrubby tree that loves sunlight and fixes nitrogen in the soil for other plants. Bud scales overlap each other. Cones are on stems that are longer than the cones.

Comments: River alder, *Alnus incana* ssp. *tenufolia*, has grayish bark, later turning reddish especially in exposed sites. Leaves are more oblong. Bud scales do not overlap and cones are on short stems (shorter than cones).

Alder cones / New buds
(Anchorage, AK)

BROOMRAPE, GROUND CONE

Boschniakia rossica

Family: Broomrape / Orobanchaceae

Habitat: A parasite growing on the roots of Mountain Alder, *Alnus crispa*, throughout the area.

Blooming Time: Late June and July

Description: The tiny reddish-brown to purple flowers grow on a heavy fleshy spike between glabrous brownish bracts. At maturity, the plant is 8 to 12" (20 to 30cm) tall and looks very much like an erect tall soft pine cone. It can be seen, dried and still standing, in the winter and early spring.

DWARF BIRCH

Betula nana

Family: Birch / Betulaceae

Habitat: Bogs and tundra in AK and YT.

Blooming Time: June

Description: A low shrub up to 30" (75cm). Twigs with resin dots that feel like sandpaper. Leaves are small (dime-sized) in clusters of 3 or 4 and toothed. Leaves turn orange in fall.

Comments: Shrub Birch, *Betula glandulosa,* may also be seen on the tundra and up into low alpine areas. Up to 8' (2.5m) tall with slightly larger, more pointed leaves that turn orange to red in the fall.

Dwarf Birch
(Tetlin Jct., AK)

SWEET GALE

Myrica gale

Family: Wax Myrtle / Myricaceae

Habitat: Bogs and margins of lakes in AK and a few scattered areas in BC.

Blooming Time: May

Description: A shrub up to 40" (1m) tall. Reddish-brown branches and some resin dots. The grayish-green leaves are oblong tapering at the base and have a few teeth at the tip. Male and female flowers are on separate shrubs.

Comments: The leaves smell much like bay leaf and may be used as a seasoning.

Sweet Gale in flower
(Northway Jct., AK)

Sweet Gale in seed
(Northway Jct., AK)

Short-stalk Sedge
(Summit Lake, BC)

SHORT-STALK SEDGE

Carex microchaeta

Family: Sedge / Cyperaceae

Habitat: Sub-alpine to alpine tundra, meadows and ridges throughout much of the area.

Blooming Time: July and August

Description: A 5 to 10" (12.5 to 25cm) tall plant with many linear basal leaves and obvious old dead stubbles. The flowering spikes are large for the plant and stamens are very showy. The top 1 or 2 spikes are staminate; the lower ones pistillate, drooping when mature. There are many sedges in the area, and it is a complex genus. This species is very common, and showy for its size. It is usually taller than other plants growing in the same area. Most sedges have a triangular stem that is solid.

Comments: Other sedges that may be seen along the way are: 1) *Carex podocarpa*, a 16 to 24" (40 to 60cm) tall plant, with long pointed, yellowish-green leaves that are up to 1/5" (5cm) broad. It is found in wet places. Flower spikes have long drooping stems. The leaf-like bract that starts at the bottom of the flowering spike barely exceeds the top flower spike. 2) *C. aquatilis* is a similar wetland species. Bracts go beyond flower spikes, which are stiff and have only short stems. 3) *Scirpus microcarpus* var. *rubrotinctus* may be seen in roadside ditches along the lower sections of the Highway. It has many long pointed leaves.

Scirpus microcarpus
(Ft. Nelson, BC)

Carex podocarpa
(Delta Jct., AK)

BUR-REED

Sparganium angustifolium

Family: Bur Reed / Sparganiaceae

Habitat: In lakes scattered throughout the area.

Blooming Time: July and August

Description: Leaves flat, long and narrow, up to 1/2" (12mm) wide and up to 24" (60cm) long, frequently lying on top of the water. Flowers in rounded heads, the upper 2 or 3 staminate and close together, the lower 2 or 3 pistillate and on long stems.

Comments: *Sparganium multipedunculatum* has broader leaves and flowering heads farther apart and may be seen in AK and BC south of the Rocky Mt. divide.

Bur-Reed
(Deadman Lake, AK)

Few-flowered Rush
(Ft. Nelson, BC)

FEW-FLOWERED RUSH

Luzula parviflora

Family: Rush / Juncaceae

Habitat: Damp places from lowlands to tundra throughout the area.

Blooming Time: July and August

Description: Tufted plants up to 16" (40cm) with flat, broad, up to 1/2" (12mm) leaves. Upperstem leaves brownish or reddish tinged. Flowering stem arched.

Comments: Other rushes which may be seen in wet areas along the Highway are: 1) Slender Rush, *Juncus filiformis*, with slender stems up to 40" (4dm) arising from a creeping root. The cluster of flowers appears to be halfway up the stem. 2) Arctic Rush, *J. arcticus*, is shorter and flower clusters nearer the top of stems. 3) Chestnut-colored Rush, *J. castanaeus*, may be seen in wet mountain areas. It has 1 to 3 heads with a bract that extends beyond the flower heads.

Slender Rush
(Ft. Nelson, BC)

Alpine Bluegrass
(Summit Lake, BC)

ALPINE BLUE GRASS

Poa alpina

Family: Grass / poaceae

Habitat: Rocky slopes and meadow margins throughout the area.

Blooming Time: July and August

Description: A tufted plant up to 16" (40cm) tall with short, bluish-green, mostly flat (occasionally folded) leaves. Many old leaves remain at the base. Upper most stem leaf is about halfway up the stem. Flowering head is triangular (about 2/3 as wide as tall) and green to purplish when young.

Star Moss / Step Moss

STAR MOSS

Polytrichum sp.

Family: Polytrichiaceae

Habitat: Woods and moist alpine slopes throughout the area.

Blooming Time: Spore bearing in late summer and fall.

Description: Individual stiff, dark green, upright branches that look like small spruce trees.

Comments: Other common moss varieties in the area are: 1) *Sphagnum* sp. which grow in wet boggy areas and have long, soft, upright branches that can be nearly white at the base to a bright green to reddish color on top. Sphagnum has the ability to wick up water and actually raise the water table. This plant was used in olden times for liners for babys' diapers as it absorbs moisture and has been used as a wound dressing because it is also antiseptic. 2) Step Moss, *Hylocomium splendens*, is a branched trailing moss with lacy branches that may be seen in moist woods. 3) Feather Moss, *Pleurozium schreberi*, is a trailing branched moss of moist woodlands. 4) *Ptilium crista-castrensis* occurs as single stalks in moist woods and looks like ostrich plumes.

Feather Moss

Sphagnum Moss
(Summit Lake, BC

Red Sphagnum with seed capsules

NET LEAF WILLOW

Salix reticulata

Family: Willow / Salicaceae

Habitat: Tundra and alpine locations throughout most of the area.

Blooming Time: May to mid-June

Description: A trailing shrub with thick, rounded (very variable), dark green leaves to 1-1/2" (4cm) with strong net veins. Leaves are very hairy when young. Catkins are long and slender on leafy stalks and reddish in flower. Seed capsules are hairy with a short style.

Comments: Other dwarf willows that may be seen are: 1) Least Willow, *Salix rotundifolia*, in AK and YT, with very small rounded leaves up to 1/2" (1.5cm). Catkins are very short and reddish. Capsules are mostly glabrous. 2) Setchell's Willow, *S. setchelliana*, found on gravelly flood plains. Leaves are long, oval, smooth, thick and frequently reddish. Catkins are reddish and on leafy stems. 3) Arctic Willow, *S. arctica*. There are 2 species in the area, mostly on the tundra. An extremely variable species. Leaves, up to 3" (7.5cm), are light to dark green, slightly hairy when young, mostly glabrous when mature. Usually broad, tapering to the base. Tip usually rounded, but sometimes pointed. Catkins are long and on a leafy stem. 4) Alaska Bog Willow, *S. fuscescens*, is common in AK in bogs and wet meadows. Leaves are oval. Catkins on leafy stems. 5) Skeleton Leaf Willow, *S. phlebophylla*, is a dwarf shrub of AK and YT with many old dead skeleton-like leaves.

Net Leaf Willow
(Summit Lake, BC)

Arctic Willow
(Destruction Bay, YT)

Skeleton Leaf Willow
(Hatcher Pass, AK)

Setchell's Willow
(Tanana River, AK)

Gray leaf Willow
(Liard Hot Springs, BC)

GRAY LEAF WILLOW

Salix glauca

Family: Willow / Salicaceae

Habitat: Woods and tundra along streams throughout most of the area.

Blooming Time: June

Description: Usually shrubby, occasionally tree-like, up to 20' (6m). Whole shrub looks grayish. Upper surface of leaves are dark green with hairs. Lower surface is whitish with hairs. Leaves are long, oval, rounded at the base and gradually come to a point at the end. Catkins are about 2" (5cm) long on leafy twigs and remain on shrub most of the summer.

Comments: Other commonly seen willows are: 1) Alaska Willow or Felt-leaf Willow, *Salix alaxensis*, is a tall shrubby tree found throughout most of the area. It grows up to 30' (9m). Leaves which are a long oval, rounded at the base and with a pointed tip are covered with hairs on the underside, thick like felt; while the upper surface is hairless. Branch tips (especially in winter) are covered with dense hairs. Catkins are very long, up to 4" (20cm), wooly and upright on leafless stalks. 2) Silver Willow, *S. candida*, up to 7' (2m), has long narrow, very silvery, wooly leaves with edges that are frequently rolled under. 3) Cherry Willow, *S. padophylla*, can be up to 12' (3.5m) tall. Leaves which have fine teeth are green, shiny and pointed. A most obvious shrubby willow in new growth areas as new leaves are reddish.

Silver Willow
(Ft. Nelson, BC)

Cherry Willow
(Liard Hot Springs, BC)

Alaska Willow
(Tanana River, AK)

SAND BAR WILLOW

Salix interior

Family: Willow / Salicaceae

Habitat: River bars in AK and northern BC.

Blooming Time: June

Description: An upright shrub, 10 to 12' (25 to 30cm) tall, with smooth, long, narrow, pointed leaves that are 2 to 4" (5 to 10cm) long and have fine teeth. Catkins are about 2" (5cm) and on leafy stalks.

Comments: Other willows that may be seen in the area are: 1) Little Tree Willow, *Salix arbusculoides* a shrubby tree up to 16' (5m) tall with long, shiny, leaves that are broad in the middle and have teeth evenly placed around their edges. Leaf veins become nearly parallel. Catkins are small and on leafless stalks. 2) Pacific Willow, *S. lasiandra*, a tall shrubby tree up to 20' (6m) tall. Leaves are broad at the base tapering to the tip, and up to 5" (12cm). Leaves are shiny green above, whitish beneath and have fine teeth. 3) Barclay Willow, *S. barclayii*, a 3 to 9' (1 to 3m), greatly branched shrub. Leaves are generally oval, pointed and yellowish-green with teeth. This shrub produced "Willow Roses" caused by insect damage at the tips of the branches. 4) Bebb Willow, *S. depressa* ssp. *rostrata*, is a tall shrub that frequently grows in dense clumps. In flower (mid to late June), the female tree is a beautiful sight, similar to a smoke tree. Seeds have unusually long stems, so catkins are spread out. Male catkins are very aromatic (early June). This is a major producer of "Diamond Willow". A fungus attacks wounds causing diamond-shaped depressions. The wood is carved into walking canes and other gift items. 5) Barren Ground Willows, *S. brachycarpa* and *S. niphoclada*, have narrow, somewhat diamond-shaped leaves with a rather blunt tip. They have yellow, upright male catkins on leafy stems that are very attractive and aromatic. 6) Diamond Leaf Willows, *S. phylicifolia* and *S. pulcha* have diamond-shaped leaves, the catkins are on leafless stems, and many old dead leaves remain attached to the stems.

Sand Bar Willow
(Tanana River, AK)

Pacific Willow

Bebb Willow

DECIDUOUS TREES

Black Cottonwood—*Populus trichocarpa*
Balsam Poplar—*Populus balsamifera*

Very large trees, 40 to 90 feet (13 to 30m) tall with deeply grooved, thick bark; young trees have smooth bark. Leaf shape is very variable. Young trees often have very large leaves. Most are large pointed, elongated, heart-shaped leaves that turn bright yellow in the Fall. Balsam Poplar is found throughout the area, and Black Cottonwood in the southern part of the Highway. Hybridization occurs where ranges overlap. They are common near rivers and near stream beds up into the mountains. The bark is used by craftsman for paintings and woodcarvings.

Quaking Aspen—*Populus tremuloides*

A medium sized, short lived, tree, 18 to 40 feet (6 to 13m) tall with smooth, greenish-gray bark becoming grooved near the base on older trees. The broad, sharply-pointed, heart-shaped leaves tremble with the slightest breeze, due the long delicate petioles. It is found throughout most of the area. The leaves turn bright yellow in the Fall. They prefer dry, sandy or rocky ground from lowlands up to alpine. They often look misshapen or gnarled, especially in exposed sites. It grows slowly, so space between growth rings on branches is short.

Paper Birch—*Betula papyrifera*

A medium sized tree, up to 50 feet (16m) tall with whitish, peeling bark and horizontal markings. The coarse-veined, sharply-toothed, pointed, heart-shaped leaves turn yellow in the Fall. They are common throughout the area at all elevations. Ssp. *humilis* has an elongated, pointed tip and is found in AK, YT and northern BC. Ssp. *commutata* has a more blunt tip and is found in BC. Birches produce salicin, a bitter chemical related to Aspirin, in their bark. This discourages animals from browsing them too heavily. Young trees produce more than older trees, whose branches are out of the reach of animals.

Tamarack / Larch —*Larix laricina*

A small tree, up to 30 feet (10m) tall found in bogs and lowlands in AK and BC. The short needles, which grow in clusters, are deciduous, so fall off in the Fall.

Willows—*Salix sp.*

There are several Willows in the area that grow to tree size, but most still grow in clumps. Most have ovate to elliptical leaves. All produce catkins, and contain salicin in varying amounts. See pages 145, 146 and 147. Scouler's Willow, *Salix scouleriana*, frequently grows tree-like up to 25' (9m). Leaves are rounded at the base, becoming broadest near the middle and have a short point. Most mature leaves have short reddish hairs on the underside.

Scouler's Willow
(Whitehorse, YT)

Cottonwood
(Bougie Creek, BC)

Aspen
(Teslin, YT)

Tamarack
(South of Teslin, YT)

Cottonwood Bark
(Bougie Creek, BC)

Tamarack
(South of Teslin, YT)

Resin glands on Birch

Birch Bark

Birch
(North Pole, AK)

EVERGREEN TREES

Black Spruce—*Picea mariana* 

Small tree, up to 30 feet (9M), found in bogs or wet areas at low elevations in AK and YT. Young branches have rusty-colored hairs. Needles are 4-angled with stomata on all sides, and are short, 1/4 to 1/2" (up to 13mm). The small, 3/4 to 1-1/4" (2 to 3cm), egg-shaped cones, which grow close to the main trunk, remain on the trees for years, usually waiting for the heat of a forest fire to release the seeds. Due to a high water table and poor growing conditions, these trees are often very deformed. They frequently lean at an angle due to frost heaving.

White Spruce—*Picea glauca*

A medium tree, 30 to 90 feet (9 to 25m), found in woodlands and into alpine throughout most of the area. Hybridization with other Spruce species is common. The needles are 3/8 to 3/4" (10 to 18mm) long and are 4-angled with stomata on all sides, and have a skunky smell. The medium sized, 1-1/4 to 2" (2 to 5cm), elongated cones, which grow on the outer branches, fall off each Spring. Alpine specimens often are stunted, and sometimes resemble Junipers.

Alpine Fir --- *Abies lasiocarpa*

This tree is found in alpine areas. Needles curve upwards. Cones are broadly oval. This tree has a very soft, full appearance.

Lodgepole Pine or Scrub Pine --- *Pinus contorta*

Grows 20 to 33 feet (6 to 10m) tall and is very common in dry areas of BC and YT. Needles are 2 in a fascicle. Cones are 1-1/2 to 2" (up to 5cm) long, nearly round and stay on trees for several years.

Lodgepole Pine
(Champagne, YT)

Black Spruce
(Tetlin Jct., AK)

Lichen on Black Spruce
(Tetlin Jct., AK)

White Spruce
(North Pole, AK)

Alpine Fir
(Fish Lake, YT)

Dawson Creek, BC to Fort Nelson, BC

Mile 0 to Mile 283

Fields of Canola (a hybrid rape that produces a low cholesterol oil) surround Dawson Creek. The warm plains and sandy bluffs produce many more different plants than the northern portion of the Highway. In this section of the Highway, there is a wide range of habitats climaxing in a large area of wetlands near Fort Nelson.

Canola Field,Watson Lake, BC

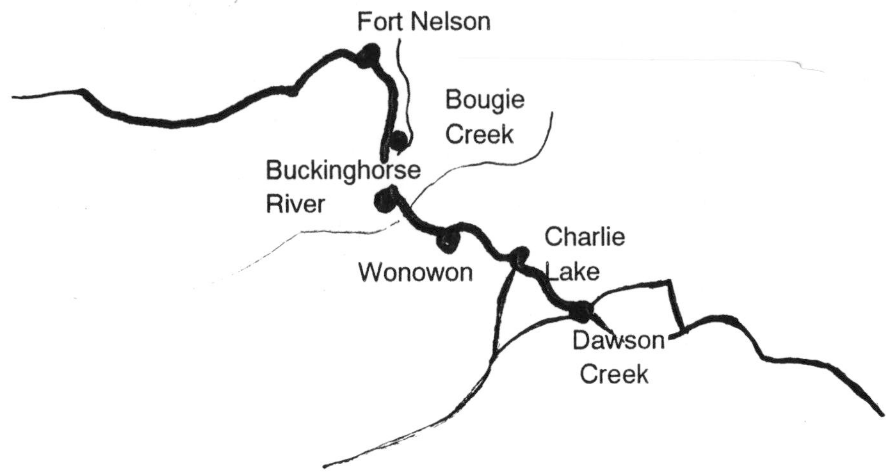

DAWSON CREEK TO FORT NELSON

___*Achillea borealis* .... Northern Yarrow
___*Aconitum delphinifolium* .... Monkshood
___*Actaea rubra* .... Baneberry
___*Allium cernua* .... Nodding Onion
___*Alnus crispa* .... Mountain Alder
___*Amelanchier alnifolia* .... Serviceberry
___*Antennaria rosea* .... Pink Pussy-toes
___*Anthemis cotula* .... Mayweed
___*Apocynum androsaemifolium* .... Dogbane
___*Aralia nudicaulis* .... Wild Sarsaparilla
___*Arctostaphylos uva-ursi* .... Kinnikinnick
___*Arnica chamissonis* ....
___*Arnica cordifolia* .... Heart-leaf Arnica
___*Artemisia frigida* .... Prairie Sagewort
___*Aster lievis* .... Smooth Aster
___*Aster modestus* .... Showy Aster
___*Astragalus alpinus* .... Alpine Milk Vetch
___*Astragalus americanus* .... American Milk Vetch
___*Astragalus ochroleucus* .... White Pea Vine
___*Betula papyrifera* .... Paper Birch
___*Brassica sp.* .... Canola (Hybrid Rape)
___*Capsella bursa-pastoris* .... Shepherd's Purse
___*Castilleja miniata* .... Indian Paintbrush
___*Centauria* sp. .... Knapweed
___*Chenopodium album* .... Lamb's Quarters, Pigweed
___*Cicuta douglasii* .... Poison Water Hemlock
___*Cirsium canadensis* .... Canada Thistle
___*Cirsium vulgare* .... Bull Thistle
___*Coeloglossum viride* .... Frog Orchid
___*Commandra umbellata pallida* .... Pale Commandra
___*Corallorhiza striata* .... Striped Coral Root Orchid
___*Corallorrhiza maculata* .... Red Coral Root Orchid
___*Corallorrhiza trifida* .... Coral Root Orchid
___*Cornus canadensis* .... Canadian Dogwood
___*Cornus stolonifera* .... Red-twig Dogwood
___*Crepis capillaris* .... Low Hawksbeard
___*Crepis tectorum* .... Tall Hawksbeard
___*Delphinium glaucum* .... Larkspur
___*Disporin trachycarpum* .... Fairy Bells
___*Dryas drummondii* .... Yellow Dryas
___*Epilobium angustifolium* .... Common Fireweed
___*Epilobium latifolium* .... Dwarf Fireweed
___*Epilobium palustris* .... Marsh Willow Herb
___*Equisetum arvense* .... Field Horsetail
___*Erigeron elatus* .... Long-leaf Fleabane
___*Erigeron philadephicus* .... Philadelphia Fleabane
___*Euphrasia disjuncta* .... Eyebright
___*Fragaria virginiana* .... Wild Strawberry
___*Galeopsis tetrahit* .... Hemp Nettle
___*Galium boreale* .... Northern Bedstraw
___*Galium triflorum* .... Sweet Scented Bedstraw
___*Gentiana amarella* ....

___ *Gentiana propinqua* .... Four-parted Gentian
___ *Geocaulon lividum* .... Timberberry
___ *Geranium bicknelli* .... Bicknell's Geranium
___ *Geum macrophyllum* .... Large-leaf Avens
___ *Geum triflorum* .... Prairie Smoke
___ *Goodyera repens* .... Rattlesnake Plantain
___ *Heracleum lanatum* .... Cow Parsnip
___ *Lathyrus palustris* .... Vetchling
___ *Ledum palustre* .... Labrador Tea
___ *Linaria dalmatica* .... Dalmatian Toadflax
___ *Linnaea borealis* .... Twinflower
___ *Linum perrenne* .... Blue Flax
___ *Lonicera dioica* .... Twining Honeysuckle
___ *Lonicera involucrata* .... Black Twinberry
___ *Lupinus arcticus* .... Arctic Lupine
___ *Maianthemum dilatatum* .... False Lily of the Valley
___ *Melilotus albus* .... White Sweet Clover
___ *Melilotus officinalis* .... Yellow Sweet Clover
___ *Mentha arvensis* .... Mint
___ *Mertensia paniculata* .... Bluebells
___ *Mitella nuda* .... Bishops' Cap
___ *Moehringia lateriflora* .... Grove Sandwort
___ *Monarda fistulosa* .... Wild Bergamot
___ *Moneses uniflora* .... Single Delight
___ *Osmorhiza depauperata* .... Sweet Cicely
___ *Oxycoccus microcarpus* .... Bog Cranberry
___ *Oxytropis deflexa* .... Small-flowered Oxytrope
___ *Oxytropis splendens* .... Showy Locoweed
___ *Oxytropis viscida* .... Sticky Oxytrope
___ *Parnassia palustris* .... Grass of Parnassus
___ *Pedicularis labradorica* .... Labrador Lousewort
___ *Pedicularis sudetica* .... Fern Leaf Lousewort
___ *Penstemon procerus* .... Slender Beardstongue
___ *Petasites palmatus* .... Palmate Leaf Coltsfoot
___ *Petasites sagittatus* .... Arrow-leaf Coltsfoot
___ *Picea glauca* .... White Spruce
___ *Pinus contorta* .... Lodgepole Pine, Jack Pine
___ *Plantago major* .... Common Plantain
___ *Platanthera hyperborea* .... Northern Green Bog Orchid
___ *Platanthera orbiculata* .... Round-leaf Rein Orchid
___ *Polemonium acutiflorum* .... Tall Jacob's Ladder
___ *Populus balsamifera* .... Cottonwood
___ *Populus tremuloides* .... Quaking Aspen
___ *Potentilla arguta* .... White Cinquefoil
___ *Potentilla fruticosa* .... Tundra Rose
___ *Potentilla norvegica* ssp. *monspeliensis* .... Norwegian Cinquefoil
___ *Prunus virginiana* .... Bird Cherry
___ *Pyrola asarifolia* .... Pink Pyrola
___ *Pyrola chlorantha* .... Green Pyrola
___ *Pyrola secunda* .... Sidebells Pyrola
___ *Rhinanthus minor* .... Rattlebox
___ *Ribes oxycanthoides* .... Purple Gooseberry
___ *Ribes triste* .... Red Currant

___*Rosa acicularis* .... Prickly Rose
___*Rubus chamaemorus* .... Cloudberry
___*Rubus idaeus* .... Raspberry
___*Rubus pubescens* .... Trailing Red Blackberry
___*Rumex fenestratus* .... Dock
___*Salix alaxensis* .... Alaska Willow
___*Salix arbusculoides* .... LittleTree Willow
___*Salix candida* .... Silver Willow
___*Salix depressa* .... Bebb Willow
___*Salix lasiandra* .... Pacific Willow
___*Salix scouleriana* .... Scouler's Willow
___*Scirpus rubrotincus* .... Small Rush
___*Scirpus validus* .... Bull Rush
___*Senecio jacobaea* .... Tall Groundsel
___*Senecio lugens* .... Black-tipped Groundsel
___*Senecio vulgaris* .... Common Groundsel
___*Shepherdia canadensis* .... Soapberry
___*Sisyrinchium montanum* .... Blue-eyed Grass
___*Smilacina stellata* .... False Solomon's Seal
___*Solidago canadensis* .... Canada Goldenrod
___*Solidago decumbens oreophila* .... Decumbent Goldenrod
___*Solidago multiradiata ssp. scopularum* .... Rocky Mt. Goldenrod
___*Sorbus scopulina* .... Green Mt. Ash
___*Spiraea betulifolia* .... Birch-leaf Spiraea
___*Spiranthes romanzoffiana* .... Hooded Ladies Tresses
___*Stellaria longifolia* .... Chickweed
___*Symphoricarpus albus* .... Snowberry
___*Taraxacum sp.* .... Dandelion
___*Thalictrum occidentalis* .... Western Meadow Rue
___*Thalictrum sparsiflorum* .... Common Meadow Rue
___*Tragopogon dubius* .... Western Salsify
___*Trifolium pratense* .... Red Clover
___*Trifolium repens* .... White Clover
___*Typha latifolia* .... Cattail
___*Vaccinium myrtilloides* .... Canada Blueberry
___*Vaccinium ovalifolium* .... Early Blueberry
___*Vaccinium uliginosum* .... Bog Blueberry
___*Vaccinium vitis-idaea* .... Low-bush Cranberry
___*Viburnum edule* .... High-bush Cranberry
___*Viola canadensis* .... Canada Violet
___*Viola selkirkii* .... Selkirk's Violet

Common Chickweed
(*Stellaria media*)

Charlie Lake Provincial Park

Mile 53.7

This excellent park area contains nice campsites, plus nature trails to the lake. The wide variety of plants visible here, that may not be seen elsewhere along the Alcan, prompted us to make this the location for a special list.

Woods, Charlie Lake, BC

Striped Coral Root

CHARLIE LAKE PROVINCIAL PARK

___*Actea rubra* .... Baneberry
___*Aralia nudicaulis* .... Wild Sarsaparilla
___*Arnica cordifolia* .... Heart-leaf Arnica
___*Astragalus ochroleucus* .... White Pea Vine
___*Centaurea* sp. .... Knapweed
___*Circuta douglassii* .... Water Hemlock
___*Corallorrhiza maculata* .... Red Coral Root Orchid
___*Corallorrhiza striata* .... Striped Coral Root Orchid
___*Corallorrhiza trifida* .... Coral Root Orchid
___*Cornus canadensis* .... Canadian Dogwood
___*Crepis capillaris* .... Hawksbeard
___*Crepis tectorum* .... Tall Hawksbeard
___*Delphinium glaucum* .... Larkspur
___*Disporum tracycarpum* .... Fairy Bells
___*Epilobium angustifolium* .... Common Fireweed
___*Fragaria virginiana* .... Wild Strawberry
___*Galium boreale* .... Northern Bedstraw
___*Galium triflorum* .... Sweet Scented Bedstraw
___*Gentiana propinqua* .... Four-parted Gentian
___*Heracleum lanatum* .... Cow Parsnip
___*Lathrus palustris* .... Vetchling
___*Linnaea borealis* .... Twinflower
___*Lonicera involucrata* .... Black Twinberry
___*Maianthemum dilatatum* .... False Lily of the Valley
___*Melilotus albus* .... White Sweet Clover
___*Mentha arvensis* .... Mint
___*Mertensia paniculata* .... Bluebells
___*Mitella nuda* .... Bishop's Cap
___*Moehringia lateriflora* .... Grove Sandwort
___*Osmorhiza depauperata* .... Sweet Cicely
___*Pedicularis sudetica* .... Fern-leaf Lousewort
___*Petasites sagittatus* .... Arrow-leaf Coltsfoot
___*Platanthera orbiculata* .... Round Leaf Rein Orchid
___*Populus balsamifera* .... Cottonwood
___*Populus tremuloides* .... Quaking Aspen
___*Potentilla norvegica* ssp. *monspeliensis* .... Norwegian Cinquefoil
___*Pyrola asarifolia* .... Pink Pyrola
___*Pyrola chlorantha* .... Green Pyrola
___*Pyrola secunda* .... Sidebells Pyrola
___*Ribes oxyacanthoides* .... Purple Gooseberry
___*Ribes triste* .... Red Currant
___*Rosa acicularis* .... Prickly Rose
___*Rubus idaeus* .... Raspberry
___*Rubus pubescens* .... Trailing Red Blackberry
___*Salix alaxensis* .... Alaska Willow
___*Salix depressa* .... Bebb Willow
___*Salix scouleriana* .... Scouler's Willow
___*Shepherdia canadensis* .... Soapberry
___*Spiraea betulifolia* .... Birch Leaf Spireae
___*Taraxacum sp.* .... Dandelion
___*Thalictrum occidentale* .... Western Meadowrue
___*Trilflorum repens* .... White Clover

___ *Vaccinium ovalifolium* .... Early Blueberry
___ *Viburnum edule* .... High-bush Cranberry
___ *Viola canadensis* .... Canada Violet
___ *Viola selkirkii* .... Selkirk's Violet

Ant Hill
(Buckinghorse River, BC)

---Be Wary---Dry, hot weather produces an abundance of these. This one was about 3 feet tall!

Fort Nelson, BC to Watson Lake, YT

Mile 283 to Mile 612.9

This is probably the most varied section of the Highway. From the wetlands of the Fort Nelson area you will travel through the moist foothills of the Rocky Mountains to Summit Lake (the highest point on the Highway). On the western descent of the Rockies, you will fully understand their name as you observe the vast area of rocky ridges and gravelly rivers, spotted with beautiful lakes.

Liard Hot Springs, BC

Devil's Club (seen only at Liard)

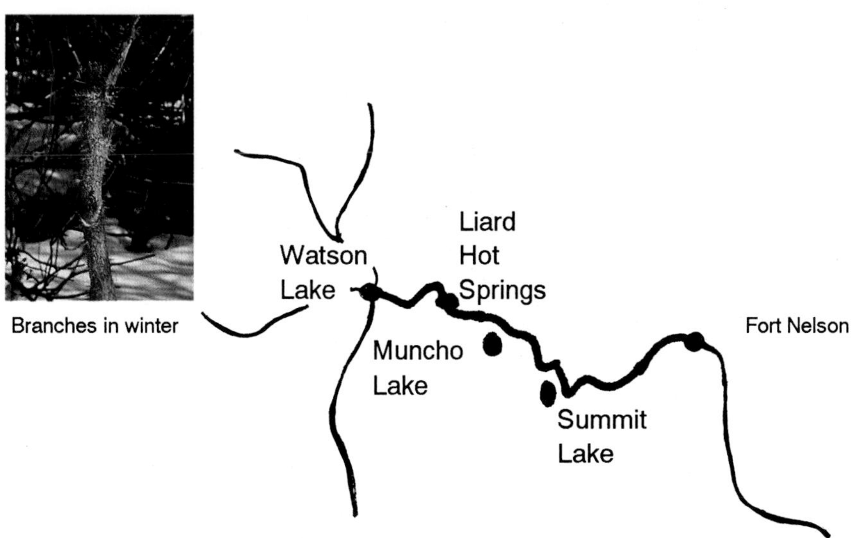

Branches in winter

FORT NELSON TO WATSON LAKE

___*Abies lasiocarpa* .... Subalpine Fir
___*Achillea borealis* .... Northern Yarrow
___*Achillea millefolium* .... Common Yarrow
___*Achillea sibirica* .... Siberian Yarrow
___*Aconitum delphinifolium* .... Monkshood
___*Actea rubra* .... Baneberry
___*Adoxa moschatellina* .... Musk Root
___*Allium schoenoprasum* .... Wild Chives
___*Alnus crispa* .... Mountain Alder
___*Alnus incana* .... Thin Leaf Alder
___*Amelanchier alnifolia* .... Alder leaf Serviceberry
___*Androsace septentrionalis* .... Northern Jasmine
___*Anemone multifida* .... Cut-leaf Anemone
___*Anemone narcissiflora* .... Narcissus-flowered Anemone
___*Anemone parviflora* .... Windflower
___*Anemone richardsonii* .... Yellow Anemone
___*Antennaria neglecta* .... White Pussy Toes
___*Antennaria monocephala* .... Cat's Paw
___*Antennaria pulcherrima* .... Tall Pussy-Toes
___*Antennaria rosea* .... Pink Pussy-toes
___*Apocynum androsaemifolium* .... Spreading Dogbane
___*Aquilegia brevistyla* .... Blue Columbine
___*Arabis holboellii* .... Holboel's Rockcress
___*Aralia nudicaulis* .... Wild Sarsaparilla
___*Arctostaphylos alpina* .... Alpine Bearberry
___*Arctostaphylos rubra* .... Red Bearberry
___*Arctostaphylos uva-ursi* .... Kinnikinnick
___*Arnica alpina* ssp. *angustifolia* .... Alpine Arnica
___*Arnica alpina* ssp. *attenuata* .... Tall Alpine Aster
___*Arnica cordifolia* .... Heart-leaf Arnica
___*Artemisia arctica* .... Arctic Wormwood
___*Artemisia frigida* .... Prairie Sagewort
___*Artemisia tilesii* .... Common Wormwood
___*Aster alpinus* .... Alpine Aster
___*Aster ciliolatus* .... Lindley Aster
___*Aster junciformis* .... Rush Aster
___*Aster laevis* .... Smooth Aster
___*Aster modestus* .... Showy Aster
___*Aster sibiricus* .... Siberian Aster
___*Aster subspicatus* .... Leafy Aster
___*Astragalus adsugens* ....
___*Astragalus alpinus* .... Alpine Milk Vetch
___*Astragalus americanus* .... American Milk Vetch
___*Astragalus drummondii* .... Drummond's Milk Vetch
___*Astragalus eucosmus* .... Elegant Milk Vetch
___*Athyrium felix-femina* .... Lady Fern
___*Betula glandulosum* .... Glandular Birch
___*Betula nana* .... Dwarf Birch
___*Betula papyrifera* .... Paper Birch
___*Boschniakia rossica* .... Broom Rape
___*Botrychium boreale* .... Northern Moonwort
___*Botrychium lunaria* .... Moonwort

___*Botrychium virginianum* .... Rattlesnake Fern
___*Calamagrostis canadensis* .... Bluejoint Grass
___*Calypso bulbosa* .... Fairy Slipper
___*Campanula aurita*... Bellflower
___*Campanula lasiocarpa*.. Mountain Harebell
___*Campanula uniflora*.. One-flowered Harebell
___*Carex aquatilis* .... Water Sedge
___*Cassiope tetragona* .... Bell Heather
___*Castilleja miniata* .... Indian Paintbrush
___*Cerastrium arvense* .... Mouse-ear Chickweed
___*Chamaerhodos erecta* .... Chamaerhodo
___*Chenopodium album*... Lamb's Quarters
___*Chenopodium capitatum* .... Strawberry Spinach
___*Chrysanthemum integrifolium*................................. Entire-leaf Chrysanthemum
___*Chrysoplenium tetrandrum* .... Northern Water Carpet
___*Cicuta douglasii* .... Poison Water-hemlock
___*Circaea alpina*... Enchanter's Nightshade
___*Corallorrhiza trifida*... Coral Root Orchid
___*Cornus canadensis* .... Canadian Dogwood
___*Cornus stolonifera*... Red-twig Dogwood
___*Corydalis aurea*... Golden Corydalis
___*Corydalis sempervirens* .... Pale Corydalis
___*Crepis capillaris*.. Hawksbeard
___*Crepis elegans*... Elegant Hawkweed
___*Crepis tectorum*... Tall Hawksbeard
___*Cypripedium calceolus* var. *pubescens*...................... Yellow Lady's Slipper
___*Cypripedium passerinum* .... Northern White Lady's Slipper
___*Cystopteris fragilis* .... Fragile Fern
___*Delphinium glaucum*... Larkspur
___*Dodecatheon frigidum* .... Frigid Shooting Star
___*Dodecatheon pauciflorum*... Few-flowered Shooting Star
___*Draba aurea* .... Golden Draba
___*Drosera anglica* .... Long-leaf Sundew
___*Drosera rotundifolia*... Round-leafed Sundew
___*Dryas drummondii*.. Yellow Dryas
___*Dryas integrifolia* .... Entire-leaf Avens
___*Dryas octopetala* .... Mt. Avens
___*Dryopteris dilatata* ssp. *americana* .... Wood Fern
___*Dryopteris fragrans* .... Fragrant Cliff Fern
___*Echinopanax horridum* .... Devil's Club
___*Elaeagnus commutata*... Silverberry
___*Empetrum nigrum* .... Crowberry
___*Epilobium adenocaulon* .... Common Willow Herb
___*Epilobium angustifolium*.. Common Fireweed
___*Epilobium latifolium*.. Dwarf Fireweed
___*Epilobium palustre* .... Marsh Willow Herb
___*Equisetum arvense*.. Field Horsetail
___*Equisetum hyemale* .... Common Scouring Rush
___*Equisetum pallustre* .... Marsh Horsetail
___*Equisetum pratense* .... Shady Horsetail
___*Equisetum scirpoides*... Sedgelike Horsetail
___*Equisetum sylvaticum* .... Horsetail
___*Equisetum variegatum* .... (variegated) Horsetail

___*Erigeron acris* .... Blue Fleabane
___*Erigeron compositus* .... Cutleaf Fleabane
___*Erigeron glabellus* .... Fringed Fleabane
___*Erigeron humilis* .... Mountain Fleabane
___*Erigeron lonchophyllus* .... Long-leaf Fleabane
___*Erigeron peregrinus* .... Coastal Fleabane
___*Erigeron philadelphicus* .... Philadelphia Daisy
___*Eriophorum angustifolium* .... Tall Cotton Grass
___*Erysimum cheiranthoides* .... Yellow Wallflower
___*Euphrasia disjuncta* .... Eye Bright
___*Fragaria virginiana* .... Wild Strawberry
___*Galium Boreale* .... Northern Bedstraw
___*Galium trifidum* .... Small Bedstraw
___*Galium triflorum* .... Sweet Scented Bedstraw
___*Gentiana prostrata* .... Moss Gentian
___*Gentiana amarella* .... Northern Gentian
___*Gentiana propinqua* .... Four-parted Gentian
___*Geocaulon lividum* .... Timberberry
___*Geranium bicknellii* .... Bicknell's Geranium
___*Geum macrophyllum* .... Large-leaf Avens
___*Goodyera repens* .... Rattlesnake Plantain
___*Gymnocarpium dryopteris* .... Oak Fern
___*Hedysarum alpinum* .... Eskimo Potato
___*Hedysarum hedysaroides* .... Alpine Pea
___*Hedysarum mackenzii* .... Wild Sweet Pea
___*Heracleum lanatum* .... Cow Parsnip
___*Hippuris vulgaris* .... Common Mare's Tail
___*Hordeum jubatum* .... Squirrel Tail Grass
___*Juncus arcticus* .... Arctic Rush
___*Juniperus communis* .... Common Juniper
___*Juniperus horizontalis* .... Creeping Savin
___*Lappula myosotis* .... Stickseed
___*Larix laricina* .... Tamarack, Larch
___*Ledum palustre* .... Labrador Tea
___*Lepidium densiflorum* .... Peppergrass
___*Linnaea borealis* .... Twinflower
___*Linum perenne* .... Wild Blue Flax
___*Listera borealis* .... Northern Twayblade
___*Listera caudata* .... Twayblade
___*Lonicera dioica* var. *glaucescens* .... Twining Honeysuckle
___*Lonicera involucrata* .... Black Twinberry
___*Lupinus arcticus* .... Arctic Lupine
___*Lycopodium annotinum* .... Stiff Clubmoss
___*Lycopodium clavatum* .... Club Moss
___*Lycopodium complanatum* .... Creeping Jenny
___*Lycopodium obscurum* .... Ground Pine
___*Lycopus uniflorus* .... Water Horehound
___*Lysimachia thyrsifolia* .... Tufted Loosestrife
___*Maianthemum dilitatum* .... Wild Lily of the Valley
___*Malaxis monophyla* ....
___*Matricaria matricarioides* .... Pineapple Weed
___*Matteuccia struthiopteris* .... Ostrich Fern
___*Medicago falcata* .... Yellow Alfalfa

___*Medicago sativa* .... Purple Alfalfa
___*Melilotus albus* .... White Sweet Clover
___*Melilotus officianalis* .... Yellow Sweet Clover
___*Mentha arvensis* .... Field Mint
___*Menyanthes trifoliata* .... Buckbean
___*Mertensia paniculata* .... Bluebells
___*Mimulus guttatus* .... Yellow Monkey Flower
___*Minuartia arctica* .... Arctic Sandwort
___*Mitella nuda* .... Bishop's Cap
___*Mitella pentandra* .... Alpine Mitrewort
___*Moehringia lateriflora* .... Grove Sandwort
___*Monesis uniflora* .... Single Delight
___*Nuphar polysepalum* .... Pond Lily
___*Orchis rotundifolia* .... Round-leafed Orchid
___*Osmorhiza depauperata* .... Blunt-fruited Sweet Cicely
___*Oxycoccus microcarpus* .... Bog Cranberry
___*Oxyria digyna* .... Mt. Sorrel
___*Oxytropis campestris* .... Northern Oxytrope
___*Oxytropis deflexa* .... Small-flowered Oxytrope
___*Oxytropis maydelliana* .... Maydell's Oxytrope
___*Oxytropis nigrescens* .... Purple or Blackish Oxytrope
___*Oxytropis splendens* .... Showy Locoweed
___*Oxytropis viscida* .... Sticky Locoweed
___*Parnassia fimbriata* .... Fringed Grass of Parnassus
___*Parnassia kotzebuei* .... Small Grass of Parnassus
___*Parnassia palustris* .... Grass of Parnassus
___*Pedicularis capitata* .... Capitate Lousewort
___*Pedicularis kanei* .... Wooly Lousewort
___*Pedicularis labradorica* .... Labrador Lousewort
___*Pedicularis oederi* .... Oeder's Lousewort
___*Pedicularis sudetica* .... Fern-leaf Lousewort
___*Penstemon gormannii* .... Yukon Beardstongue
___*Petasites frigida* .... Frigid Coltsfoot
___*Petasites hyperboreus* .... Northern Coltsfoot
___*Petasites palmatus* .... Palmate-leaf Coltsfoot
___*Petasites sagittatus* .... Arrow-leaf Coltsfoot
___*Phacelia franklinii* .... Franklin's phacelia
___*Picea glauca* .... White Spruce
___*Picea mariana* .... Black Spruce
___*Pinguicula vulgaris* .... Common Butterwort
___*Pinus contorta* .... Lodgepole Pine, Jack Pine
___*Plantago major* .... Common Plantain
___*Platanthera dilitata* .... White Bog Orchid
___*Platanthera hyperborea* .... Northern Green Bog Orchid
___*Platanthera obtusata* .... One Leaf Rein Orchid
___*Platanthera orbiculata* .... Round Leaf Rein Orchid
___*Poa alpina* .... Alpine Bluegrass
___*Polemonium acutiflorum* .... Tall Jacob's Ladder
___*Polemonium pulcherrimum* .... Beautiful Jacob's Ladder
___*Polygonum viviparum* .... Alpine Meadow Bistort
___*Populus balsamifera* .... Cottonwood
___*Populus tremuloides* .... Quaking Aspen

___ *Potentilla anserina* .... Silverweed
___ *Potentilla arguta* .... White Potentilla
___ *Potentilla biflora* .... Two-flowered Cinquefoil
___ *Potentilla diversifolia* ....
___ *Potentilla fruiticosa* .... Tundra Rose
___ *Potentilla gracilis* ....
___ *Potentilla hookeriana* .... Hooker's Cinquefoil
___ *Potentilla norvegica* ssp. *monspeliensis* .... Norwegian Cinquefoil
___ *Potentilla palustris* .... Marsh Cinquefoil
___ *Potentilla uniflora* .... One-flowered Cinquefoil
___ *Primula mistassinica* .... Bird's Eye Primrose
___ *Prunus virginiana* .... Common Chokecherry
___ *Pulsatilla patens* ssp. *multifida* .... Pasque Flower
___ *Pyrola asarifolia* .... Pink Pyrola
___ *Pyrola chlorantha* .... Green Pyrola
___ *Pyrola grandiflora* .... Large-flowered Wintergreen
___ *Pyrola minor* .... Small-flowered Wintergreen
___ *Pyrola secunda* .... Sidebells Pyrola
___ *Ranunculus hyperboreus* .... Dwarf Creeping Buttercup
___ *Ranunculus repens* .... Creeping Buttercup
___ *Ranunculus sceleratus* .... Cursed Crowfoot
___ *Rhinanthus minor* .... Rattlebox
___ *Rhododendron lapponicum* .... Lapland Rosebay
___ *Ribes glandulosum* .... Skunk Currant
___ *Ribes hudsonianum* .... Northern Black Currant
___ *Ribes lacustre* .... Swamp Gooseberry
___ *Ribes oxyacanthoides* .... Purple Gooseberry
___ *Ribes triste* .... Red Currant
___ *Rosa acicularis* .... Prickly Rose
___ *Rosa woodsii* .... Wood's Rose
___ *Rubus arcticus* .... Nagoonberry
___ *Rubus idaeus* .... Raspberry
___ *Rubus pubescens* .... Trailing Red Blackberry
___ *Rumex salicifolius* .... Narrow leaved Dock
___ *Salix alaxensis* .... Alaska Willow
___ *Salix arbusculoides* .... Little Tree Willow
___ *Salix arctica* .... Arctic Willow
___ *Salix barclayii* .... Barclay Willow
___ *Salix candida* .... Silver Willow
___ *Salix depressa* .... Bebb Willow
___ *Salix glauca* .... Grayleaf Willow
___ *Salix lasiandra* .... Pacific Willow
___ *Salix padophylla* .... Park Willow
___ *Salix polaris* .... Polar Willow
___ *Salix reticulata* .... Netted Willow
___ *Salix scouleriana* .... Scouler Willow
___ *Salix setchelliana* .... Setchel's Willow
___ *Sanguisorba stipulata* .... Sitka Burnet
___ *Sanicula marilandica* .... Black Snakeroot
___ *Saxifraga aiziodes* .... Golden Saxifrage
___ *Saxifraga flagellaris* .... Spider Saxifrage
___ *Saxifraga oppositifolia* .... Purple Mt. Saxifrage

___*Saxifraga tricuspidata* .... Prickly Saxifrage
___*Scirpus caespitosus* .... Tufted Club Rush
___*Scirpus rubrotincus* .... Small Bull Rush
___*Scirpus validus* .... Great Bull Rush
___*Scutellarea galericulata* .... Marsh Skullcap
___*Senecio cymbalariodes* ....
___*Senecio fuscatus* ....
___*Senecio lugens* .... Black-tipped Groundsel
___*Senecio pauciflorus* .... Few-flowered Groundsel
___*Senecio paupercaulis* .... Groundsel
___*Senecio vulgaris* .... Common Groundsel
___*Shepherdia canadensis* .... Soapberry
___*Smilacina stellata* .... Star-flowered False Solomon's Seal
___*Solidago canadensis* .... Canada Goldenrod
___*Solidago decumbens* ssp. *oreophila* .... Decumbent Goldenrod
___*Solidago multiradiata* ssp. *scopularia* .... Rocky Mt. Goldenrod
___*Sorbus scopulina* .... Green Mountain Ash
___*Spiraea betulifolia* .... Birch Leaf Spiraea
___*Spiranthes romanzoffiana* .... Hooded Ladies' Tresses
___*Stellaria calycantha* .... Northern Starwort
___*Stellaria longipes* .... Longstalk Starwort
___*Streptopus amplexifolius* .... Watermelon Berry
___*Taraxacum* sp. .... Dandelion
___*Taraxicum alaskanum* .... Native Dandelion
___*Thalictrum occidentale* .... Western Meadowrue
___*Thalictrum sparsiflorum* .... Common Meadowrue
___*Tofieldia glutinosa* .... Sticky Asphodel
___*Tofieldia pusilla* .... False Asphodel
___*Triflorum pratense* .... Red Clover
___*Triflorum repens* .... White Clover
___*Triglochin maritimum* .... Seaside Arrow-grass
___*Triglochin palustre* .... Marsh Arrow-grass
___*Typha latifolia* .... Cattail
___*Urtica dioica* .... Stinging Nettle
___*Urtica lyallii* .... Lyall Nettle
___*Utricularia intermedia* .... Bladderwort
___*Vaccinium ovalifolium* .... Early Blueberry
___*Vaccinium uliginosum* .... Bog Blueberry
___*Vaccinium vitis-idaea* .... Low-bush Cranberry
___*Veronica americana* .... American Brook Lime
___*Veronica serphyllifolia* .... Brook Lime
___*Viburnum edule* .... High-bush Cranberry
___*Vicia americana* .... American Vetch
___*Viola adunca* .... Western Dog Violet
___*Viola canadensis* .... Canada Violet
___*Viola nephrophylla* .... Northern Bog Violet
___*Viola renifolia* .... White Wood Violet
___*Woodsia ilvensis* .... Rusty Woodsia
___*Zygadenus elegans* .... Death Camas

Summit Lake Provincial Park, BC

Mile 373.6

This alpine lake, with a small campground, can be a jumping-off point for hikes for wildflower enthusiasts. This is the only place along the Highway with easy access to alpine plants. This area is easy to explore and produces many different plants.

Tundra, Summit Lake, BC
Senecio fuscatus

SUMMIT LAKE PROVINCIAL PARK, BC

___*Achillea borealis* .... Northern Yarrow
___*Aconitum delphinifolium* .... Monkshood
___*Alnus crispa* .... Green Mountain Alder
___*Anemone narcissiflora* .... Narcissus-flowered Anemone
___*Anemone parviflora* .... Windflower
___*Antennaria neglecta* .... White Pussy Toes
___*Antennaria monocephala* .... Cat's Paw
___*Antennaria pulcherrima* .... Tall Pussy Toes
___*Antennaria rosea* .... Pink Pussy-toes
___*Aquilegia brevistyla* .... Blue Columbine
___*Arctostaphylos alpina* .... Alpine Bearberry
___*Arctostaphylos rubra* .... Red Bearberry
___*Arctostaphylos uva-ursi* .... Kinnikinnick
___*Artemisia arctica* .... Arctic Wormwood
___*Artemisia tilesii* .... Common Wormwood
___*Aster sibiricus* .... Siberian Aster
___*Astragalus adsurgens* ....
___*Astragalus alpinus* .... Alpine Milk Vetch
___*Astragalus americanus* .... American Milk Vetch
___*Betula nana* .... Dwarf Birch
___*Campanula aurita* .... Bell Flower
___*Campanula lasiocarpa* .... Mountain Harebell
___*Campanula uniflora* .... One-flowered Harebell
___*Carex microchaeta* .... Short-stalked Sedge
___*Cassiope tetragona* .... Bell Heather
___*Castilleja miniata* .... Indian Paintbrush
___*Cerastrium beeringianum* ssp. *beeringianum* .... Bering Sea Chickweed
___*Chenopodium capitatum* .... Strawberry Spinach
___*Chrysanthemum integrifolium* .... Entire Leaf Chrysanthemum
___*Chrysosplenum tetrandrum* .... Northern Water Carpet
___*Coeloglossum viride* .... Frog Orchid
___*Cornus canadensis* .... Canadian Dogwood
___*Cypripedium passerinum* .... Northern Orchid
___*Cystopteris fragilis* .... Fragile Fern
___*Dodecatheon frigidum* .... Frigid Shooting Star
___*Dryas drummondii* .... Yellow Dryas
___*Dryas integrifolia* .... Entire-leaf Avens
___*Dryas octopetala* .... Mountain Avens
___*Empetrum nigrum* .... Crowberry
___*Epilobium angustifolium* .... Common Fireweed
___*Equisetum arvense* .... Field Horsetail
___*Erigeron humilis* .... Mountain Fleabane
___*Fragaria virginiana* .... Wild Strawberry
___*Galium boreale* .... Northern Bedstraw
___*Gentiana propinqua* .... Four-parted Gentian
___*Gentiana prostrata* .... Moss Gentian
___*Geocaulon lividum* .... Timberberry
___*Hedysarum alpinum* .... Eskimo Potato
___*Hedysarum hedysaroides* .... Alpine Eskimo Potato
___*Hedysarum mackenzii* .... Wild Sweet Pea
___*Juniperus communis* .... Common Juniper
___*Ledum palustre* .... Labrador Tea

___ *Lesquella arctica* .... Bladderpod
___ *Linnaea borealis* .... Twinflower
___ *Lupinus arcticus* .... Arctic Lupine
___ *Melandrium apetalum* .... Bladder Campion
___ *Melilotus albus* .... White Sweet Clover
___ *Melilotus officianalis* .... Yellow Sweet Clover
___ *Mertensia paniculata* .... Bluebells
___ *Minuartia arctica* .... Arctic Sandwort
___ *Mitella pentandta* .... Alpine Mitrewort
___ *Moneses uniflora* .... Single Delight
___ *Oxyria digyna* .... Mt. Sorrel
___ *Oxytropis deflexa* .... Small-flowered Oxytrope
___ *Oxytropis maydelliana* .... Maydell's Oxytrope
___ *Oxytropis nigrescens* .... Purple Oxytrope
___ *Oxytropis splendens* .... Showy Locoweed
___ *Parnassia fimbriata* .... Fringed Grass of Parnassus
___ *Parnassia kotzebuei* .... Small Grass of Parnassus
___ *Parnassia palustris* .... Grass of Parnassus
___ *Pedicularis capitata* .... Capitate Lousewort
___ *Pedicularis kanei* .... Wooly Lousewort
___ *Pedicularis labradorica* .... Labrador Lousewort
___ *Pedicularis oederi* .... Oeder's Lousewort
___ *Pedicularis sudetica* .... Fern-leaf Lousewort
___ *Petasites palmatus* .... Palmate-leaf Coltsfoot
___ *Petasites sagittatus* .... Arrow-leaf Coltsfoot
___ *Picea glauca* .... White Spruce
___ *Pinguicula vulgaris* .... Common Butterwort
___ *Pinus contorta* .... Lodgepole Pine, Jack Pine
___ *Platanthera hyperborea* .... Northern Green Bog Orchid
___ *Platanthera obtusata* .... One-leaf Rein Orchid
___ *Polemonium acutiflorum* .... Tall Jacob's Ladder
___ *Polygonum viviparum* .... Alpine Meadow Bistort
___ *Potentilla biflora* .... Two-flowered Cinquefoil
___ *Potentilla fruiticosa* .... Tundra Rose
___ *Potentilla gracilis* ....
___ *Potentilla norvegica* ssp. *monspeliensis* .... Norwegian Cinquefoil
___ *Potentilla uniflora* .... One-flowered Cinquefoil
___ *Pyrola asarifolia* .... Pink Pyrola
___ *Pyrola chlorantha* .... Green Pyrola
___ *Pyrola grandiflora* .... Large-flowered Wintergreen
___ *Pyrola minor* .... Small-flowered Pyrola
___ *Pyrola secunda* .... Sidebells Pyrola
___ *Rhinanthus minor* .... Rattlebox
___ *Rhododendron lapponicum* .... Lapland Rosebay
___ *Rubus arcticus* .... Nagoonberry
___ *Salix alaxensis* .... Alaska Willow
___ *Salix arctica* .... Arctic Willow
___ *Salix barclayii* .... Barclay Willow
___ *Sanguisorba stipulata* .... Sitka Burnet
___ *Saxifraga aiziodes* .... Golden Saxifrage
___ *Saxifraga flagellaris* .... Spider Saxifrage
___ *Saxifraga oppositifolia* .... Purple Mt. Saxifrage

___*Saxifraga tricuspidata* .... Prickly Saxifrage
___*Senecio fuscatus* ....
___*Senecio lugens* .... Black-tipped Groundsel
___*Senecio resedifolius* .... Dwarf Arctic Butterweed
___*Shepherdia canadensis* .... Soapberry
___*Silene acaulis* .... Moss Campion
___*Solidago decumbens ssp. oreophila* .... Decumbent Goldenrod
___*Solidago multiradiata ssp. multiradiata* .... Northern Goldenrod
___*Solidago multiradiata ssp. scopularia* .... Rocky Mt. Goldenrod
___*Taraxacum alaskanum* .... Native Dandelion
___*Tofieldia pusilla* .... False Asphodel
___*Triflorum pratense* .... Red Clover
___*Triflorum repens* .... White Clover
___*Vaccinium uliginosum* .... Bog Blueberry
___*Vaccinium vitis-idaea* .... Low-bush Cranberry
___*Zygadenus elegans* .... Death Camas

Lamb's Quarters, Pigweed
(*Chenopodium album*)

Liard Hot Springs, BC

Mile 477.7

This refreshing oasis in the north country is reached by a very short side trip, and is a must for everyone. Many warm climate plants are exclusive to the area.

"Hanging Gardens" at Liard Hot Springs, BC

LIARD HOT SPRINGS PROVINCIAL PARK, BC

___*Abies lasiocarpa* .... Subalpine fir
___*Achillea millefolium* .... Common Yarrow
___*Achillea sibirica* .... Siberian Yarrow
___*Actea rubra* .... Baneberry
___*Adoxa moschatellina* .... Musk Root
___*Allium schoenoprasum* .... Wild Chives
___*Alnus incana* .... Thin Leaf Alder
___*Amelanchier alnifolia* .... Alder-leaf Serviceberry
___*Androsace septentrionalis* .... Northern Jasmine
___*Anemone multifida* .... Cut-leaf Anemone
___*Anemone parviflora* .... Windflower
___*Anemone richardsonii* .... Yellow Anemone
___*Antennaria pulcherrima* .... Tall Pussy Toes
___*Antennaria rosea* .... Pink Pussy-toes
___*Apocynum androsaemifolium* .... Spreading Dogbane
___*Aquilegia brevistyla* .... Blue Columbine
___*Arabis holboellii* .... Holboell's Rockcress
___*Aralia nudicaulis* .... Wild Sarsaparilla
___*Arctostaphylos rubra* .... Red Bearberry
___*Arctostaphylos uva-ursi* .... Kinnikinnick
___*Arnica alpina* ssp. *angustifolia* .... Alpine Arnica
___*Arnica cordifolia* .... Heart-leaf Arnica
___*Artemisia frigida* .... Prairie Sagewort
___*Artemisia tilesii* .... Common Wormwood
___*Aster alpinus* .... Alpine Aster
___*Aster ciliolatus* .... Lindley Aster
___*Aster junciformis* .... Rush Aster
___*Aster laevis* .... Smooth Aster
___*Aster modestus* .... Showy Aster
___*Aster sibiricus* .... Siberian Aster
___*Aster subspicatus* .... Leafy Aster
___*Astragalus alpinus* .... Alpine Milk Vetch
___*Astragalus eucosmus* .... Elegant Milk Vetch
___*Athyrium felix-femina* .... Lady Fern
___*Betula papyrifera* .... Paper Birch
___*Botrychium lunaria* .... Moonwort
___*Botrychium virginianum* .... Rattlesnake Fern
___*Calamagrostis canadensis* .... Bluejoint Grass
___*Calypso bulbosa* .... Fairy Slipper
___*Campanula aurita* .... Bell Flower
___*Carex aquatilis* .... Water Sedge
___*Cerastrium arvense* .... Mouse-ear Chickweed
___*Chamaerhodos erecta* .... Chamaerhodo
___*Chenopodium album* .... Lamb's Quarters
___*Chenopodium capitatum* .... Strawberry Blite
___*Chrysoplenium tetrandrum* .... Northern Water Carpet
___*Cicuta douglassii* .... Poison Water Hemlock
___*Circaea alpina* .... Enchanter's Nightshade
___*Corallorrhiza trifida* .... Coral Root Orchid
___*Cornus canadensis* .... Canadian Dogwood
___*Cornus stolonifera* .... Red-twig Dogwood

___ *Corydalis aurea* .... Golden Corydalis
___ *Corydalis sempervirens* .... Pale Corydalis
___ *Crepis capillaris* .... Hawksbeard
___ *Cypripedium calceolus* var. *pubescens* .... Yellow Lady's Slipper
___ *Cypripedium passerinum* .... Northern White Lady's Slipper
___ *Cystopteris fragilis* .... Fragile Fern
___ *Dodecatheon pauciflorum* .... Few-flowered Shooting Star
___ *Draba aurea* .... Golden Draba
___ *Drosera anglica* .... Long-leafed Sundew
___ *Drosera rotundifolia* .... Round-leafed Sundew
___ *Dryas drummondii* .... Yellow Dryas
___ *Dryopteris dilatata* .... Wood Fern
___ *Dryopteris fragrans* .... Fragrant Fern
___ *Echinopanax horridum* .... Devil's Club
___ *Elaeagnus commutata* .... Silverberry
___ *Empetrum nigrum* .... Crowberry
___ *Epilobium adenocaulon* .... Common Willow Herb
___ *Epilobium angustifolium* .... Common Fireweed
___ *Epilobium latifolium* .... Dwarf Fireweed
___ *Epilobium palustre* .... Marsh Willow Herb
___ *Equisetum arvense* .... Field Horsetail
___ *Equisetum hyemale* .... Common Scouring Rush
___ *Equisetum palustre* .... Marsh Horsetail
___ *Equisetum scirpoides* .... Sedge-like Horsetail
___ *Equisetum sylvaticum* .... Horsetail
___ *Equisetum variegatum* .... Variegated Horsetail
___ *Erigeron acris* .... Blue Fleabane
___ *Erigeron compositus* .... Cutleaf Fleabane
___ *Erigeron glabellus* .... Fringed Fleabane
___ *Erigeron peregrinus* .... Coastal Fleabane
___ *Erigeron philadelphicus* .... Philadelphia Daisy
___ *Erysimum cheiranthoides* .... Yellow Wallflower
___ *Fragaria virginiana* .... Wild Strawberry
___ *Galium boreale* .... Northern Bedstraw
___ *Galium trifidum* .... Small Bedstraw
___ *Galium triflorum* .... Sweet Scented Bedstraw
___ *Gentiana amarella* .... Northern Gentian
___ *Geocaulon lividum* .... Timberberry
___ *Geranium bicknellii* .... Bicknell's geranium
___ *Geum macrophyllum* .... Large-leaf Avens
___ *Goodyera repens* .... Rattlesnake Plantain
___ *Gymnocarpium dryopteris* .... Oak Fern
___ *Hedysarum alpinum* .... Eskimo Potato
___ *Hedysarum mackenzii* .... Wild Sweet Pea
___ *Heracleum lanatum* .... Cow Parsnip
___ *Hippuris vulgaris* .... Mare's Tail
___ *Hordeum jubatum* .... Squirrel Tail Grass
___ *Juniperus communis* .... Common Juniper
___ *Juniperus horizontalis* .... Creeping Savin
___ *Lappula myosotis* .... Stickseed
___ *Larix laricina* var. *alaskensis* .... Tamarack, Larch
___ *Ledum palustre* .... Labrador Tea

___*Linnaea borealis* .... Twinflower
___*Linum perenne* .... Wild Blue Flax
___*Listera borealis* .... Northern Twayblade
___*Listera cordata* .... Heart-leaf Twayblade
___*Lobelia kalmii* .... Brook Lobelia
___*Lonicera dioica* var. *glaucescens* .... Twining Honeysuckle
___*Lonicera involucrata* .... Black Twinberry
___*Lupinus arcticus* .... Arctic Lupine
___*Lycopodium annotinum* .... Stiff Club Moss
___*Lycopodium complanatum* .... Creeping Jenny
___*Lycopodium obscurum* .... Ground Pine
___*Lycopus uniflorus* .... Water Horehound
___*Lysimachia thyrsifolia* .... Tufted Loosestrife
___*Maianthemum canadense* .... Wild Lily of the Valley
___*Malaxis monophyllos* .... Malaxis
___*Matricaria matricarioides* .... Pineapple Weed
___*Matteuccia struthiopteris* .... Ostrich Fern
___*Mentha arvensis* .... Field Mint
___*Mertensia paniculata* .... Bluebells
___*Mimulus guttatus* .... Yellow Monkey Flower
___*Mitella nuda* .... Bishop's Cap
___*Moehringia lateriflora* .... Grove Sandwort
___*Monesis uniflora* .... Single Delight
___*Orchis rotundifolia* .... Round-leafed Orchid
___*Osmorhiza depauperata* .... Blunt-fruited Sweet Cicely
___*Oxycoccus microcarpus* .... Bog Cranberry
___*Oxytropis campestris* .... Northern Oxytrope
___*Oxytropis deflexa* .... Small-flowered Oxytrope
___*Oxytropis splendens* .... Showy Locoweed
___*Oxytropis viscida* .... Sticky Locoweed
___*Parnassia fimbriata* .... Fringed Grass of Parnassus
___*Parnassia palustris* .... Grass of Parnassus
___*Penstemon gormannii* .... Yukon Beardstongue
___*Petasites palmatus* .... Palmate-leaf Coltsfoot
___*Petasites sagittatus* .... Arrow-leaf Coltsfoot
___*Phacelia franklinii* .... Franklin's Phacelia
___*Picea glauca* .... White Spruce
___*Picea mariana* .... Black Spruce
___*Pinguicula vulgaris* .... Common Butterwort
___*Pinus contorta* .... Lodgepole Pine, Jack Pine
___*Plantago major* .... Common Plantain
___*Platanthera hyperborea* .... Northern Green Bog Orchid
___*Platanthera obtusata* .... One-leaf Rein Orchid
___*Platanthera orbiculata* .... Round-leaved Rein Orchid
___*Polemonium acutiflorum* .... Tall Jacob's Ladder
___*Polemonium pulcherrimum* .... Beautiful Jacob's Ladder
___*Populus balsamifera* .... Cottonwood
___*Populus tremuloides* .... Quaking Aspen
___*Potentilla arguta* .... White Potentilla
___*Potentilla diversifolia* ....
___*Potentilla fruiticosa* .... Tundra Rose
___*Potentilla hookeriana* .... Hooker's Cinquefoil

___ *Potentilla norvegica* ssp. *monspeliensis*...................... Norwegian Cinquefoil
___ *Primula mistassinica*.. Bird's eye Primrose
___ *Prunus virginiana*... Common Chokecherry
___ *Pulsatilla patens* ssp. *multifida*.................................... Pasque Flower
___ *Pyrola asarifolia*... Pink Pyrola
___ *Pyrola chlorantha*.. Green Pyrola
___ *Pyrola grandiflora*... Large-flowered Wintergreen
___ *Pyrola secunda* .... Sidebells Pyrola
___ *Ranunculus hyperboreus*.. Dwarf Creeping Buttercup
___ *Ranunculus sceleratus*.. Cursed Crowfoot
___ *Ribes glandulosum* .... Skunk Currant
___ *Ribes hudsonianum*... Northern Black Currant
___ *Ribes lacustre*... Swamp Gooseberry
___ *Ribes oxyacanthoides* .... Northern Gooseberry
___ *Ribes triste*.. Red Currant
___ *Rosa acicularis* .... Prickly Rose
___ *Rosa woodsii* .... Wood's Rose
___ *Rubus arcticus* .... Nagoonberry
___ *Rubus idaeus* .... Raspberry
___ *Rubus pubescens* .... Trailing Red Blackberry
___ *Rumex salicifolius* .... Narrow-leaved Dock
___ *Salix alaxensis* .... Alaska Willow
___ *Salix arbusculoides* .... Little Tree Willow
___ *Salix candida* .... Silver Willow
___ *Salix depressa* .... Bebb Willow
___ *Salix glauca*.. Grayleaf Willow
___ *Salix lasiandra* .... Pacific Willow
___ *Salix scouleriana* .... Scouler's Willow
___ *Sanicula marilandica* .... Black Snakeroot
___ *Saxifraga tricuspidata* .... Prickly Saxifrage
___ *Scirpus caespitosus* .... Tufted Club Rush
___ *Scutellaria galericulata* .... Marsh Skullcap
___ *Senecio cymbalarioides*..
___ *Senecio lugens*.. Black-tipped Groundsel
___ *Senecio pauciflorus* .... Few-flowered Groundsel
___ *Shepherdia canadensis*.. Soapberry
___ *Smilacina stellata* .... Star-flowered False Solomon's Seal
___ *Smilacina trifolia*... Siberian False Solomon's Seal
___ *Solidago canadensis*.. Canada Goldenrod
___ *Solidago decumbens ssp. oreophila*............................. Decumbent Goldenrod
___ *Solidago multiradiata ssp. scopularia* .... Rocky Mt. Goldenrod
___ *Sorbus scopulina* .... Greene Mountain Ash
___ *Spiraea betulifolia* .... Birch Leaf Spiraea
___ *Spiranthes romanzoffiana*... Hooded Ladies' Tresses
___ *Stellaria calycantha* .... Northern Starwort
___ *Stellaria longipes*... Longstalk Starwort
___ *Streoptopus amplexifolius*.. Watermelon Berry
___ *Taraxacum sp.*... Dandelion
___ *Thalictrum occidentale* .... Western Meadowrue
___ *Thalictrum sparsiflorum* .... Common Meadowrue
___ *Tofieldia glutinosa* .... Sticky Asphodel
___ *Tofieldia pusilla*... False Asphodel
___ *Trifolium repens* .... White Clover

__ *Triglochin maritimum* .... Seaside Arrow-grass
__ *Triglochin palustre* .... Marsh Arrow-grass
__ *Typha latifolia* .... Cattail
__ *Urtica dioica* ssp. *gracilis* .... Stinging Nettle
__ *Urtica lyallii* .... Lyall Nettle
__ *Utricularia intermedia* .... Bladderwort
__ *Vaccinium ovalifolium* .... Early Blueberry
__ *Vaccinium uliginosum* .... Bog Blueberry
__ *Vaccinium vitis-idaea* .... Low-bush Cranberry
__ *Veronica americana* .... American Brook Lime
__ *Viburnum edule* .... High-bush Cranberry
__ *Vicia americana* .... American Vetch
__ *Viola adunca* .... Western Dog Violet
__ *Viola canadensis* .... Canada Violet
__ *Viola nephrophylla* .... Blue Violet
__ *Viola renifolia* .... Kidney-leaved Violet
__ *Woodsia ilvensis* .... Rusty Woodsia
__ *Zygadenus elegans* .... Death Camas

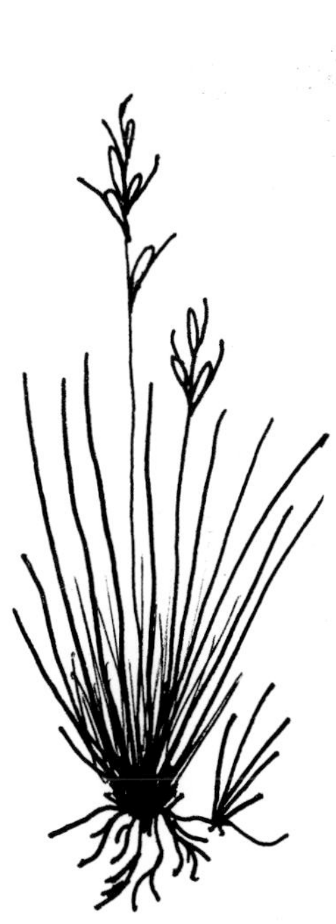

Sedges
Solid stems,
usually triangular
Leaves usually
stiff

Rushes
Solid stems,
round
Leaves usually
not stiff

Grasses
Hollow stems,
round
Leaves usually
flexible

Watson Lake, YT to Whitehorse, YT

Mile 612.9 to Mile 884

Here the road travels mostly through low elevations following rivers, finally arriving at Whitehorse with its dry sandy hillsides. We recommend that the traveler visit the Yukon Gardens, just south of Whitehorse, which is a very nice mixture of native plants and horticultural specimens.

Roadside, Muncho Lake, BC

Fireweed Seed Head

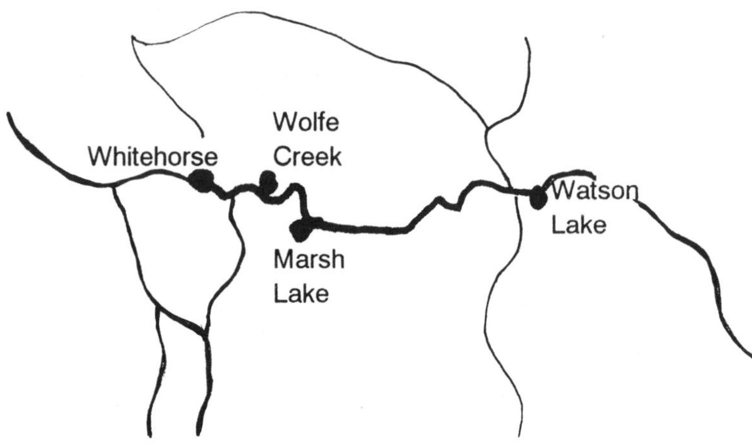

WATSON LAKE, YT TO WHITEHORSE, YT

___*Achillea borealis* .... Northern Yarrow
___*Actea rubra* .... Baneberry
___*Alnus crispa* .... Green Mountain Alder
___*Alnus incana* .... Thin Leaf Alder
___*Amelanchier alnifolia* .... Alder-leaf Serviceberry
___*Androsace septentrionalis* .... Northern Jasmine
___*Anemone multifida* .... Cut-leaf Anemone
___*Anemone parviflora* .... Windflower
___*Antennaria media* .... White Pussy Toes
___*Antennaria pulcherrima* .... Tall PussyToes
___*Antennaria rosea* .... Pink Pussy-toes
___*Aquilegia formosa* .... Western Columbine
___*Arctostaphylos rubra* .... Red Bearberry
___*Arctostaphylos uva-ursi* .... Kinnikinnick
___*Arnica alpina* ssp. *attenuata* .... Tall Alpine Arnica
___*Arnica chamissonis* .... Tall Meadow Arnica
___*Arnica cordifolia* .... Heart-leaf Arnica
___*Arnica frigida* .... Frigid Arnica
___*Arnica lonchophylla* .... Narrow Leaf Arnica
___*Artemisia alaskana* .... Alaska Wormwood
___*Artemisia arctica* .... Arctic Wormwood
___*Artemisia canadensis* .... Canada Wormwood
___*Artemisia dracunculus* .... Common Wormwood
___*Artemisia frigida* .... Prairie Sagewort
___*Artemisia tilesii* .... Common Wormwood
___*Aster laevis* .... Smooth Aster
___*Aster sibiricus* .... Siberian Aster
___*Astragalus alpinus* .... Alpine Milk Vetch
___*Astragalus americanus* .... American Milk Vetch
___*Betula papyrifera* .... Paper Birch
___*Calamagrostis canadensis* .... Bluejoint Grass
___*Castilleja caudata* .... Yellow Paintbrush
___*Chenopodium album* .... Lamb's Quarters
___*Chenopodium capitatum* .... Strawberry Spinach
___*Cornus canadensis* .... Canadian Dogwood
___*Cornus stolonifera* .... Red-twig Dogwood
___*Crepis capillaris* .... Hawksbeard
___*Crepis elegans* .... Elegant Hawksbeard
___*Crepis tectorum* .... Tall Hawksbeard
___*Delphinium glaucum* .... Larkspur
___*Dryas drummondii* .... Yellow Dryas
___*Elaeagnus commutata* .... Silverberry
___*Epilobium adenocaulin* .... Tall Willow Herb
___*Epilobium angustifolium* .... Common Fireweed
___*Epilobium latifolium* .... Dwarf Fireweed
___*Epilobium palustre* .... Marsh Willow Herb
___*Equisetum arvense* .... Field Horsetail
___*Equisetum sylvaticum* .... Woodland Horsetail
___*Erigeron acris* .... Blue Fleabane
___*Erigeron lonchiphyllus* .... Long Leaf Fleabane
___*Eriophorum angustifolium* .... Tall Cotton Grass
___*Eriophorum* sp. .... Cotton Grass

___*Fragaria virginiana* .... Wild Strawberry
___*Galium Boreale* .... Northern Bedstraw
___*Gentiana armarella* .... Northern Gentian
___*Gentiana propinqua* .... Four-parted Gentian
___*Geocaulon lividum* .... Timberberry
___*Geum macrophyllum* .... Large-leaf Avens
___*Goodyera repens* .... Rattlesnake Plantain
___*Hedysarum alpinum* .... Eskimo Potato
___*Heracleum lanatum* .... Cow Parsnip
___*Hordeum jubatum* .... Squirrel Tail Grass
___*Juniperus scopulina* .... Rocky Mt. Juniper
___*Lathyrus palustris* .... Vetchling
___*Ledum palustre* .... Labrador Tea
___*Linnaea borealis* .... Twinflower
___*Lupinus arcticus* .... Arctic Lupine
___*Lycopodium annotinum* .... Stiff Club Moss
___*Lycopodium complanatum* .... Creeping Jenny
___*Matricaria matricarioides* .... Pineapple Weed
___*Medicago falcata* .... Yellow Alfalfa
___*Medicago sativa* .... Purple Alfalfa
___*Melilotus albus* .... White Sweet Clover
___*Melilotus officianalis* .... Yellow Sweet Clover
___*Menyanthes trifoliata* .... Buckbean
___*Mertensia paniculata* .... Bluebells
___*Moehringia lateriflora* .... Grove Sandwort
___*Moneses uniflora* .... Single Delight
___*Onobrychis viciaefolia* .... Sand Fain
___*Oxycoccus microcarpus* .... Bog Cranberry
___*Oxytropis campestris* .... Northern Oxytrope
___*Oxytropis deflexa* ssp. *foliolosa* .... Small-flowered Locoweed
___*Oxytropis deflexa* ssp. *sericea* .... Small-flowered Oxytrope
___*Oxytropis splendens* .... Showy Locoweed
___*Oxytropis viscida* .... Sticky Locoweed
___*Parnassia palustris* .... Grass of Parnassus
___*Pedicularis labradorica* .... Labrador Lousewort
___*Pedicularis sudetica* .... Fern-leaf Lousewort
___*Penstemon gormanii* .... Yukon Beardstongue
___*Petasites hyperboreus* .... Alpine Coltsfoot
___*Petasites palmatus* .... Palmate-leaf Coltsfoot
___*Petasites sagittatus* .... Arrow-leaf Coltsfoot
___*Picea glauca* .... White Spruce
___*Picea mariana* .... Black Spruce
___*Pinus contorta* .... Lodgepole Pine, Jack Pine
___*Plantago major* .... Common Plantain
___*Platanthera dilitata* .... Bog Candle
___*Platanthera hyperborea* .... Northern Green Bog Orchid
___*Platanthera obtusata* .... One-leaf Rein Orchid
___*Polemonium acutiflorum* .... Tall Jacob's Ladder
___*Polemonium pulcherrimum* .... Beautiful Jacob's Ladder
___*Polygonum* sp. .... Knotweed
___*Populus balsamifera* .... Cottonwood
___*Populus tremuloides* .... Quaking Aspen

___ *Potentilla fruiticosa* .... Tundra Rose
___ *Potentilla norvegica* ssp. *monspeliensis* .... Norwegian Cinquefoil
___ *Potentilla palustris* .... Marsh Cinquefoil
___ *Pulsatilla patens* ssp. *multifida* .... Pasque Flower
___ *Pyrola asarifolia* .... Pink Pyrola
___ *Pyrola chlorantha* .... Green Pyrola
___ *Pyrola secunda* .... Sidebells Pyrola
___ *Ranunculus gmelini* .... Creeping Crowfoot
___ *Ranunculus lapponicus* .... Lapland Buttercup
___ *Rhinanthus minor* ssp. *borealis* .... Rattlebox
___ *Ribes oxyacanthoides* .... Purple Gooseberry
___ *Ribes triste* .... Red Currant
___ *Rosa acicularis* .... Prickly Rose
___ *Rubus arcticus* .... Nagoonberry
___ *Rubus idaeus* .... Raspberry
___ *Rumex arcticus* .... Arctic Dock
___ *Rumex maritimus* .... White Dock
___ *Salix alaxensis* .... Alaska Willow
___ *Salix arbusculoides* .... Little Tree Willow
___ *Salix depressa* .... Bebb Willow
___ *Salix glauca* .... Grayleaf Willow
___ *Salix phylicifolia* ssp. *planifolia* .... Diamond Leaf Willow
___ *Sanguisorba stipulata* .... Sitka Burnet
___ *Saxifraga aiziodes* .... Golden Saxifrage
___ *Saxifraga tricuspidata* .... Prickly Saxifrage
___ *Sedum lanceolatum* .... Yellow sedum
___ *Senecio cymbalarioides* ....
___ *Senecio lugens* .... Black-tipped Groundsel
___ *Senecio pauciflorus* .... Few-flowered Groundsel
___ *Senecio vulgaris* .... Common Groundsel
___ *Shepherdia canadensis* .... Soapberry
___ *Solidago decumbens* ssp. *oreophila* .... Decumbent Goldenrod
___ *Solidago multiradiata* ssp. *multiradiata* .... Northern Goldenrod
___ *Solidago multiradiata* ssp. *scopularia* .... Rocky Mt. Goldenrod
___ *Sphagnum* sp. .... Red Sphagnum
___ *Spiraea betulifolia* .... Birch Leaf Spiraea
___ *Spiranthes romanzoffiana* .... Hooded Ladies Tresses
___ *Taraxacum* sp. .... Dandelion
___ *Tofieldia glutinosa* .... Sticky Asphodel
___ *Tofieldia pusilla* .... False Asphodel
___ *Trifolium pratense* .... Red Clover
___ *Trifolium repens* .... White Clover
___ *Vaccinium vitis-idaea* .... Low-bush Cranberry
___ *Viola adunca* .... Western Dog Violet
___ *Viola canadensis* .... Canada Violet
___ *Zygadenus elegans* .... Death Camas

Marsh Lake Campground, YT

Mile 859.9

This is a very nice Yukon Government campground south of Whitehorse, that has a lovely nature trail. This list consists of only the plants seen along the boardwalk trail to the lake.

Mixed woodlands in fall, Marsh Lake, YT
Canadian Dogwood

MARSH LAKE

___*Arctostaphylos rubra* .... Red Bearberry
___*Aster sibiricus* .... Siberian Aster
___*Crepis tectorum* .... Tall Hawksbeard
___*Empetrum nigrum* .... Crowberry
___*Epilobium palustris* .... Marsh Willow Herb
___*Equisetum arvense* .... Field Horsetail
___*Erigeron lonchophyllus* .... Narrow Leaf Erigeron
___*Eriophorum* sp. .... Cotton Grass
___*Gentiana propinqua* .... Four-parted Gentian
___*Geocaulon lividum* .... Timberberry
___*Hedysarum alpinum* .... Eskimo Potato
___*Ledum decumbens* .... Narrow-leaf Labrador Tea
___*Ledum palustre* .... Labrador Tea
___*Linnaea borealis* .... Twinflower
___*Moneses uniflora* .... Single Delight
___*Oxycoccus microcarpus* .... Bog Cranberry
___*Pedicularis sudetica* .... Fern-leaf Lousewort
___*Petasites sagittatus* .... Arrow-leaf Coltsfoot
___*Picea glauca* .... White Spruce
___*Picea mariana* .... Black Spruce
___*Platanthera hyperborea* .... Northern Green Bog Orchid
___*Platanthera obtusata* .... One Leaf Rein Orchid
___*Polemonium acutiflorum* .... Tall Jacob's Ladder
___*Pyrola asarifolia* .... Pink Pyrola
___*Pyrola chlorantha* .... Green Pyrola
___*Pyrola secunda* .... Sidebells Pyrola
___*Ranunculus gmelini* .... Creeping Crowfoot
___*Ribes oxyacanthoides* .... Purple Gooseberry
___*Rubus arcticus* .... Nagoonberry
___*Rumex arcticus* .... Arctic Dock
___*Salix phylicifolia* ssp. *planifolia* .... Diamond Leaf Willow
___*Senecio lugens* .... Black-tipped Groundsel
___*Senecio paupercaulis* .... Groundsel
___*Shepherdia canadensis* .... Soapberry
___*Spiranthes romanzoffiana* .... Hooded Ladies Tresses
___*Tofieldia glutinosa* .... Sticky Asphodel
___*Vaccinium vitis-idaea* .... Low-bush Cranberry

Wolfe Creek Campground, YT
Mile 876.8

This excellent Yukon Government campground , just south of Whitehorse, has an interesting variety of plants. This list was compiled from walks around the campground and on the steep sandy bluff adjacent to the campground.

Roadside, Wolfe Creek, YT
Prickly Rose

WOLFE CREEK CAMPGROUND, YT

___*Achillea borealis* .... Northern Yarrow
___*Alnus crispa* .... Green Mountain Alder
___*Anemone multifida* .... Cut-leaf Anemone
___*Antennaria media* .... White Pussy Toes
___*Antennaria rosea* .... Pink Pussy-toes
___*Arctostaphylos uva-ursi* .... Kinnikinnick
___*Arenaria capillaris* .... Tall Sandwort
___*Artemisia alaskana* .... Alaska Wormwood
___*Artemisia canadensis* .... Canada Wormwood
___*Artemisia frigida* .... Prairie Sagewort
___*Artemisia tilesii* .... Common Wormwood
___*Aster sibiricus* .... Siberian Aster
___*Astragalus alpinus* .... Alpine Milk Vetch
___*Betula papyrifera* .... Paper Birch
___*Castilleja caudata* .... Yellow Paintbrush
___*Equisetum arvense* .... Field Horsetail
___*Erigeron acris* .... Blue Fleabane
___*Galium Boreale* .... Northern Bedstraw
___*Geocaulon lividum* .... Timberberry
___*Geum macrophyllum* .... Large-leaf Avens
___*Juniperus horizontalis* .... Creeping Savin
___*Lathrus palustris* .... Vetchling
___*Ledum palustre* .... Labrador Tea
___*Linnaea borealis* .... Twinflower
___*Lupinus arcticus* .... Arctic Lupine
___*Mertensia paniculata* .... Bluebells
___*Oxytropis campestris* .... Northern Oxytrope
___*Penstemon gormanii* .... Yukon Beardstongue
___*Picea glauca* .... White Spruce
___*Pinus contorta* .... Lodgepole Pine, Jack Pine
___*Plantago major* .... Common Plantain
___*Polemonium acutiflorum* .... Tall Jacob's Ladder
___*Populus balsamifera* .... Cottonwood
___*Populus tremuloides* .... Quaking Aspen
___*Potentilla fruiticosa* .... Tundra Rose
___*Potentilla hookeriana* .... Hooker's Potentilla
___*Potentilla virgulata* ....
___*Pulsatilla patens* ssp. *multifida* .... Pasque Flower
___*Pyrola asarifolia* .... Pink Pyrola
___*Pyrola chlorantha* .... Green Pyrola
___*Pyrola secunda* .... Sidebells Pyrola
___*Ribes hudsonium* .... Northern Black Currant
___*Ribes triste* .... Red Currant
___*Rosa acicularis* .... Prickly Rose
___*Rubus idaeus* .... Raspberry
___*Salix glauca* .... Grayleaf Willow
___*Sanguisorba stipulata* .... Sitka Burnet
___*Saxifraga nivalis* .... Snow Saxifrage
___*Saxifraga tricuspidata* .... Prickly Saxifrage
___*Sedum lanceolatum* .... Yellow sedum
___*Senecio cymbalarioides* .... Small Groundsel
___*Solidago decumbens* ssp. *oreophila* .... Decumbent Goldenrod
___*Solidago multiradiata* ssp. *multiradiata* .... Northern Goldenrod
___*Stellaria media* .... Common Chickweed
___*Triflorum repens* .... White Clover
___*Vaccinium vitis-idaea* .... Low-bush Cranberry
___*Zygadenus elegans* .... Death Camas

Whitehorse, YT to Port Alcan, AK (Alaska Border)

Mile 884 to Mile 1221.8

This stretch of the Highway is mostly very dry, but includes beautiful Kluane Lake and Destruction Bay (a unique sub-alpine area). Kluane Lake is a great place for the avid hiker — weather permitting. Access to alpine areas is possible for the rugged hiker. (It is not uncommon to have the snow remain into mid-June, and re-appear in mid-August). Be wary that seemingly small creeks can become rushing rivers when sudden storms arrive.

Kluane Lake
Dwarf Fireweed

WHITEHORSE TO PORT ALCAN

___*Achillea borealis* .... Northern Yarrow
___*Aconitum delphinifolium* .... Monkshood
___*Alnus crispa* .... Green Mountain Alder
___*Alnus incana* .... Thin Leaf Alder
___*Amelanchier alnifolia* .... Alder-leaf Serviceberry
___*Amerorchis rotundifolia* .... Round Leaf Orchid
___*Andromeda polifolia* .... Bog Rosemary
___*Androsace chamaejasme* .... Rock Jasmine
___*Androsace septentrionalis* .... Northern Jasmine
___*Anemone multifida* .... Cut-leaf Anemone
___*Anemone narcissiflora* .... Narcissus-flowered Anemone
___*Anemone parviflora* .... Windflower
___*Anemone richardsonii* .... Yellow Anemone
___*Antennaria pallida* .... Pussy Toes
___*Antennaria rosea* .... Pink Pussy-toes
___*Aquilegia formosa* .... Western Columbine
___*Arabis divaricarpa* ....
___*Arabis holboellii* .... Holboell's Rockcress
___*Arabis lyrata* .... Kamchatka Rockcress
___*Arctostaphylos rubra* .... Red Bearberry
___*Arctostaphylos uva-ursi* .... Kinnikinnick
___*Arnica alpina* ssp. *attenuata* .... Tall Alpine Arnica
___*Arnica alpina* ssp. *vestita* .... Wooly Alpine Arnica
___*Arnica frigida* .... Frigid Arnica
___*Arnica lonchophylla* .... Narrow Leaf Arnica
___*Artemisia arctica* .... Arctic Wormwood
___*Artemisia borealis* .... Northern Wormwood
___*Artemisia canadensis* .... Canada Wormwood
___*Artemisia frigida* .... Prairie Sagewort
___*Artemisia tilesii* .... Common Wormwood
___*Aster alpinus* .... Alpine Aster
___*Aster sibiricus* .... Siberian Aster
___*Astragalus alpinus* .... Alpine Milk Vetch
___*Astragalus americanus* .... American Milk Vetch
___*Barbarea orthoceras* .... Winter Cress
___*Betula glandulosa* ....
___*Betula nana* .... Dwarf Birch
___*Betula papyrifera* .... Paper Birch
___*Boschniakia rossica* .... Broom Rape
___*Botrichium boreale* .... Northern Moonwort
___*Botrychium lunaria* .... Moonwort
___*Bupleurum triradiatus* .... Thoroughwort
___*Calamagrostis canadensis* .... Bluejoint Grass
___*Calla palustris* .... Wild Calla Lily
___*Caltha palustris* .... Marsh Marigold
___*Capsella bursa-pastoris* .... Shepherd's Purse
___*Cardamine pratensis* .... Cuckoo Flower
___*Carex aquatilis* .... Water Sedge
___*Castilleja caudata* .... Yellow Paintbrush
___*Castilleja hyperborea* .... Northern Paintbrush
___*Castilleja unalaschcensis* .... Coastal Paintbrush

___ *Castilleja yukonensis* .... Yukon Paintbrush
___ *Cerastrium arvense* .... Mouse-ear Chickweed
___ *Cerastrium beeringianum* .... Bering Sea Chickweed
___ *Chamaerhodos erecta* .... Chamaerhodo
___ *Cicuta mackenzieana* .... Poison Water Hemlock
___ *Cnidium cnidiifolium* ....
___ *Coeloglossum viride* .... Frog Orchid
___ *Corallorrhiza trifida* .... Coral Root Orchid
___ *Cornus canadensis* .... Canadian Dogwood
___ *Corydalis aurea* .... Golden Corydalis
___ *Crepis elegans* .... Elegant Hawksbeard
___ *Cypripedium passerinum* .... Northern White Lady's Slipper
___ *Delphinium glaucum* .... Larkspur
___ *Drosera rotundifolia* .... Round Leaf Sundew
___ *Dryas drummondii* .... Yellow Dryas
___ *Dryas integrifolia* .... Entire-leaf Avens
___ *Elaeagnus commutata* .... Silverberry
___ *Empetrum nigrum* .... Crowberry
___ *Epilobium angustifolium* .... Common Fireweed
___ *Epilobium hornemannii* .... Willow Herb
___ *Epilobium latifolium* .... Dwarf Fireweed
___ *Equisetum arvense* .... Field Horsetail
___ *Equisetum scirpoides* .... Small Horsetail
___ *Equisetum sylvaticum* .... Woodland Horsetail
___ *Equisetum variegatum* ssp. *alaskanum* .... Horsetail
___ *Erigeron acris* .... Blue Fleabane
___ *Erigeron caespitosa* .... Tufted Fleabane
___ *Erigeron compositus* .... Cutleaf Fleabane
___ *Erigeron glabellus* ssp. *pubescens* .... Fringed Fleabane
___ *Erigeron lonchophyllus* .... Narrow Leaf Erigeron
___ *Eriophorum angustifolium* .... Tall Cotton Grass
___ *Eriophorum brachyantherum* .... Cotton Grass
___ *Erysimum cheiranthoides* .... Yellow Wall Flower
___ *Fragaria virginiana* .... Wild Strawberry
___ *Galium Boreale* .... Northern Bedstraw
___ *Gentiana propinqua* .... Four-parted Gentian
___ *Gentiana prostrata* .... Moss Gentian
___ *Geocaulon lividum* .... Timberberry
___ *Geranium bicknellii* .... Bicknell's Geranium
___ *Geum macrophyllum* ssp. *macrophyllum* .... Large-leaf Avens
___ *Geum macrophyllum* ssp. *perincisum* .... Large Leaf Aven
___ *Hedysarum alpinum* .... Eskimo Potato
___ *Hedysarum mackenzii* .... Wild Sweet Pea
___ *Hippuris vulgaris* .... Mare's Tail
___ *Hordeum jubatum* .... Squirrel Tail Grass
___ *Juncus alpinus* .... Alpine Rush
___ *Juniperus communis* .... Common Juniper
___ *Juniperus horizontalis* .... Creeping Savin
___ *Lappula myosotis* .... Stickseed
___ *Lappula occidentalis* .... Western Stickseed
___ *Ledum palustre* .... Labrador Tea
___ *Linnaea borealis* .... Twinflower

___*Linum perenne* .... Blue Flax
___*Lupinus arcticus* .... Arctic Lupine
___*Luzula parviflora* .... Few-flowered Wood Rush
___*Matricaria matricarioides* .... Pineapple Weed
___*Melilotus albus* .... White Sweet Clover
___*Melilotus officianalis* .... Yellow Sweet Clover
___*Menyanthes trifoliata* .... Buckbean
___*Mertensia paniculata* .... Bluebells
___*Moehringia lateriflora* .... Grove Sandwort
___*Moneses uniflora* .... Single Delight
___*Nuphar polysepalum* .... Pond Lily
___*Oxycoccus microcarpus* .... Bog Cranberry
___*Oxytropis campestris* .... Northern Oxytrope
___*Oxytropis deflexa* .... Small-flowered Oxytrope
___*Oxytropis splendens* .... Showy Locoweed
___*Parnassia palustris* .... Grass of Parnassus
___*Pedicularis kanei* .... Wooly Lousewort
___*Pedicularis labradorica* .... Labrador Lousewort
___*Pedicularis sudetica* .... Fern-leaf Lousewort
___*Petasites sagittatus* .... Arrow-leaf Coltsfoot
___*Phacelia franklini* .... Franklin's Scorpion Weed
___*Phacelia mollis* .... Scorpion Weed
___*Picea glauca* .... White Spruce
___*Picea mariana* .... Black Spruce
___*Pinguicula vulgaris* .... Common Butterwort
___*Pinus contorta* .... Lodgepole Pine, Jack Pine
___*Plantago major* .... Common Plantain
___*Platanthera hyperborea* .... Northern Green Bog Orchid
___*Platanthera obtusata* .... One Leaf Rein Orchid
___*Polemonium acutiflorum* .... Tall Jacob's Ladder
___*Polemonium pulcherrimum* .... Beautiful Jacob's Ladder
___*Polygonum alaskanum* .... Wild Rhubarb
___*Polygonum viviparum* .... Alpine Meadow Bistort
___*Populus balsamifera* .... Cottonwood
___*Populus tremuloides* .... Quaking Aspen
___*Potentilla anserina* .... Silverweed
___*Potentilla arguta* .... White Potentilla
___*Potentilla fruiticosa* .... Tundra Rose
___*Potentilla hookeriana* .... Hooker's Potentilla
___*Potentilla norvegica* ssp. *monspeliensis* .... Norwegian Cinquefoil
___*Potentilla palustris* .... Marsh Cinquefoil
___*Potentilla virgulata* .... Cut-leaf Cinquefoil
___*Primula stricta* .... Mealy Primrose
___*Pulsatilla patens ssp. multifida* .... Pasque Flower
___*Pyrola asarifolia* .... Pink Pyrola
___*Pyrola chlorantha* .... Green Pyrola
___*Pyrola grandiflora* .... Large-flowered Wintergreen
___*Pyrola secunda* .... Sidebells Pyrola
___*Ranunculus gmelini* .... Creeping Crowfoot
___*Ranunculus lapponicus* .... Lapland Buttercup
___*Rhinanthus minor* .... Rattlebox
___*Rosa acicularis* .... Prickly Rose

___ *Rubus arcticus* .... Nagoonberry
___ *Rubus chamaemorus* .... Cloudberry
___ *Rubus idaeus* .... Raspberry
___ *Rumex acetosella* .... Sheep Sorrel
___ *Rumex arcticus* .... Arctic Dock
___ *Salix alaxensis* .... Alaska Willow
___ *Salix arbusculoides* .... Little Tree Willow
___ *Salix barclayii* .... Barclay Willow
___ *Salix brachycarpa* .... Barren Ground Willow
___ *Salix depressa* .... Bebb Willow
___ *Salix glauca* .... Grayleaf Willow
___ *Salix interior* .... Sandbar Willow
___ *Salix lasiandra* .... Pacific Willow
___ *Salix monticola* .... Park Willow, Cherry Willow
___ *Salix phylicifolia* ssp. *planifolia* .... Diamond Leaf Willow
___ *Sedum lanceolatum* .... Yellow sedum
___ *Senecio congestus* .... Marsh Fleabane
___ *Senecio cymbalarioides* ....
___ *Senecio lugens* .... Black-tipped Groundsel
___ *Senecio paupercaulis* .... Groundsel
___ *Senecio vulgaris* .... Common Groundsel
___ *Shepherdia canadensis* .... Soapberry
___ *Solidago decumbens ssp. oreophila* .... Decumbent Goldenrod
___ *Solidago multiradiata ssp. multiradiata* .... Northern Goldenrod
___ *Solidago multiradiata ssp. scopularia* .... Rocky Mt. Goldenrod
___ *Sorbus scopulina* .... Greene Mountain Ash
___ *Sparganium angustifolium* .... Bur-reed
___ *Spiraea betulifolia* .... Birch Leaf Spiraea
___ *Taraxacum sp.* .... Dandelion
___ *Tofieldia glutinosa* .... Sticky Asphodel
___ *Trientalis europaea* .... Star Flower
___ *Trifolium pratense* .... Red Clover
___ *Trifolium repens* .... White Clover
___ *Vaccinium uliginosum* .... Bog Blueberry
___ *Vaccinium vitis-idaea* .... Low-bush Cranberry
___ *Valeriana capitata* .... Capitate Valerian
___ *Viburnum edule* .... High-bush Cranberry
___ *Zygadenus elegans* .... Death Camas

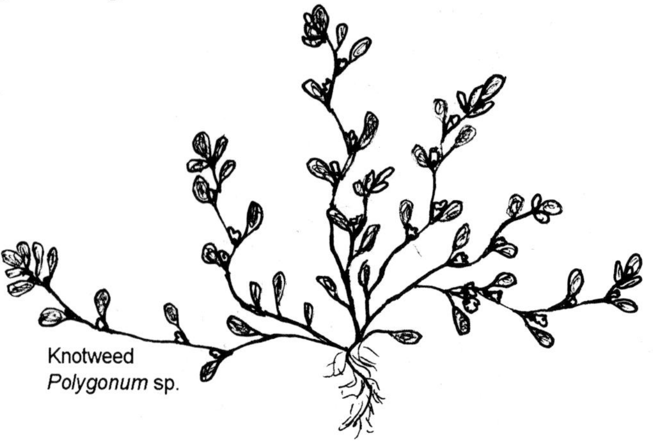

Port Alcan, AK to Delta Junction, AK and on to Fairbanks, AK

Mile 1221.8 to Mile 1520

This section of the Highway runs through bogs and wetlands intermixed with dry fields. The farm lands of the Delta Junction area are well worth exploring, as is the Hawk's Nursery with its attractive grounds. As you near Fairbanks, wide rivers and windy, sandy bluffs support very different plants.

1991 Burn area, Tok, AK

Cottongrass

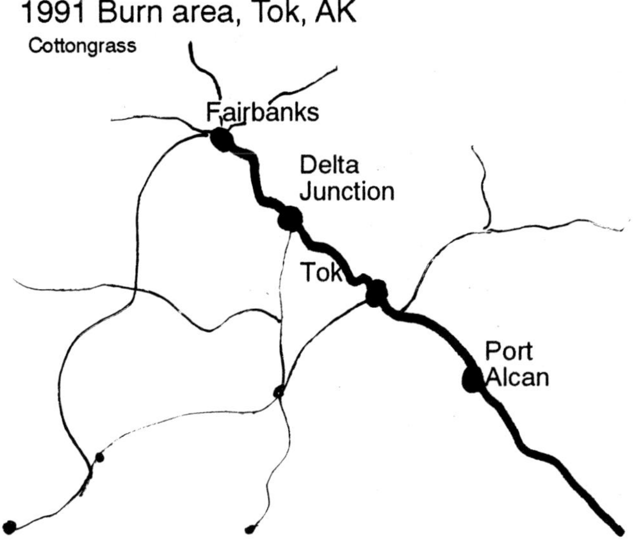

PORT ALCAN, AK TO DELTA JUNCTION, AK AND ON TO FAIRBANKS, AK

___*Achillea borealis* .... Northern Yarrow
___*Achillea sibirica* .... Siberian Yarrow
___*Aconitum delphinifolium* .... Monkshood
___*Adoxa moschatellina* .... Moschatel
___*Alnus crispa* .... Green Mountain Alder
___*Amelanchier alnifolia* .... Alder-leaf Serviceberry
___*Androsace chamaejasme* .... Rock Jasmine
___*Androsace septentrionalis* .... Northern Jasmine
___*Anemone multifida* .... Cut-leaf Anemone
___*Anemone parviflora* .... Windflower
___*Antennaria pulcherrima* .... Tall Pussy Toes
___*Antennaria rosea* .... Pink Pussy-toes
___*Aquilegia formosa* .... Western Columbine
___*Arabis hirsuta* ssp. *pycnocarpa* .... Hairy Rock Cress
___*Arabis holboellii* .... Holboell's Rock Cress
___*Arabis lyrata* .... Lyre-leaf Rockcress
___*Arctostaphylos rubra* .... Red Bearberry
___*Arctostaphylos uva-ursi* .... Kinnikinnick
___*Arnica alpina* .... Alpine Arnica
___*Arnica alpina* ssp. *attenuata* .... Tall Alpine Arnica
___*Arnica frigida* .... Frigid Arnica
___*Arnica lonchophylla* .... Narrow Leaf Arnica
___*Artemisia arctica* .... Arctic Wormwood
___*Artemisia borealis* .... Northern Wormwood
___*Artemisia frigida* .... Prairie Sagewort
___*Artemisia tilesii* .... Common Wormwood
___*Aster junciformis* .... White Rush Aster
___*Aster sibiricus* .... Siberian Aster
___*Astragalus alpinus* .... Alpine Milk Vetch
___*Astragalus umbellatus* .... Hairy Arctic Milk Vetch
___*Betula glandulosa* ....
___*Betula nana* .... Dwarf Birch
___*Betula papyrifera* .... Paper Birch
___*Boschniakia rossica* .... Broom Rape
___*Botrychium lunaria* .... Moonwort
___*Bupleurum triradiatum* .... Thoroughwax
___*Calamagrostis canadensis* .... Bluejoint Grass
___*Calla palustris* .... Wild Calla Lily
___*Capsella bursa-pastoris* .... Shepherd's Purse
___*Castilleja caudata* .... Yellow Paintbrush
___*Cerastrium arvense* .... Mouse-ear Chickweed
___*Cerastrium beeringianum* .... Bering Sea Chickweed
___*Chenopodium album* .... Lamb's Quarters
___*Chenopodium capitatum* .... Strawberry Spinach
___*Cicuta mackenzieana* .... Poison Water Hemlock
___*Cnidium cnidiifolium* ....
___*Corallorrhiza trifida* .... Coral Root Orchid
___*Cornus canadensis* .... Canadian Dogwood
___*Corydalis aurea* .... Golden Corydalis

___*Corydalis pauciflora* .... Few-flowered Corydalis
___*Crepis elegans* .... Elegant Hawksbeard
___*Cypripedium passerinum* .... Northern White Lady's Slipper
___*Delphinium glaucum* .... Larkspur
___*Dodecatheon pauciflorum* .... Few-flowered Shooting Star
___*Drosera rotundifolia* .... Round Leaf Sundew
___*Dryas drummondii* .... Yellow Dryas
___*Dryopteris fragrans* .... Fragrant Shield Fern
___*Elaeagnus commutata* .... Silverberry
___*Empetrum nigrum* .... Crowberry
___*Epilobium angustifolium* .... Common Fireweed
___*Epilobium latifolium* .... Dwarf Fireweed
___*Epilobium palustris* .... Marsh Willow Herb
___*Equisetum arvense* .... Field Horsetail
___*Equisetum fluvatile* .... Water Horsetail
___*Equisetum pratense* ....
___*Equisetum variegatum* .... Variegated Horsetail
___*Erigeron acris* .... Blue Fleabane
___*Erigeron lonchophylus* .... Narrow Leaf Fleabane
___*Eriophorum angustifolium* .... Tall Cotton Grass
___*Eriophorum* sp. .... Cotton Grass
___*Fragaria virginiana* .... Wild Strawberry
___*Galium boreale* .... Northern Bedstraw
___*Gentiana propinqua* .... Four-parted Gentian
___*Geocaulon lividum* .... Timberberry
___*Geum macrophyllum* ssp. *macrophyllum* .... Large-leaf Avens
___*Gymnocarpium dryopteris* .... Oak Fern
___*Hedysarum alpinum* .... Eskimo Potato
___*Hedysarum mackenzii* .... Wild Sweet Pea
___*Hordeum jubatum* .... Squirrel Tail Grass
___*Juniperus communis* .... Common Juniper
___*Juniperus horizontalis* .... Creeping Savin
___*Lappula myosotis* .... Stickseed
___*Lappula occidentalis* .... Western Stickseed
___*Larix laricina* ssp. *alaskensis* .... Larch / Tamarack
___*Ledum palustre* .... Labrador Tea
___*Linnaea borealis* .... Twinflower
___*Listera borealis* .... Twayblade
___*Lupinus arcticus* .... Arctic Lupine
___*Luzula multiflora* .... Wood Rush
___*Lycopodium complanatum* .... Creeping Jenny
___*Matricaria matricarioides* .... Pineapple Weed
___*Mertensia paniculata* .... Bluebells
___*Moehringia lateriflora* .... Grove Sandwort
___*Myrica gale* .... Sweet Gale
___*Nuphar polysepalum* .... Pond Lily
___*Oxytropis campestris* .... Northern Oxytrope
___*Oxytropis campestris* ssp. *gracilis* .... White Northern Oxytrope
___*Oxytropis deflexa* .... Small-flowered Oxytrope
___*Oxytropis deflexa* ssp. *sericea* .... Small-flowered oxytrope
___*Papaver lapponicum* .... Lapland Poppy
___*Papaver nudicauli* .... Iceland Poppy

___ *Parnassia palustris* .... Grass of Parnassus
___ *Pedicularis labradorica* .... Labrador Lousewort
___ *Pedicularis sudetica* .... Fern-leaf Lousewort
___ *Penstemon gormanii* .... Yukon Beardstongue
___ *Petasites frigidus* .... Frigid Coltsfoot
___ *Petasites sagittatus* .... Arrow-leaf Coltsfoot
___ *Picea glauca* .... White Spruce
___ *Picea mariana* .... Black Spruce
___ *Plantago major* .... Common Plantain
___ *Platanthera hyperborea* .... Northern Green Bog Orchid
___ *Polemonium acutiflorum* .... Tall Jacob's Ladder
___ *Polemonium pulcherrimum* .... Beautiful Jacob's Ladder
___ *Populus balsamifera* .... Cottonwood
___ *Populus tremuloides* .... Quaking Aspen
___ *Potentilla fruiticosa* .... Tundra Rose
___ *Potentilla norvegica* ssp. *monspeliensis* .... Norwegian Cinquefoil
___ *Potentilla palustris* .... Marsh Cinquefoil
___ *Potentilla virgulata* .... Cut-leaf Cinquefoil
___ *Primula incana* .... Long leaf Mealy Primrose
___ *Pulsatilla patens ssp. multifida* .... Pasque Flower
___ *Pyrola asarifolia* .... Pink Pyrola
___ *Pyrola chlorantha* .... Green Pyrola
___ *Pyrola secunda* .... Sidebells Pyrola
___ *Ribes hudsonium* .... Northern Black Currant
___ *Ribes triste* .... Red Currant
___ *Rosa acicularis* .... Prickly Rose
___ *Rubus arcticus* .... Nagoonberry
___ *Rubus chamaemorus* .... Cloudberry
___ *Rubus idaeus* .... Raspberry
___ *Rumex acetosella* .... Sheep Sorrel
___ *Salix alaxensis* .... Alaska Willow
___ *Salix arbusculoides* .... Little Tree Willow
___ *Salix brachycarpa* .... Barren Ground Willow
___ *Salix depressa* .... Bebb Willow
___ *Salix glauca* .... Grayleaf Willow
___ *Salix interior* .... Sandbar Willow
___ *Sanguisorba stipulata* .... Sitka Burnet
___ *Saxifraga nivalis* .... Snow Saxifrage
___ *Saxifraga tricuspidata* .... Prickly Saxifrage
___ *Senecio eremophilus* ....
___ *Senecio lugens* .... Black-tipped Groundsel
___ *Senecio paucerflorus* .... Few-flowered Groundsel
___ *Senecio paupercaulis* .... Groundsel
___ *Shepherdia canadensis* .... Soapberry
___ *Silene menziesii* .... Menzies's Campion
___ *Solidago canadensis* .... Canada Goldenrod
___ *Solidago decumbens* ssp. *oreophila* .... Decumbent Goldenrod
___ *Solidago multiradiata* ssp. *multiradiata* .... Northern Goldenrod
___ *Sparganium minimum* .... Bur Reed
___ *Spiraea betulifolia* .... Birch Leaf Spiraea
___ *Stellaria crassifolia* .... Marsh Chickweed
___ *Stellaria longifolia* .... Small-flowered Chickweed

___*Stellaria longipes* .... Stiff Chickweed
___*Taraxacum sp.* .... Dandelion
___*Thelypteris phegopteris* ....
___*Tofieldia glutinosa* .... Sticky Asphodel
___*Trientalis europaea* .... Star Flower
___*Typha latifolia* .... Cattail
___*Utricularia intermedia* .... Bladder Pod
___*Viola epipsela* .... Marsh Violet
___*Zygadenus elegans* .... Death Camas

Corolla or flower parts

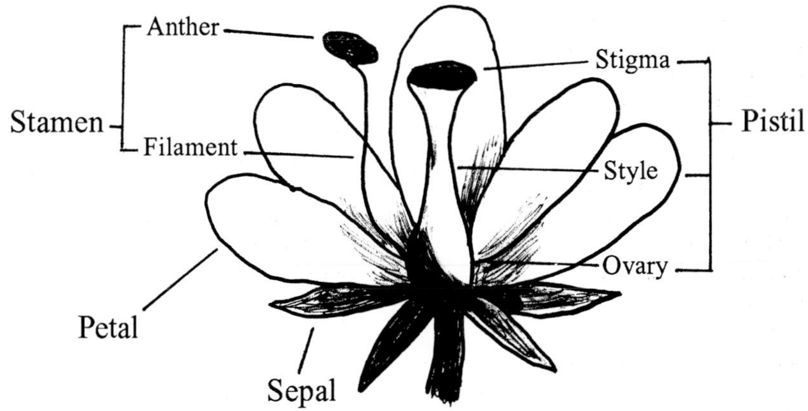

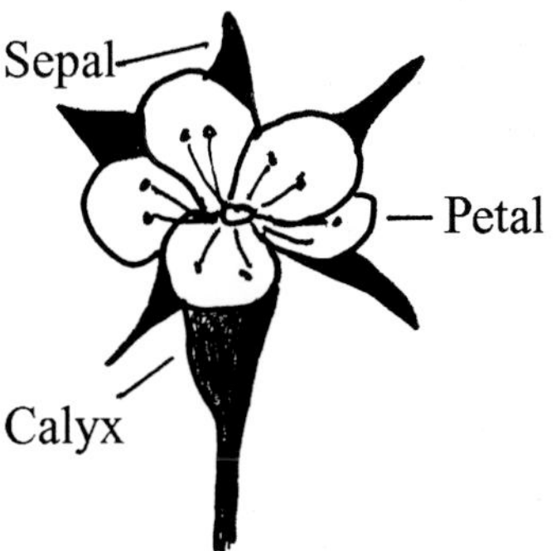

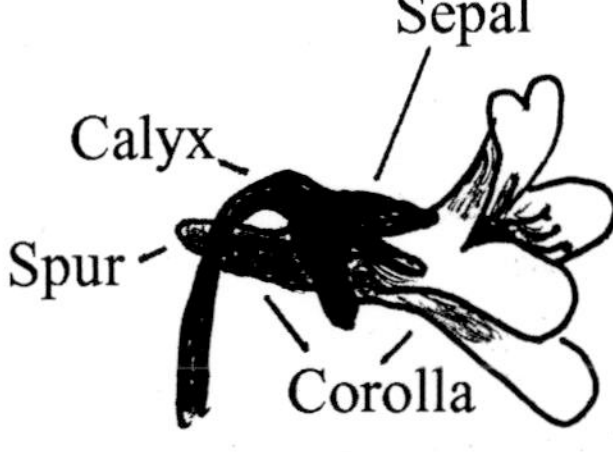

Showing:
6 colorful purple sepals
Erect purplish pistil
Large cluster of yellow stamens
Long dense hairs on tips of sepal

Pasque Flower (Denali Park)

COROLLA (FLOWER) TYPES

Regular or Symmetrical

Campanulate

Bell

Irregular

Funnel

Urn

Papilionaceous

Tube

Salverform

Labiate

Spurred

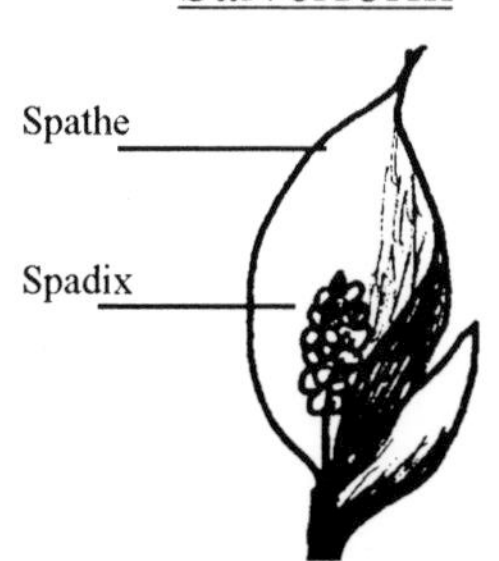

Floral-like Bract

INFLORESCENCES

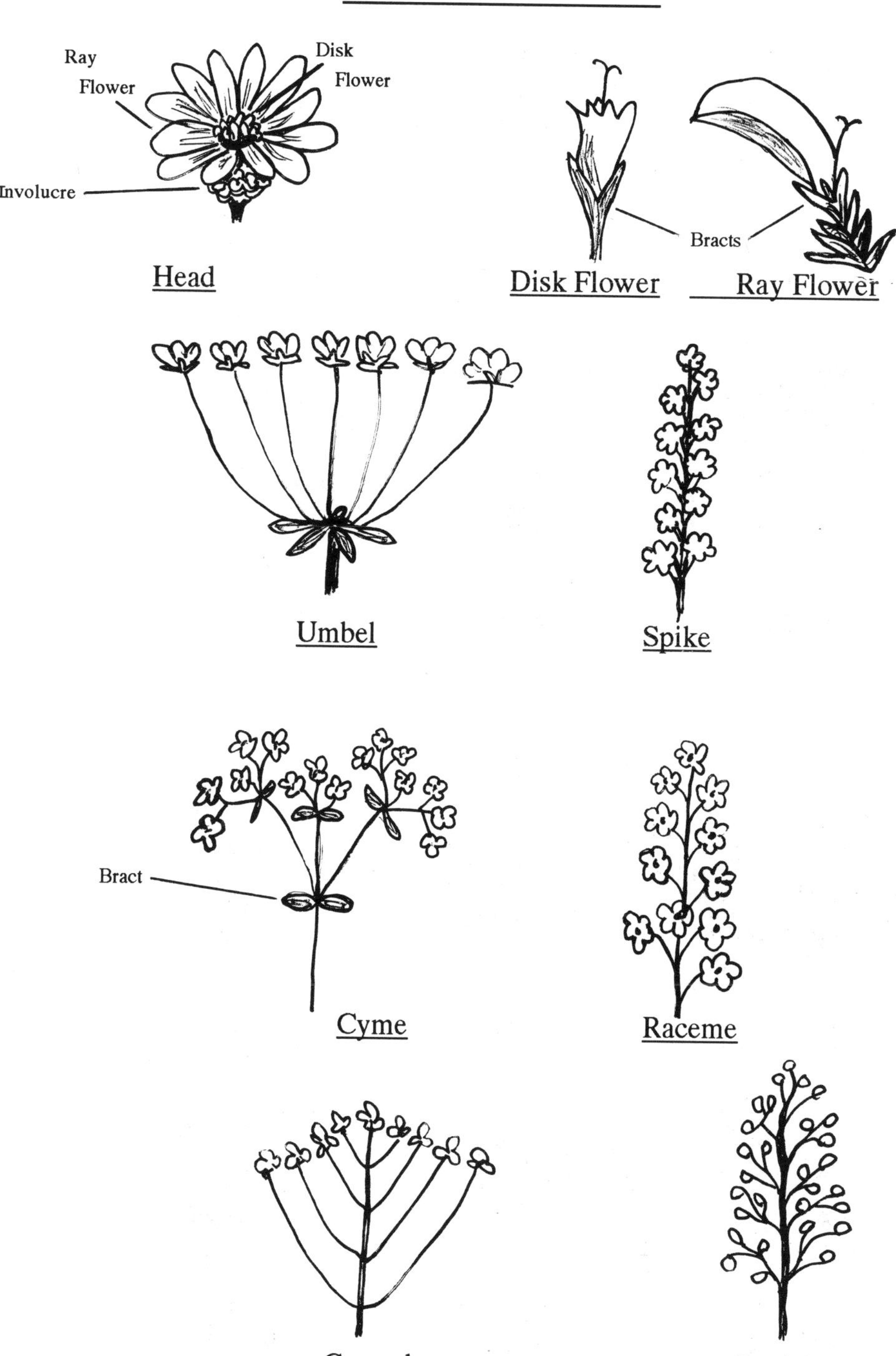

LEAF ARRANGEMENTS

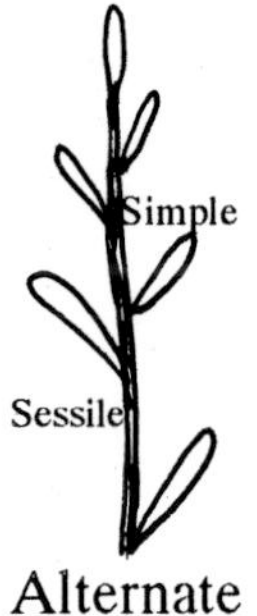

Alternate

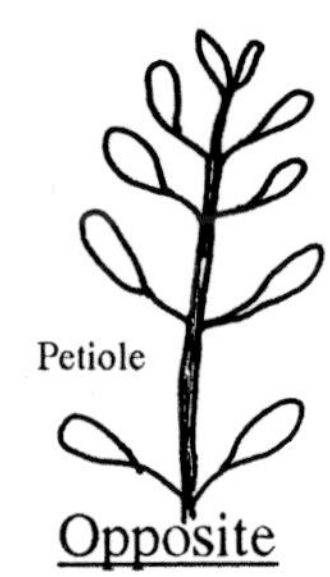

Opposite

Palmate

Basal

Whorled

Stipule

Pinnate

Clasping

Dissected

Lobed

Compound Leaves

Sheathing

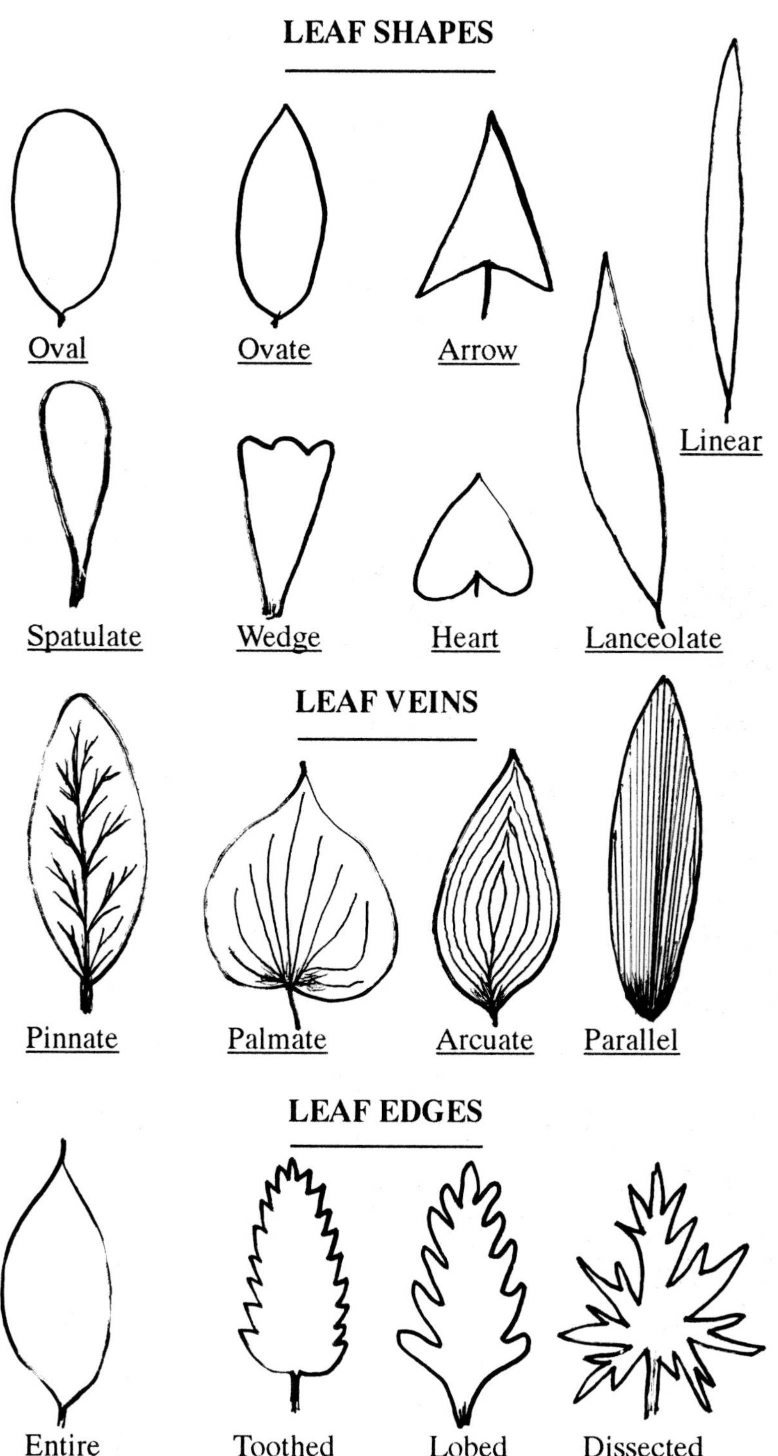
LEAF SHAPES
Oval
Ovate
Arrow
Linear
Spatulate
Wedge
Heart
Lanceolate
LEAF VEINS
Pinnate
Palmate
Arcuate
Parallel
LEAF EDGES
Entire
Toothed
Lobed
Dissected

PLANT FAMILY CHARACTERISTICS

Plants are divided into families by differences of reproductive parts; such as, number and placement of stamens, how the ovaries are divided, placement of seeds within the ovaries, manner of seed disbursement, etc. However, these characteristics are not always available nor easily noticed, so I have listed below some other, more obvious, characteristics to look for. In botany, there are a lot of "usually"s, some families vary greatly, and many oddities do occur. The characteristics listed are aimed at the genera that occur in this area..

(1) Aster / Asteraceae---formerly the daisy or Composite/ Compositae. Herbaceous plants or shrubs having a head of flowers (composed of many flowers), usually disk flowers, surrounded by showy ray flowers (sometimes incorrectly called petals) with a circle of bracts (involucre) at the base. Leaf shape and placement variable according to genus.

(2) Bladderwort / Lentibulareaceae---insectivorous plants of wet areas having a short spike of irregularly shaped flowers with 2 to 5 sepals, 5 united petals, and 2 stamens. Terrestrial plants have a rosette of leaves, while aquatic varieties have finely dissected leaves on long, floating stems.

(3) Bluebell / Campanulaceae---herbaceous plants with a few flowers having 5 sepals, 5 petals (united at base and, frequently, bell-shaped), 5 stamens, and 1 ovary. Leaves are simple and alternate on stems.

(4) Borage / Boraginaceae---herbaceous plants with branched stems with many flowers having 5 united sepals, 5 united petals (bell-shaped or salverform), 5 stamens, and an ovary divided into 2 parts (often times lobed, giving the appearance of 4 parts). Leaves are alternate, simple, often hairy and frequently buds are in a curled cyme.

(5) Buckwheat / Polygonaceae---herbaceous plants with a spike of many small flowers having 5 sepals, no petals; and, usually, 8 stamens. Leaves are simple, sometimes basal. but usually on the stem.

(6) Bur-reed / Sparganiaceae---aquatic plants with long, flat, linear leaves, some erect, some floating. Flower heads are round. Male flowers have 3 or 6 sepals and 3 or 6 stamens and are above the female heads.

(7) Buttercup or Crowfoot / Ranunculaceae---herbaceous plants with 1 to many common flowers usually having 5 sepals, 5 petals, many stamens (tight cushion effect) divided into 1 to many sections. (this is a very variable family having unusual numbers of petals; and, sometimes completely lacking petals). Leaves are frequently divided into a lobed or dissected crowfoot (birdfoot) pattern, have long stems, and are predominantly basal. Many members of this family are poisonous.

(8) Cattail / Typhaceae---monocot plants of marshes and lakes, with a creeping rhizome. Leaves are basal, long, and erect with linear veins. Male flowers have 2 to 5 stamens and are on the end of a long spike. The female flowers are on a long dense spadix just below.

(9) Calla / Araceae---herbaceous plants having large, simple leaves and a large floral type leaf below a spike of inconspicuous flowers having no petals and 6 stamens. The fruit is a berry, frequently poisonous.

(10) Crowberry / Empetraceae--------evergreen shrubs having inconspicuous flowers of 3 bracts, 3 to 6 sepals (sometimes in whorls and confused as petals) and 2 to 4 stamens. The ovary is divided into many parts and produces a round berry. Leaves are simple and heath-like.

(11) Dogbane / Apocynaceae---usually woody with opposite simple leaves and stems with a milky juice. Flowers are bell-shaped or tubular and have 4 or 5 united sepals, 5 united petals, 4 or 5 stamens. The fruit is a berry or capsule with 2 sections.

(12) Dogwood / Cornaceae---shrubs having clusters of very small flowers consisting of 4 showy bracts, 4 sepals, 4 petals, 4 stamens, and 1 ovary which produces a soft drupe. The 4 large, whitish, showy bracts are often confused with petals. The simple leaves have arcuate veins.

(13) Earthsmoke / Fumariaceae---herbaceous plants having delicately branched stems of small, irregular flowers having 2 sepals, 4 united petals (forming a spur), 6 stamens, and a two-parted ovary. Some leaves are basal, some on the stems, and they are finely dissected. The stems are very soft and watery.

(14) Evening Primrose / Onagraceae---herbaceous plants having spikes of showy flowers with 4 narrow sepals, 4 petals, and an ovary seen distinctly as a branched stigma. Leaves are simple and on the main stems, arising from deep horizontal roots.

(15) Figwort or Snapdragon / Scrophulariaceae---herbaceous plants with spikes or racemes of many irregularly shaped flowers having 5 united sepals, 5 united petals, 4 (sometimes 2) stamens, and 1 ovary. Most leaves are simple, except for Pedicularis, which is pinnately divided.

(16) Flax / Linaceae---herbaceous plants with simple stem leaves. Common flowers having 5 sepals, 5 petals, and 5 stamens.

(17) Gentian / Gentianaceae---herbaceous plants with stout stems having opposite, simple, entire leaves. Flowers are tubular or salverform having 4 or 5 sepals (sometimes united), 4 or 5 united petals, 4 or 5 stamens, and 1, obviously protruding, ovary.

(18) Geranium / Geraniaceae---herbaceous plants with branched stems having flowers with 5 sepals, 5 clawed petals, 10 stamens, and a 5-parted extruded ovary that resembles a Crane's bill. Leaves are long-stemmed, palmately-divided and mostly basal.

(19) Ginseng / Araliaceae---spiny shrubs with spikes of very small flowers having 5 sepals, 5 petals, 5 stamens, and 1 ovary that forms a berry. Very large maple-like, palmate leaves.

(20) Gooseberry / Grossulariaceae---shrubs sometimes with thorns, having small flowers with 4 or 5 sepals, 5 very small petals, 5 stamens, and a 2-parted ovary in the form of a berry. Leaves are usually lobed with teeth.

(21) Goosefoot / Chenopodiaceae---herbaceous plants with spikes of small, mostly green, inconspicuous clusters of flowers with 5 sepals, no petals, 5 stamens, and 1 ovary. These are mostly weedy plants usually with opposite leaves.

(22) Heath / Ericaceae---mostly shrubs, frequently evergreen, and often with bell or urn-shaped flowers. Flowers have 4 or 5 (sometimes united) sepals, 4 or 5 (usually united) petals, 4 or 5 stamens, and 1 ovary. The leaves are entire, simple and, usually, narrow.

(23) Honeysuckle / Caprifoliaceae---shrubs with tubular or salverform flowers having 5 sepals, 5 united petals, 5 stamens, and 1 ovary. Leaves are opposite.

(24) Iris / Iridaceae---herbaceous plants growing from rhizomes and having stout stems. Flowers have 3 sepals, 3 petals, 3 stamens, and a 3-parted ovary. Leaves are long and blade-like with linear (parallel) veins.

(25) Lily / Liliaceae---frequently bulbous plants usually with a stout flower stalk. Flowers have 6 tepals (3 sepals, 3 petals), 6 stamens, and a 3-parted ovary. Flowers are in a raceme or umbel. Leaves have parallel veins and, frequently, clasp the stem.

(26) Mustard / Brassicaceae---herbaceous plants with branched inflorescences of flowers having 4 sepals, 4 petals, 6 stamens (4 high and 2 low), and a one-parted ovary. Leaves are mostly basal, but, frequently, continue up the flower stalk. Distinct seed stalk as silicle or silique. Most members have edible leaves.

(27) Madder / Rubiaceae---herbaceous plants having a panicle of small salverform flowers with 4 sepals, 4 united petals, 4 stamens, and one 2-parted ovary. Some varieties have square stems, all have entire leaves that are opposite of in a whorl.

(28) Mint / Lamiaceae---herbaceous plants with irregular flowers with 4 united petals, (a 2-lobed upper lip, and 3 petals joined as a lower lip). Stems are usually square, leaves are simple and toothed.

(29) Moschatel / Adoxaceae---herbaceous plants. There is one small member in the area having one 4-petalled flower at the end of the stem and four 5-petalled flowers surrounding it. The basal leaves are thin, yellowish-green with broad, toothed lobes. Blooms very early and is very small.

(30) Nettle / Urticaceae---herbaceous upright plants having limp spikes of inconspicuous unisexual flowers. Leaves are opposite. Stems are sometimes square and frequently fibrous. Plants are often equipped with stinging hairs.

(31) Oleaster / Elaeagnaceae---shrubs having salverform flowers with 4 sepals, no petals, 4 stamens, and 1 ovary in the form of a berry. Leaves are simple, entire, and have scales.

(32) Orchid / Orchidaceae---herbaceous plants with irregularly shaped flowers having 3 sepals, 3 petals (the lower are "sac-like"). Flower stalks are stout, leaves usually alternate (sometimes opposite), simple with parallel veins.

(33) Parsley / Apiaceae---herbaceous plants with umbels of small flowers having 5 sepals, 5 petals, 5 stamens, and a 2-parted ovary. Most leaves are pinnately divided and finely dissected or toothed. Many plants have hollow stems and leaves with petioles that clasp the stems.

(34) Pea / Fabaceae---herbaceous plants having irregular flowers, with 5 united sepals, 5 petals (the lower 2 joined to form a keel), 10 stamens, and 1 pistil. Leaves are entire, pinnately divided, often with stipules, sometimes with tendrils.

(35) Phlox / Polemoniaceae---herbaceous plants having flowers with 5 united sepals, 5 rounded united petals, 5 stamens and a 3-parted ovary. Leaves are entire and can be simple or pinnately divided.

(36) Pink / Caryophyllaceae---herbaceous plants with 5 sepals, 5 rounded united petals, 10 stamens, and a 5-parted ovary. The entire, simple leaves are placed opposite on the stems which are swollen at the joints.

(37) Poppy / Papaveraceae---herbaceous plants having flowers with 2 deciduous sepals, 4 large petals, many stamens, and a large, many-seeded ovary. The leaves having petioles are mostly basal, usually hairy and pinnately divided.

(38) Primrose / Primulaceae---herbaceous plants with flowers having 5 sepals, 5 united petals, 5 stamens, and a 5-parted ovary. Leaves are mostly basal and, usually, glabrous.

(39) Rose / Rosaceae---plants or shrubs with flowers having 5 sepals, usually 5 petals, many stamens. Many have fruits. Leaves have stipules and most are divided or lobed with teeth.

(40) Sandlewood / Santalaceae---plants, sometimes parasitic, with 3 to 5 sepals and no petals. Leaves are usually simple and alternate.

(41) Saxifrage / Saxifragaceae---plants usually with mostly simple basal leaves and reduced, alternate stem leaves. Flowers have 5 sepals, 5 petals (often clawed), 10 stamens, and a pronounced (often cone-shaped) ovary that is usually 2-parted.

(42) Stonecrop, Sedum / Crassulaceae---small succulent plants with many thick, succulent, stalkless, undivided, stem leaves. Flowers have 4 or 5 sepals, 4 or 5 petals, and 8 or 10 stamens.

(43) Sundew / Doseraceae---insectivorous glandular plants often in acidic bogs. Leaves are usually basal and have either hairs or sticky glands. Flowers have 5 united sepals, 5 petals, 5 stamens and a 2, 3 or 5-parted ovary.

(44) Valerian / Valerianaceae---plants with opposite stem leaves and sometimes basal leaves. Sepals are inconspicuous. Flowers have 5 joined petals, are bell-shaped or salverform and have 1 to 4 epipetalous stamens.

(45) Violet / Violaceae---small plants with long-stemmed, heart-shaped leaves. Flowers are irregular, have 5 sepals, 5 petals, and a spur.

(46) Waterleaf / Hydrophyllaceae---Herbaceous plants often glandular. Leaves can be alternate or opposite, often in rosettes. They can be entire or pinnately lobed. Flowers have 5 united sepals, 5 united petals, 5 epipetalous stamens and a 2-parted ovary.

(47) Wintergreen / Pyrolaceae---small plants with simple, petiolate, evergreen leaves. Flowers are usually on a heavy stalk, often showing the color of the flowers. The flowers have 5 sepals, 5 somewhat waxy petals, 10 stamens, and a 5-parted ovary with a protruding style.

EDIBLE PLANTS

included in this book

(See keys to Type, Part Used, Preparation Method, and Use at end of listing)

Name	Type	Part	Prep	Use
Bearberry	S	B	R,C	J
Bedstraw	P	Sd	D,R	D
Bee Balm	P	L	R,C,D	D,S
Birch	T	F,St,L,S	R,C,D	V,G
Bistort	P	L	R,C	V
Bluebell	P	L	R,C	V
Blueberries	S	B	R,C	D,J,Fr
Brook Lime	P	L	R,C	V
Bull Thistle	P	R,L	R,C,D	V,G
Bunchberry	P	B	R,C	Fr
Canola	p	L,S	R,C	V,S
Cattail	P	F,S,St	R,C	V
Celery, Wild	P	L,R,St	R,C	V,S
Chives	P	L,R	R,C	V,S
Choke Cherry	S,T	B	R,C	D,J,Fr,M
Cloudberry	S	B	R,C	D,J,Fr
Clover	P	F,L,St,R	C	D
Coltsfoot	P	L	C,D	V,S
Cottonwood	T	Bud	C	V
Cow Parsnip	P	St,R	R,C	V
Cranberry, Bog	S	B	R,C	D,J
Cranberry, High-bush	S	B	R,C	D,J
Cranberry, Low-bush	S	B	R,C	D,J
Cresses	P	L,St	R.C	V
Crowberry	S	B	R,C	L,Fr
Currants	S	B	R,C	J
Dandelion	P	L,F,R	R,C,D	V,D
Devil's Club	S	St*2	R,C	M
Dock	P	L,St	R,C	V
Eskimo Potato	P	R	C	V
Fairy Bells	P	B	R,C	Fr
Fern species	P	R,St *1	R,C	V
Fireweed	P	St,L,F	R,C	V,J
Gooseberry	S	B	R,C	D,J,Fr
Great Burnet	P	L	R,C	V

Name	Type	Part	Prep	Use
Huckleberry	S	B	R,C	D,J,Fr
Juniper, Common	S	Fr	D	S
Kinnikinnick	S	B	C	J
Labrador Tea	S	L	C	D
Lamb's Quarters	P	L,St	R,C	V
Lily, Pond	P	R,Sd	C,D	G
Lousewort	P	R	C	V
Mare's Tail	P	St	C	V
Marigold, Marsh	P	L*3,St*3	C	V
Monkey Flower	P	L,St	R,C	V
Moonwort	P	L	R,C	V
Mountain Ash	T	B	C	Fr
Mustard Weed	P	L,St	R,C,D	V,S
Nagoonberry	S	B	R,C	D,J,Fr
Nettle	P	L,St	C	V
Orchid, Calypso	P	R	R	V
Pepper Grass	P	L,S	R,C	V,S
Pineapple Weed	P	F	C	D
Plantain	P	L	R	V,M
Raspberry	S	B,L	R,C,D	D,J,Fr
Rhubarb, Wild	P	R	R,C	V,M
Rose	S	F,L,Fr*4	R,C,D	J,Fr,D
Roseroot, Rosewort	P	L,St,R	R,C	V
Rough Fruited Fairy Bells	P	B	R	Fr
Salsify	P	L	R,C	V,D
Serviceberry	S	B	R,C,D	J,Fr
Shepherd's Purse	P	L	R,C	V
Silverberry	S	B	C	V
Silverweed	P	R	C	V
Soapberry	S	B	R	Fr
Sorrel	P	L,St	R,C	V
Spruce	T	L,S	C	D
Strawberry	P	B,L	R,C,D	D,J,Fr
Strawberry Spinach	P	L,St,F	R,C	V.J
Sundew	P	L	R	V
Sweet Cicely	P	S	R	S
Sweet Gale	S	L	D	S
Thimbleberry	S	B	R,C	D,J,Fr
Timberberry	P	B	R	Fr
Trailing Red Blackberry	P	B	R,C	Fr,J
Violet	P	L,St,F	R,C	V
Water Horehound	P	R,L	R,C	V,S,P
Watermelon Berry	P	B,L,St	R,C	V,J,D

Name	Type	Part	Prep	Use
Wild Mint	P	L	C,D	S,J,D
Wild Onion	P	R	R,C,D	V
Wild Sarsaparilla	P	R	C,D	D,M
Willows	S,T	L,St,F	R,C	M,V
Willows, Dwarf	S	R	R,C	V
Wormwood	P	L	R,C	S
Yarrow	P	St,L	C	S,D

KEYS:

Plant Type	Part Used	Preparation	Use
S---Shrub	R---Root	R---Raw	V---vegetable
P---Plant	St---Stem	C---Cooked	G---Grain
T---Tree	L---Leaf	D---Dried	D---Drink
	S---Sap		J---Jellies
	F---Flower		S---Seasoning
	B---Berry		P---Pickles
	Sd---Seed		Fr---Fruit
	Fr---Fruit		M---Medicinal
	Sh---Shoots		

SPECIAL ATTENTION:

*1-----Use with caution
*2-----Underground Stem
*3-----Contains poison that is broken down by boiling
*4-----Spit out seeds

POISONOUS PLANTS

ALL ANEMONES (*Anemone* species)---All contain extremely poisonous anemonin.

BANEBERRY (*Actaea rubra*)---Both red and white-berried plants very poisonous. Six berries have been known to kill a small child.

BOG ROSEMARY (*Andromeda polifolia*)---Contains Andromedotoxin---causes lowered blood pressure, difficult breathing, vomiting, diarrhea and cramps. In past times, it was used medicinally with careful control.

BUTTERCUP (*Ranunculus* species)---For emergency food use only, poison can be broken down by boiling and changing water.

CHOKE CHERRY (*Prunus virginiana*)---The bark, seeds and dried leaves contain hydrocyanic acid, which is very poisonous.

DEATH CAMAS (*Zygadenus elegans*)---Very poisonous. Extremely bitter. Death results from respiratory depression and asphyxia.

DEVIL'S CLUB (*Echinopanax horridum*)---Berries contain a toxin and are considered inedible.

DOGBANE (*Apocynum androsaemifolium*)---Milky juice of this plant is very poisonous.

FALSE LILY OF THE VALLEY (*Maianthemun dilatatum*)---Contains cardiac glycosides (alkaloids).

FIR CLUB MOSS (*Lycopodium selago*)---Contains a poisonous alkaloid causing pain in mouth, vomiting and diarrhea.

LABRADOR TEA (*Ledum palustre*)---Has cathartic effect if too much tea is consumed. The robustly aromatic leaves, however, make it one of the most famous teas in the North Country.

LARKSPUR (*Delphinium* species)---Poisonous like Monkshood, but not quite as active.

LUPINE (*Lupinus* species)---Leaves and seeds poisonous.

MARSH MARIGOLD (*Caltha palustris*)---Poisonous when raw, but poison is broken down by boiling.

MONKSHOOD (*Aconitum* species)---All parts poisonous. Once called Wolfbane.

WATER HEMLOCK (*Cicuta mackenzieana & Cicuta douglasii*)---Considered by many authorities to be the most virulent poisonous plant in the North Temperate Zone. Death has been known to occur within 20 minutes of ingestion.

WILD CALLA (*Calla palustris*)---Entire plant, especially berries, contains poisonous acids and burning saponin-like substances, neutralized by drying or boiling.

WILD IRIS (*Iris setosa*)---Irritant substance in leaves. Non-flowering plant mistaken for Cattail. Rhizome poisonous. Powdered rhizome called "Orris Root" formerly used in cosmetics; it is EXTREMELY allergenic!

WILD SWEET PEA (*Hedysarum mackenzii*)---Edibility very questionable.

IMPORTANT NOTES: Impress upon your family and friends to never eat any unknown plant or berry. Birds and other animals often eat berries that are poisonous to humans. Our digestive systems are entirely different. In case of poisoning, contact medical personnel and be prepared to tell them the name of the plant involved, and try to collect a sample of the plant. Better to be safe, even if embarrassed, than sorry! Remember, it takes less poison to be fatal to a small child than an adult.

GLOSSARY

Acute: Sharply pointed.

Alpine: Growing above timberline.

Alternate: Leaf or branch arrangement on stem, not opposite each other.

Annual: A plant growing from seed, blooming, setting seed and then dying all in one growing season.

Arcuate: Usually referring to veins in a leaf; bowed or following a curve looking nearly parallel.

Axil: The upper angle formed by the junction of a main stem and a leaf stalk or branch.

Basal: Situated at, or pertaining to, the base.

Bearded: A line or tuft of hairs.

Berry: A soft, fleshy, multi-seeded fruit.

Bi-pinnately divided: Describing a pinnate leaf in which the leaflets are further divided in a pinnate fashion.

Biennial: Of two seasons' duration from seed to maturity and death.

Binomial: The botanical nomenclature, or scientific name of a plant; consisting of the genus name and the species name.

Blade: The expanded part of a leaf, petal or sepal.

Bloom: A whitish coating on a fruit that, usually, can be rubbed off. Often waxy looking.

Bog: A low, very wet area. Soil is often acidic, and standing water is common.

Bract: A reduced or modified leaf, usually below a flower. Often petal-like.

Bracteoles: A small bract on top of a pedicel instead of below it.

Bristles: Long, stiff hairs.

Calyx: The outermost circle of the floral parts. The external portion, usually green. The group of sepals.

Campanulate: Bell-shaped.

Capitate: Having a dense, head-like cluster.

Capsule: A dry fruit composed of more than 1 seed cavity.

Carpel: The structure of the plant that holds the seeds.

Catkin: A tight spike of petalless flowers (usually either male or female).

Caudex: The woody base of a perennial plant.

Ciliate: Having hairs along the edges.

Clasping: Partially surrounding the stem (usually referring to a leaf petiole).

Clawed: Narrow, stalk-like base of some petals or sepals.

Cluster: A tight grouping, or bunch.

Cyme: A flat-topped flower cluster, with central flowers opening first.

Deciduous: Not persistent, said of leaves falling in Autumn or of floral parts falling after flowering.

Decumbent: Sprawling on the ground with upturned ends.

Dentate: Having a margin or edge cut with sharp teeth directed outward.

Dissected: Cut or divided into sections.

Drupe: A fleshy fruit having one seed inside a tough shell.

Elliptical: Mostly oval, tapering to both ends equally.

Entire: Without divisions, lobes, or teeth. With even or smooth margin or edge.

Epipetalous: Referring to stamens that are attached on the petals, not at the base of them.

Ethnic: Pertaining to a person, or group of people, who are native to, or have traditionally lived in, an area.

Evergreen: Remaining green all year.

Fall: A term for the large, petal-like sepals of the Iris family.

Farinose: Covered with a powdery substance.

Fascicle: A tight bundle, cluster or clump.

Fleshy: Soft or puffy.

Frond: Leaf of a fern. (Also, a large leaf).

Genus: A group of closely related plants. The first part of a binomial or scientific name.

Glabrous: Having a smooth, even surface without hairs.

Glandular: Having a substance (often sticky) that is released from the plant by way of pores or hairs.

Glaucous: Having a waxy, grayish-blue appearance.

Heath: Open wasteland, with usually acidic soil.

Herbaceous: A non-woody, perennial plant, with above ground parts dying to the ground each year.

Hummock: A rounded rise of vegetation Usually in a wet area; such as, a bog or marsh.

Hybrid: A cross between 2 species or subspecies, usually of the same genus.

Incisions: Sharp cuts or indentations, usually referring to leaf edges.

Inflorescence: A flower cluster, or grouping on a stem.

ing upcurved at the end.

Insectivorous: Referring to plants that capture insects; and absorb nutriment from them.

Introduced: Said of plants that were not originally native to an area. Becoming established after escaping from farmlands or in reseeding projects.

Involucre: A group of bracts beneath a flower cluster, as in the heads of the Aster Family.

Lanceolate: Narrow, tapering to both ends.

Lateral: Situated to the side.

Leaflet: A single part of a compound leaf.

Linear: Long and narrow. Usually having mostly parallel edges.

Lobed: Describing a leaf that is divided into curved or rounded parts connected to each other by an undivided central area.

Lyrate: Lyre shaped. A pinnatifid leaf with a larger end lobe, like a Dandelion leaf.

Margin: Edge.

Meadow: A moist, open area, usually free of shrubs and trees.

Native Plant: Any plant that grows naturally in the area orf concern, not placed there in either plant or seed form.

Nectaries: A structure giving off a sweet substance, usually sticky.

Node: A joint in a stolon or stem, or the point on a stem where the leaf starts.

Nut: A dry, hard, one-seeded fruit.

Nutlet: A small nut.

Oblanceolate: Similar to lanceolate, but broader at base.

Oblong: Much longer than broad, with nearly parallel margins and a rounded tip.

Opaque: Not letting light through, not transparent nor translucent.

Ovary: The lower swollen portion of the reproductive part of a plant, containing the seeds.

Ovate: Egg-shaped, with a point.

Ovoid: Egg-shaped.

Palmate: Lobed, divided or ribbed so as to resemble the outstretched fingers of a hand.

Parasitic: An organism obtaining food and/or shelter at the expense of another.

Pedicel: The stalk attaching individual flowers to the main stem of the inflorescence.

Perennial: Living for more than two years; and, usually, flowering each year after the first.

Petal: Usually the colorful part of the corolla, the row of floral parts above the sepals..

Petiolate: Having a petiole.

Petiole: The stalk that attaches the leaf to the stem.

Pinnate: Describing a compound leaf in which the leaflets are arranged in two rows, one on each side of the midrib.

Pinnatifid: Divided in a pinnate fashion.

Pistil: A term used ambiguously to describe either a single carpel (simple pistil) or a group of fused carpels (compound pistil).

Pistillate: A flower that has only the female reproductive parts.

Prickle: A short woody pointed outgrowth from the epidermis of a plant.

Raceme: An inflorescence in which the flowers are formed on individual pedicels attached to the main stem.

Ray Flower: The flat outer flowers of the Aster family, often incorrectly referred to as petals of a Daisy.

Reflexed: Bent abruptly downward or backward.

Revegetate: To plant again. Usually an attempt to restore to original or acceptable condition.

Rhizome: An underground stem or rootstalk, usually rooting at the nodes, becoming upcurved at the end.

Rosette: A crowded cluster of leaves, appearing to rise from one point in the ground.

Runner: A stolon or trailing stem.

Sac-like: Having a swollen pouch.

Saline: Containing salt.

Salverform: A tube-shaped flower, with petals that flatten out at right angles from the tube.

Sepal: One of the outer group of floral parts. Usually green .

Serrated: Having sharply pointed teeth or indentations.

Sessile: Without a stalk or stem.

Sheath: A tubular (often thin) plant structure that surrounds a plant part. Often at a connection where petiole meets stem. Typical of many members of the Parsley family.

Shrub: A woody perennial, smaller than a tree, usually with several basal stems.

Silicle: The seed capsule of some members of the Mustard family, usually no more than twice as long as wide.

Silique: The seed capsule of many members of the Mustard family, more than twice as long as wide.

Simple: Not branched or divided.

Sinus: An indentation or depression between 2 lobes of a leaf, or where the leaf meets the petiole.

Spadix: A thick fleshy stem (like a spike) that bears many flowers and fruits of a plant.

Spathe: A large bract, or pair of bracts, often petal-like, enclosing a flower cluster or spadix.

Spatulate: Describing structures that have a broad end and a long narrow base, such as the leaves of the Daisy.

Species: A further division of plants beyond genus, showing slight differences. More specifically, the specific epithet, or second part of the binomial or scientific name.

Spike: An inflorescence like a raceme, but without individual flower stems.

Spine: The stiff mid-portion of a leaf, or a long pointed end or thorn.

Spore: The small, dust-like, asexual, unicellular reproductive body of flowerless plants.

Spur: A tubular or sac-like part of a flower. It usually contains a nectar secreting gland.

Stamen: The male organ of the flower, consisting of a filament and an anther, the latter bearing the pollen.

Staminate: A flower that has only the male reproductive part.

Stellate: Star-shaped.

Stigma: The top part of a pistil or style, often hairy and/or sticky, which receives the pollen at pollination time and on which the pollen grain germinates.

Stigmatic Rays: Ridges on the top of a seed capsule, radiating from the center, as in the Poppy family.

Stipe: The stalk beneath the ovary. The leaf stalk of a fern.

Stipule: A part of the leaf where it attaches to the stem (especially common in the Rose and Pea families). A broadening on either side of the stem that could be mistaken for a bract.

Stolons: Runners or trailing stems.

Stomata (singular stoma): Small openings or pores in the surface of a leaf through which gaseous exchange takes place between the internal tissues and the atmosphere.

Style: The tubular part of the reproductive portion of a plant that connects the stigma to the ovary.

Subshrub: A very low shrub.

Succulent: Fleshy, juicy.

Tap Root: The main root of some species reaching down deep into the soil to gain nutrients or moisture.

Teeth: Notches along the margins of leaves.

Tendril: A long thread-like part of a plant stem that supports it by twining around other objects. Notable in members of the Pea family.

Terminal: At the end.

Toxin: A soluble toxic product of a bacterial cell which is capable of diffusing out of the living cell into the surrounding medium.

Transluscent: Allowing some light through without being able to see inside.

Tubular: Having the form of, or consisting of, a tube or tubes.

Tundra: Treeless Arctic plain, often times damp and having mounds.

Umbel: An inflorescence, more or less flat-topped, in which all of the pedicels arise at the same point, like the ribs of an umbrella.

Unisexual: A single sexplant. One that bears only stamens or carpels, not both.

Waste Places: Areas where soil has been stripped of its naturally occurring vegetation. Usually lack of humus, soil and care causes it to develop into a different environment and plant community than it was originally. Generally referring to roadside pull-offs, old road-beds, around old buildings and townsites.

Watery: Juicy. Said of plants with a non-fibrous stem.

Whorl: An arrangement of leaves, etc., in a circle around the stem, radiating from a node. Three or more leaves or flowers at one node, in a circle.

BIBLIOGRAPHY

Britton, Nathaniel Lord, and Brown, Hon. Addison. *An Illustrated Flora of the Northern U.S. and Canada.* Dover Books. 3 volumes. 637 pp.

Clark, Lewis J. *Wild Flowers of the Pacific Northwest..* Gray's Publishing Limited, 602 pp.

Hitchcock, S. Leo. and Cronquist, Arthur. *Flora of the Pacific Northwest..* University of Washington Press. 730 pp.

Hultén, Eric. 1968. *Flora of Alaska and Neighboring Territories.* Stanford University Press. 1008 pp.

Kari, Priscilla R. *1987. Tanaina Plantlore. Dena'ina K'et'una.* National Park Service, Alaska Region. 205 pp.

Peterson, Roger Tory. *Wildflowers---Northeastern / Northcentral North America.* Houghton-Mifflin Co. 420 pp.

Scotter, George W. *Wildflowers of the Canadian Rockies. Hurtig Publishers. 170 pp.*

Smith, James P., Jr. 1977. *Vascular Plant Families.* Mad River Press, Eureka, California. 321 pp.

Viereck, Leslie A. , and Little, Elbert L., Jr. *1972. Alaska Trees and Shrubs.* Forest Service, U.S. Dept. of Agriculture. Washington, D.C. 266 pp.

Welsh, Stanley L. 1974. *Anderson's Flora of Alaska and Adjacent Parts of Canada.* Brigham Young University Press, Provo, Utah. 724 pp.

Index

Note: Common names in UPPER CASE indicate full descriptions and photos, while lower case indicates other information.

A

B

C

G

H

I

J

K

L

M

N

O

P

Q

R

S

For your Notes

For your Notes

For your Notes

For your Notes

For your Notes

For your Notes

For your Notes